Kalinga and Southeast Asia: A Saga of Shared Civilizations

Kalinga and Southeast Asia: A Saga of Shared Civilizations

Patit Paban Mishra

BLACK EAGLE BOOKS
Dublin, USA | Bhubaneswar, India

 Black Eagle Books
USA address:
7464 Wisdom Lane
Dublin, OH 43016

India address:
E/312, Trident Galaxy, Kalinga Nagar,
Bhubaneswar-751003, Odisha, India

E-mail: info@blackeaglebooks.org
Website: www.blackeaglebooks.org

First International Edition Published by
Black Eagle Books, 2025

**KALINGA AND SOUTHEAST ASIA:
A SAGA OF SHARED CIVILIZATIONS**
by **Patit Paban Mishra**

Copyright © Patit Paban Mishra

All rights reserved. No part of this publication may be reproduced, stored in a retrieval system, or transmitted, in any form or by any means, electronic, mechanical, photocopying, recording or otherwise without the prior permission of the publisher.

Cover & Interior Design: Ezy's Publication

ISBN- 978-1-64560-696-3 (Paperback)

Printed in the United States of America

Dedication

To the families of my brother, my sister, and my own--
You are the tender threads in the fabric of my life,
woven with moments that linger,
with laughter that heals,
and with love that asks for nothing, yet gives everything.

You are the hands that hold,
the voices that soothe,
the hearts that keep the past alive
while nurturing the future with quiet grace.

In each of you, I see the light of generations reborn.
In your presence, I feel the pulse of those we've lost—
a soft, enduring echo that reminds me:
family is not bound by time,
but by love, by memory,
and by the way, we carry one another forward.

This book is for you—
for the countless ways you walk beside me,
for the love you give without needing to be seen.
You are my home,
my quiet strength,
and the living legacy I cherish most.

Patit Paban Mishra

Contents

Foreword	09
Preface	13
Chapter-I Political, Socio-Economic and Cultural Milieu of Odisha	19
Chapter-II Cultural Profile Of Southeast Asia	68
Cahpter-III Odisha's Cultural Rapprochement with Myanmar and Thailand	106
Chapter- IV Odisha and Indo-China: Cultural Connect	137
Chapter-V Odisha and Malayo-Indonesian Region: Exploring Age Old Linkages	173
Chaptr-VI Conclusion	219
Select Bibliography	232
Maps & Visuals	247

FOREWORD

Lalit Mansingh

The writing of history is often hazardous, especially when there is societal pressure on historians to be motivational and lend credibility to the beliefs of interested groups. Of the many such groups, three are easily identified: the Ideologues who expect a validation of their political or economic theories; the Nationalists who seek a glorification of the nation's past history and the Parochialists who plead for an embellishment of the history of a province or region. The task of any historian who deals with India and South East Asia is particularly challenging because of these expectations.

In his book "Kalinga and Southeast Asia: a Saga of Shared Civilizations", Prof Patit Paban Mishra has confronted the issue head on. After a lifetime of meticulous research and field experience, he has produced a cohesive and authoritative history of Kalinga's role in South East Asia from a mass of fragmentary and diverse data. He has provided the most rational answers to the frequently asked questions on the subject. This is a book, which will be cherished by students of history as much as by the wider public for the sweep of its coverage and authenticity.

Prof Mishra has courageously refuted many of the

conclusions reached by earlier historians, both Indian and foreign, which shaped public perceptions in the past. By mid-20th Century, when India achieved independence, our national leaders declared solidarity with a host of nations in Asia and Africa, which were still under colonial rule. Many of these were in South East Asia. Turning the searchlight on our eastern neighbours, several historians were struck by the similarity of religion, language, art and culture between India and the region. It led to an erroneous conclusion that India was undoubtedly the major source of their civilisation and culture. It was common to use terms like "colonisation" and "Indianisation", which were not only factually incorrect but deeply insensitive and offensive to the citizens of these countries. Starting with the sub-title of his book: "A Saga of Shared Civilizations", Prof Mishra has firmly asserted that the cultural heritage of South East Asia was not a gift from India. It was in reality a process of mutual assimilation.

"The material and cultural base of autochthonous society of Southeast Asia", he writes, "was already developed at the time of contact with external forces.... An interaction between local and external cultures went on. A rapport was established and as acculturation proceeded, elements of culture were absorbed."

It is time we understood and accepted that India has benefitted vastly, both culturally and economically, from its eastern neighbours over nearly two thousand years of continuous contacts.

Kalinga, a powerful kingdom on the eastern seaboard, had a community of intrepid and adventurous maritime traders called the *Sadhabas*. It is to their credit that the trading routes flourished from 5th Century BCE until the 15th Century CE, when the kingdom disintegrated.

Prof Mishra has delivered valuable service in decisively rejecting a number of speculative assertions by earlier scholars. There is no truth, according to him, in reports of large-scale migration of people from Kalinga after Asoka's invasion in the 3rd Century BCE, or in any other period of political upheaval in Kalinga. There is no conclusive evidence either of the claims that the Sailendra Dynasty of Java was an offshoot of the Sailodbhaba rulers of Odisha.

It may be noted, however, that recent archaeological excavations at ancient port sites like Tamralipti, Pithunda, Palur, Kalinganagara and Khalkapatna have revealed rouletted ware, coins, beads, potsherds and other items which reveal Kalinga's chain of external trade stretching from the ancient Roman empire in the west to China in the east.

A host of questions still remain about Kalinga's cultural influence in South East Asia. How much did Kalinga influence the language and literature in the region? How significant a factor was Kalinga in the spread of Hinduism and Buddhism in the region? Did Kalinga have substantial influence on art and architecture, especially on the majestic sites of Borobudur, Ankur Wat and on the numerous ancient temples, stupas and pagodas scattered across South East Asia?

Prof Mishra has used his historian's instinct and discretion to suggest that Odisha "perhaps" had a dominant role.

There is enough in the book to bring pride to the heart of Odias. The fact that Indians in general are still referred to as *Kling* or *Kelang* in the region is a significant acknowledgement of Kalinga's soft power.

There is a fleeting reference in the book to the

importance given in India's foreign policy to South East Asia. Embedded in this is an important message for Odisha. While it is understandable to feel proud and celebrate Kalinga's influence in past centuries, it will be sobering to remember that the defeat of Mukunda Deb, the last Gajapati, at the hands of Sultan Suleiman Karmani of Bengal in the 16th Century CE sent Odisha into virtual oblivion for the next five hundred years. Kalinga ceased to be of consequence in South East Asia.

Odisha is currently in the midst of a cultural and economic renaissance. It is today a fast-growing economy. By coincidence, the Indo-Pacific has once again emerged as the *Subarna Bhumi* of the past. It is recognised as the geopolitical as well as the geo-economic centre of gravity of the world. Odisha can once again carve out a role for itself in seeking investments and markets for its products in the region.

The second phase of the history of Kalinga and South East Asia has begun and today's Kalinga must seize this opportunity.

Former Foreign Secretary
Ambassador to the USA and High Commissioner to the UK
Founder Chairman, Kalinga International Foundation

PREFACE

The present book is a revised version of the D.Litt thesis of Rabindra Bharati University, entitled, **"Orissa in Trans-National Migration: A Study of Culture in Transit"**. As the culture of India consists of plurality of traditions, the part played by this eastern state of India is portrayed in proper perspective. This is a region where cultural influences from different directions have been synthesized to produce a unique type of culture. Having a long maritime tradition, the people of Kalinga/Odisha/ Orissa had gone to Southeast Asia and left a cultural legacy. A number of similarities between Orissa and Southeast Asia could be found in different fields. The impact of Orissan religion, philosophy, social custom, art and architecture upon various countries of Southeast Asia is abundantly evident. The present author is not tempted too much to stress the claim of Orissa in cultural diffusion to Southeast Asia, but has taken an objective view in pointing out Orissa's contribution to the whole gamut of Indo- Southeast Asian relations. As a part of Indian subcontinent, it had created extensive commercial ties and trade networks with various parts of Asia. Through its numerous ports on the long coastline, Orissan contact had flowed out in successive waves to different countries. As the study of west coast of India is inadequate without a special reference to the Konkan coast lying between

Malabar and Gujrat coast; so as also study of eastern coast of India is incomplete without thorough study of Orissan coast adjoining Bengal and Coromandel coast.

The term 'Southeast Asia' is designated to include the area to the east of Indian subcontinent and to the south of People's Republic of China. It consists of two broad groups in a geographical sense; mainland comprising Myanmar (Burma), Thailand, Laos, Cambodia, Vietnam and island consisting of Indonesia, Malaysia, Singapore, Brunei and the Philippines. A region of ethnic, cultural, linguistic, historical and physical mosaic; external influences like Indian, Chinese, Islamic and European civilizations have left deep imprints on the indigenous culture of Southeast Asia. Although it has received transfusion of these cultures adding nuances and shades of meaning through centuries, the region has not lost its idiom. The data from India and Southeast Asia is inseparably linked and a comprehensive study of one is meaningless without a thorough knowledge of the other. Beginning from prehistoric times, Indian culture flowed to Southeast Asia in gush and sometimes in tickles until the western hegemony was established in both the regions. Orissa immensely contributed to this process. The autochthonous society of Southeast Asia was of such a standard that it could assimilate elements of Indian culture. It has been claimed that Southeast Asians were pioneers in metal tools industry, rice cultivation, marine technology etc. Southeast Asia also did not forsake its own cultural identity in spite of nourishing external cultural expression.

The author has taken interest in study of Southeast Asia from his Delhi University days, where he took up Southeast Asia as a special paper in MA. The M.Phil. and Ph.D. degrees of Jawaharlal Nehru University, New Delhi awarded to him were on subjects not related to the present work. The topics for M.Phil. and Ph.D. were, "The Pathet Lao Movement" and "The Problem of Laos: Its International Dimensions since the Geneva Conference" respectively. Indo-Southeast Asian relations have received attention of scholars a great deal and a number of articles, monographs and books have been published. However, there is no integrated and systematic work on Orissan contact with Southeast Asia. The author has taken up this challenging task. There are number of articles by scholars like A.K. Pattanaik, K.S. Behera, K.K. Basa, N. Ping, N.K. Sahu, R.M. Sahu, S.K. Panda etc throwing some light on maritime past of Orissa. Starting from an article entitled, "Cultural Contact between Orissa and Southeast Asia in Ancient times" in *The Journal of Orissan History* (Vol. I, July 1980), the author has published a couple of articles on the subject in national and international journals. The archaeological excavations in Orissa, Thailand and Indonesia have thrown new light on the subject. Evidences of people of Orissa going to distant lands are found in literary texts. Folklore, oral traditions, legends and festivals etc form important source materials and their authenticity is ascertained from other sources. Some palm leaf manuscripts and inscriptions are strong indicators of Orissa's contact with Southeast Asia. Field study in both the regions has also opened new angles.

The book consists of five chapters. Chapter-I entitled; "Political, Socio-Economic and Cultural Milieu of Orissa" deals with territorial extent, social structure, overseas trade, folklore, festivals, art and architecture of Orissa. The archaeological excavations conducted recently in various parts of Orissa have been highlighted. The second chapter, "Cultural Profile of Southeast Asia" delineates external influences, prehistoric culture, maritime tradition and religion. The theories of Indianization and recent interpretations have been analyzed. Chapter-III deals with Orissa's relations with Myanmar and Thailand. The discussions on political and cultural developments have been followed by similarities in religion, literature, art and architecture between Orissa and Southeast Asia. The coastal trade of Orissa in seventeenth and eighteenth centuries has been discussed. Various facets of Orissan cultural influence on Laos, Cambodia and Vietnam have been discussed in Chapter-IV. The legends of Kaundinya, Devaraja cult and cultural development in Campa have also been discussed. In Chapter-V entitled "Orissa's relations with Malay-Indonesia region," cultures of Malay Peninsula, Java and Bali are analyzed. Conclusion, select bibliography and maps have followed it.

In completing the book, I have taken assistance from number of persons and institutions. My friend Professor S.K. Panda of Berhampur University suggested me to take this topic and he has remained a source of inspiration to me. Words are inadequate to express my deep sense of gratitude to Prof. Ranjit Sen, Prof. P.N. Chakrabarti and late Prof. Ranjit Roy for their valuable suggestions and encouragement. I am grateful to persons, who have helped me in my field trips in Orissa and Southeast Asia. The librarian and staff of the following institutions were very much helpful to me: J.N.U., I.C.W.A., National Museum, National Archives (New Delhi); National Library (Calcutta); Centre for Southeast Asian Studies (Chennai); P.G. Department of History and Sambalpur University (JyotiVihar); Siam Society, National Research Council and Chaulalongkorn University (Bangkok); Chieng Mai University (Chieng Mai); Social Sciences and National Library (Hanoi) and National Library (Vietnam). My special thanks go to Professor Upebdra Padhi, Shri Satya Patanaik and Shri Ashok Parida for bringing out the book at an early date.

Lastly, I am indebted to my family members and friends whose love and affection have been of invaluable help in completing the thesis.

Prof Patit Paban Mishra,
Former Professor Sambalpur University and Northern University of Malaysia Senior Academic Fellow of ICHR. Senior Academic Consultant of OSOU Sambalpur. e-mail. ppmishra7@yahoo.com / mishra.patit@gmail.com

CHAPTER-1

Political, Socio-Economic and Cultural Milieu of Orissa

Situated in the eastern zone of India, the state of Orissa extends from 17° 49′ to 22° 34′ north latitude and from 81° 27′ to 87° 29′ east of Greenwich. Bihar is situated on its north, Madhya Pradesh on the west, Andhra Pradesh on the south, the Bay of Bengal on the east and West Bengal on its northeast. Extending over an area of 155,842 square kilometers, Orissa emerged as a separate province in 1936. With a recorded history of nearly two thousand and five hundred years, the Orissan civilization is one of the oldest in India. Forging a link between north and south India, Orissa had long experience of commercial, cultural and military expansion. Its sea-faring life linked Indian cultural activities with those of Southeast Asia. At the height of imperial Orissa's expansion, the territorial and cultural unity of Orissa prevailed over the area extending from Ganga on the north to Godavari in the south, and from Bay of Bengal in the east to Amarakantaka on the west. The long coast of Bay of Bengal had facilitated sea voyages to distant countries for trade and commerce.

Territorial Extent of Orissa through Ages

With the passage of time, the territorial extent of Orissa had undergone remarkable changes. It had four distinct political units in earlier days; Odra, Utkala, Kalinga and Kosala.

The *Bhagavata Purana* mentions that Dirghatamas had six sons Anga, Vanga, Kalinga, Pundra, Sumta and Odra by queen Sudesna[1]. According to this tradition, Odra country was named after this son. The territory of Odra along with those of Paundra, Utkala Mekala, Kalinga and Andhra are mentioned in the *Mahabharata*. The early Greek writers like Pliny refers to a people called *Oretes*, which has been equated with Sanskrit Odras[2]. The earliest epigraphic reference to Odra could be found in the Soro copper plates of Somodatta of first quarter of seventh century AD, where there is mention of Odra Visaya[3]. The Chinese traveler Hsuan Tsang, who visited Orissa in 638 C.E. mentions vividly about *Wu-tu* country, located between the rivers Suvarnarekha and Mahanadi[4]. Al-Biruni, who came with Mahmud of Ghazni mentions in his *Tarikhu'1 Hind* about *Urdabishau*[5], which signifies *Oddavisaya* in the Tirumalai inscription (1025 C.E.) of Rajendra Cola[6]. Minhaj refers the area as Jajnagar in the thirteenth century[7]. At the time of

---

1   *Bhagavata Purana*, IX, XXIII, (Bombay, 1889), 5.
2   N.K. Sahu, *History of Orissa*, Vol. I (Cuttack, 1981), P. 140.
3   *Epigraphia Indica*, XIXXI, P. 202.
4   A. Cunningham, *Ancient Geography of India* (New Delhi, 1964), P.585.
5   E.J. Sachau, trans, *Albiruni's India* (New Delhi, 1964), P. 318.
6   P.P. Mishra, "Orissa as reflected in Al-Biruni's Tarikhul Hind" in *Proceedings of Orissa History Congress*, XII (Jyoti Vihar, 1986), P.79.
7   H.G. Raverty, trans, *Tabakat-i-Nasiri*, Vol.I, (New Delhi, 1970), Pp. 590ff.

imperial Gangas, Odra was denoted as the entire speaking Oriya region and Sarala Das made *Odisa* synonymous with *Odrarastra*. From fifteenth century onwards, the term Odisa (Orissa) was used in common parlance for the entire land of Oriya people.

According to the Puranic tradition, Utkala was located southwest of Bengal and to the south of Gaya in Bihar. It existed as a political entity during the time of Buddha as *Utkala Janapada*. Tapassu and Bhalika, the two merchant brothers went from here to *Majjimadesa* on trade. The epigraphic records of Somavamsis and Bhaumakaras point that Odra and Utkala were two distinct territories. The Dirghasi inscription of 1075 C.E. mentions their separate identities[8]. The Bhaumakaras styled themselves as Utkala *Kula* and at the time of Somavamsis the region was designated as Utkala[9]. Yayati II annexed Utkala in his domain and named his empire comprising Tosali Kosala, Kalingas as Utkala. The territory of Kosala Ananthavarman Chodagangadeva, stretching from Ganga in the north to Godavari in the south was known as empire of whole Utkala or *Sakalotkala Samarajaya*. Utkala lost its pre-eminence after the decline of Gangas and the empire of Gajapatis was designated as *Odisarajya*.

Kosala is well known in Indian tradition and literature as the country of Rama. The kingdom after Rama's death was divided between his two sons, Lava and Kusa, the former getting the northern half and the later southern half. This southern Kosala or *Daksina* Kosala roughly comprises the present Raipur and Bilaspur districts of Madhya Pradesh and some areas of Sambalpur, Bargarh, Sonepur, Patna,

---

8   *Epigraphica Indica*, IV, pp. 316ff.
9   S.N. Rajguru, ed. *Inscriptions of Orissa*, Vol.IV (Bhubaneswar, 1966), Pp. 281ff.

Sundargarh and Kalahandi of western Orissa. Kosala of Allahabad pillar inscription of Samudragupta is identical with *Daksina* Kosala of the Somavamsi inscriptions. The Chinese pilgrim Hsuan-Tsang visited Utkala and Kongoda and journeying for about 1800 li or 500 kilometres in the northwestern direction reached Kosala[10]. The civilization in the region flourished chiefly on the bank of river Mahanadi. It remained under the suzerainty of imperial Gangas until the middle of fourteenth century and later the Chauhans established their rule over the region.

Like the origin of Utkala, the *Puranas* mention the mythical origin of Kalinga. Anga, Vanga, Kalinga, Pundra and Suhma were five sons of Bali[11]. Kalinga was a part of Nanda Empire in the fourth century B.C.E. It became prominent at the time of Ashok, when the famous Kalinga war was fought in 261 B.C.E. Kalinga's imperial glory reached its pinnacle in the first century B.C.E., when the Kharavela extended his sway over a considerable portion of India. From Gupta period onwards, the size of Kalinga shrank and it corresponded to districts of Vizagpatnam and Srikakulam of Andhra and Ganjam in Orissa. The eastern Ganga rulers set up a powerful kingdom in the region and were known as the Lords of Kalinga or Kalingadhipati. Kalinga, which in ancient times covered a far-flung empire from Ganga to Godavari, denoted from seventh century onwards to the small kingdom of the eastern Gangas. Besides Kalinga proper, a separate political identity known as Trikalinga is found in epigraphical records. Pliny mentions three divisions of Kalinga known as Gangarides Calinigae,

---

10 T. Watters, *On Yuan Chwyang's Travels in India*, Vol II (London, 1908),Pp.193-200.

11 G.E. Pargiter, *Ancient Indian Historical Tradition* (London, 1913), P. 158.

Macco Calingae and Calingae[12]. Trikalinga might be same as Triglypton or Trilingon mentioned by Ptolemy[13]. Some of the earlier Ganga kings like Indravarman I and Samanta Varman styled themselves as the Lord of Trikalinga or Trikalingadhipati[14]. Trikalinga at the time of eastern Gangas covered parts of Kalahandi and Koraput districts of Orissa.

The territorial extent of Odra, Utkala, Kosala and Kalinga had frequent changes in course of time. Anantavarman Chodgangadeva (1077-1147 C.E.) amalgamated Utkala and Kalinga into one political entity and Kosala was added to this at the time of Anangabhima III (1211-1238 C.E.). Thus emerged an imperial structure stretching from the river Ganga in the north to Godavari in the south with its capital at Abinava Varanasi Kataka or modern Cuttack. The Gajapati rulers consolidated their power in this region but from the time of Prataparudra Dev (1497-1509 C.E.); the rulers of Bengal, Bahamani and Vijayanagar posed danger and consequently Orissa lost much of its territory. In 1568, Sulamain Karrni of Bengal occupied Orissa. The recurring invasion from outside, political instability with the successive rule of Afghans, Moghuls and the Marathas for over two hundred-year spelt eternal gloom in the shape of political disintegration and dismemberment. Orissa became an easy prey to the East India Company. The British forces occupied northern and southern parts of Orissa in 1765 and 1768 respectively; the coastal region in 1803 and western Orissa by 1849. There was further dismemberment of Orissa, when parts of it

---

12 Cunningham, n. 4, P. 594.
13 J.W. Mc Crindle, *Ancient India as described by Ptolemy* (Calcutta, 1885), P.234
14 Epigraphia Indica, XXVII, Pp. 216ff.

remained under Bengal, Madras and Central provinces. The search for identity of Orissa remained unabated and eventually it emerged as a separate province in 1936.

Social Structure

Ancient and medieval Orissa saw the rise and fall of powerful empires of the Chedis, Matharas, Bhaumakaras, Somavamsis, Gangas, Gajapatis etc. ruling over long periods and keeping their domain well integrated. Apart from this political strength, which helped the growth of Orissan culture, diverse social elements and different social groups played an important role. The Proto-Australoid and the Western Brachycephals form the major racial elements. Comprising the majority of the population of Orissa, the former group with long head and rather broad nose belong to scheduled tribes and lower castes. They inhabit the hilly areas of western, southern and northern Orissa. The latter group with broad head narrower nose is found among higher castes. This racial distribution and component in the population is not surprising as in ancient times the non-Aryan tribesmen predominated. The generic term *savara* was applied to all tribal folk. Apart from the *savara*, the other important tribes were *Gond, Khand, Oraon, Kisan, Koya* etc. According to tradition, Jagannatha was originally a *savara* deity and a group of the priests in the Jagannatha temple known as *daitas* originated from *savaras*. Likewise, a section of priests worshipping in the Lingaraja temples were descendants of *savaras*.

Orissa has proved to be an area where cultural winds from different parts of India have been synthesized to produce typical Orissan art form and life styles. The coming of different type of cultural forms have enriched Orison culture and when people of Ores migrated to different places in India and abroad, the cultural influence of Ores is evident. The *Brahmans* who were ranked highest in the order of four Vargas were living in Orissa at the time of Kalinga war and enjoyed the patronage of Jain king Kharavela. However, certain s*astric* prejudices to *brahmans* of Orissa are evident[15]. A large-scale migration of *Brahmans* took place from the period of fourth century C.E. onwards, which accelerated the process of brahmanization. Large scale land grants along with immunities from taxation by ruling dynasties such as Matharas, eastern Gangas, Sailodbhavas, Nalas, Bhaumakaras etc attracted the might *brahmans*. The other factors were growing competition among themselves in various parts of India and shortage of clients after disintegration of central empires in northern India[16]. From the epigraphic records, it is evident that the *brahmana* families migrated from places like Ahichchhatra, Daksinapatha, Madhyadesha, Radha, Sravasti, Takari etc.[17]. A tradition credits Yayati Kesari of bringing ten thousand *Brahmans* from Kanauj to Jajpur to perform Asvamedha sacrifice.

The main function performed by the *Brahmans* were priesthood and teaching of the Vedas. Another important role was helping the process of royal legitimation[18]. The tribes were peasantized and *brahmanas* indoctrinated the

---

15   The *Matsya Purana* mentions that *brahmans* residing in *Mlechchha* countries like Odra, Andhra, Konkona are not be invited in funeral ceremony. See *Matsya Purana*, XIV, P. 23.

16   R.N. Nandi, "Client, Ritual and Conflict in Early Brahmanical Order" in *Indian Historical Review*, Vol. 6, Nos. 1-2, Pp. 82ff.

17   *Epigraphia Indica*, Vol. XXXV, P.102; XI, P.96; IV, P.258 and XXVIII, P. 323.

18   For details see, H. Kulke, "Early State Formation and Royal Legitimation in Late Ancient India, M.N. Das, ed, *Sidelights on History and Culture of Orissa* (Cuttack, 1977), Pp. 104ff.

tribals through the process of acculturation and integration. Thus, the loyalty of the tribals was ensured. The tribals deities were upgraded and military duties were assigned to the tribals. The legendary accounts of the origins of some dynasties illustrate the relationship of the rulers with various tribes with *brahmanas* playing not an insignificant role. The Gangas acknowledged the deity of *Savara* tribe on the Mahendragiri mountain under the name of Siva-Gokarnasvamin. Stambheswari or Goddess of Pillar was the tutelary deity of Sulki dynasty. Thus, the *brahmans* both both of royal court and donee of land grants served the useful purpose of maintaining Hindu law and royal order and in the process 'Hinduizing' the tribals. This phenomenon occurred in not a dissimilar fashion when the *brahmanas* legitimized the rule of kings of Southeast Asia and autochthonous people learned about Indian mode of life. There were also deviation from traditional profession by the *brahmans*. They were taking recourse to cultivation and trade sometimes. The *Balaramagosthi brahamans* played an important role by introducing plough agriculture in place of slash-and-burn type of cultivation in tribal areas[19]. Occupying of administrative and military posts was not uncommon.

The *kshatriyas* were next to the *brahmans* in the social hierarchy. Generally, the kings and royal families were known as *kshatriyas*. Hsuan Tsang mentions the existence

---

19   G. Pfeffer, "Puri's Vedic Brahmins : Continuing and Change in their traditional Institutions", in Anncharlott Eschmann and others, ed, *The Cult of Jagannath and the Regional Tradition of Orissa* (Delhi, 1978), P. 425. Two inscriptions of the Ganga period dated 1245 A.D. mention about the son of Prayaga Upadhyaya, Risidasa Nayaka as trader in horses See, Rajguru, n. 9, Vol, V,P. 886.

of *kshatriya* rulers by stating that the ruler of Kosala was a *kshatriya* and follower of Buddhism[20]. The rulers of Ganga and Bhanja dynasties claim their descent from lunar race. Tracing their lineage to mythical ancestry, the ruling families endeavoured to achieve *kshatriya* status for legitimizing their rule. The Somavamsis and Bhanjas traced their origin from lunar race, though they had tribal origin. The brahmans prepared their genealogy. They observed rituals like *asvamedhyajna* and hiranyagarbhadana, established matrimonial relations with other *kshatriya* powers and highlighted the kingly qualities. Some of the rulers of early kingdom in Southeast Asia adopted this means also, which point to the cultural influence of Orissa and other parts of India[21]. The *kayasthas* and *karanas* were class of writers. This group arose as there was need of scribes due to frequent transfer of land and land revenue by the ruling class[22]. They functioned as high dignitaries of state also.

The main occupation of the *vaisyas* was agriculture and trade. Forming the backbone of economic life of Orissa, they indulged in trade and commerce and in the process became an important vehicle in transmitting Orissan culture abroad. With titles like *shreshitin sadhu praja*, they enjoyed social prestige and sometimes received villages as grants. The ruler of Chakrakotte Mandala, Madhukar Arnadeva's vassal Laksmana Ramadeva conferred three villages into a *vaisyagrahara* and donated these to *vaisya* named Erapa Nayaka. During the Ganga rule, there were

---

20 S. Beal, *Buddhist Records of the Western World* (London, 1906), Vol. II, P. 209.
21 This has been dealt in Chapters III & IV.
22 R.S. Sharma, *Perspectives in Social and Economic History of Early India* (New Delhi, 1983), P. 14.

royal grants of land called *vaisyagraharas* and traders from Kalinga were known as *Kalinga Vyapari*[23]. Apart from being landowners and traders, the *Vaisyas* were engaging themselves as *kumbhakaras* (potters) and telikas (oilmen) [24]. The *vaisyas* were major group among persons going in ships for trading purpose. They were known as *sadhabas* and their descendants are still residing as *Kumuti* caste in coastal areas of southern Orissa and eastern Andhra Pradesh[25]. They are Saivites and trade and commerce are their main profession. The worship of Siva had a historical background as the *sadhabas* were worshipping him before the onset of journey. The *vaisyas* were also known as *saudagaras* while taking journey to distant lands[26].

Specific reference to the *sudra* caste could be found in the Arasavalli plates of Vajrahasta-III[27]. They subsisted on service to the higher caste and were living on the outskirts of villages and cities. Various professional and artisan groups came under this fold: blacksmith or *lauhakara*, goldsmith or *suvarnakara*, brazier or *kamsakara*, coppersmith or *tamrakara*,

---

23 Rajguru, n.9, Vol II, P. 75 and Vol V, P. 850.
24 *Epigraphia India*, XXXI, Pp. 17ff.
25 H. Qanungo, "Odiya Sahityare Naubimanakara Jibanadhara" in K.S. Behera ed, *Sagara O Sahitya* in Oriya (Cuttack, 1993), P. 220. Some of the inscriptions mention the word *Kumuti*. The grant of Narasimha II dated 1296 A.D. says about a *Kumuti* merchant Mankusresthi living in Tuchuda village. See Rajguru, n.9, Pp. 293ff. The Ganga inscriptions of 11th century mention this word while referring to the *vaisya* caste. See K. Sundaram, "The vaisya Community in Medieval Andhra" in *Journal of the Andhra Historical Research Society*, XXX, P. 11.
26 G. Giri and N. Mahapatra, *Dhaneswara Saudagara Suanga* in Oriya (Cuttack, 1901), referred in Qanungo, n. 25, P. 215.
27 *Epigraphia Indica*, XXXII, P. 310.

carpenter or *patakara,* mason *or sutradhara,* stonecutter or *silakuta,* milkmen or *gopala,* fisherman or *kaivartta* etc.[28] The last mentioned caste was playing an important role in making boats and ships engaged in trade and commerce. In the month of *Chaitra* (March to April), on the fool moon day, the *Kaivirttas* worship Goddess Baseli with elaborate ritual. She is also known as *bandareswari* or protector of ports. In the folklore of Orissa, life of *Kaivartta* is amply reflected[29].

Overseas Trade

Due to flourishing trade and commerce since ancient days, the economic condition of Orissa was strong. It was producing goods and commodities like paddy, cereal, cotton, sugar cane, medicinal herbs, ivory, timber, iron ores, precious stones etc. in such abundance that after satisfying domestic needs, some of these items were being exported. The Orissan merchants collected those items through internal trade. There used to be market or *hatta* serving a number of areas as evident from the inscription of Jaipur of 7th-8th century C.E. and the Puri copper-plate inscription of Ganga king Bhanudeva II dated 1312 C.E.[30] The Kalibhana plates of Janmejaya (882.922 C.E.) of the Somavamsis refer to *Vipani* or bazar[31]. Through commercial activities certain places developed as trading centres like Angulaka, Dantapura, Suvarnapura, Vinitapura, Murasimapattana and Varanasi Kataka. Hsuan-tsang had mentioned that Kalinga was connected with Tamralipti and Karnasubarna in the north and Andhra in the south[32].

28　*Ibid,* xxviii, P. 256.
29　Qanungo, n. 25, Pp. 215ff.
30　*Epigraphia Indica,* XXVIII, P. 256.
31　Rajguru, n.9, IV, Pp. 100-104.
32　Watters, n. 10, Pp. 193ff.

The overseas trade of Orissa was carried by merchants through maritime activities by venturing into distant land since early times. Navigation in the Bay of Bengal had been carried out since pre-historic time. Orissa has a long seacoast stretching about kilometres, which has been exploited for establishing long distance maritime contacts. Dotted with ports like Dantapura, Pithunda, Palura, Tamralipti etc; the glory of Orissa as a maritime power was so great that Kalidasa, referred to the king of Kalinga as 'lord of the sea' or *mahodadhipati* in his *Raghuvamsa*. Though no definite evidence is there as regards the motive behind maritime activities, it could be safely presumed that commercial zeal and love of foreign trade were the compelling forces. Under royal patronage, there was acceleration of trade and commerce. The art of navigation formed a part of curriculum of princes of Kalinga. Migration of population from Orissa at the time of political turmoil might have been also there. Existence of seaports and availability of materials for export gave impetus to overseas trade. Due to major role played by the people of Kalinga, the migrants in Southeast Asia are still known as *Keling* or *Kling* and this has been varified by the author in his field trip to the region.

Ample information regarding Orissa's maritime activities could be known from literary sources. As the merchants of Orissa had not left records of their oceanic voyages, the author has to depend upon scattered references in Indian and foreign literary sources. The eastern sea or modern Bay of Bengal was known sometimes s the 'Kalinga Sea' as evident from the Mahayana Buddhist text, *Aryamanjusrimulakalpa*, which mentions about *Kalingodresu* or all islands in the Kalinga sea. Asoka's invasion of Kalinga in 261 B.C.E. was to gain dominance over trade centres and natural resources of the region. The great strength of

Kalinga was derived from its maritime trade. Kalinga's importance as a maritime power could be gleaned from classical texts like Periplus, Pliny's Natural History and Potelmy's Geography. Pliny places Kalinga on the seacoast and the anonymous author of the *Periplus of the Erythrean Sea* mentions about the availability of best quality of ivory in coastal Orissa[33]. Ptolemy refers about several ports of eastern coast including Palura, which acted as point of departure for sea voyages to Southeast Asia[34]. The Chines pilgrim Hsuan-tsang has referred to the city named Che-li-ta-lo situated on the shore of the ocean, which was a resting-place for sea-going traders and strangers from distant lands[35]. The chronicles like *Dipavamsa, Mahavamsa, Culavamsa, Manimekalai* etc mention about close political, cultural and commercial contacts between Kalinga and Sri Lanka[36]. The Orissan sailors were very much acquianted with sea route to Sri Lanka. Some stray references about Orissa's maritime activities are there in *Majjahima Nikaya, Mahabhaga, Jatak* stories, *Kathakosa* etc. There are some indigenous Oriya literary sources[37] giving references to role of Orissa in navigation of the Bay of Bengal. However, these are written after fourteenth century and evidences mentioned there in should be corroborated by other sources like epigraphic, archaeological, architectural etc which has been mentioned subsequently in this chapter. In the *Mahabharata* of Sarala Das, who was a contemporary

---

33   W.H.Schoff, *The Periplus of the Erythrean Sea* (London, 1912), Pp. 42 ff.
34   McCrindle, n. 13, Pp. 22ff.
35   Watters, n. 10, P. 194.
36   K.K. Pillay, *South India and Sri Lanka* (Madras, 1975), Pp. 71, 119, 121 & 132.
37   K.C. Sahu, "Oriya Sahityare Boita Banijara Smruti" in Behera, n. 25, Pp. 44-46.

of Gajapati king Kapilendradeva, there is reference to Java and Sumatra. In the *Lavanyavati* of Upendrabhanja, it has been mentioned that ships were going to the island of Sri Lanka[38].

The maritime activities and cultural transmission of Orissa are things of past, but its reminiscences are there in folklore and festivals. People still recollect with a sense of nostalgia about oceanic voyages. A number of stories are there in folklore's which speak of *sadhabas* or merchants going to distant countries with their flotlla or *boita* and coming back with lots of treasure. The most popular legend relates to the story of Tapoi[39], who suffered a lot at the hands of her sister-in-laws. Her seven brothers belonging to a rich *sadhaba* family had gone to distant lands for trade and commerce by seven ships. When her brothers returned with treasure, wives were suitably punished. This story is commemorated in the festival of *Khudurukuni* in the month of August-September or *Bhadra*. One important aspect of this ritual observed by women folk is worship of ships. The people of coastal Orissa, particularly the fishermen and cultivators celebrate a festival known as *Dutibahana Usa* which speaks of important role played by the *sadhabas*[40].

---

38   *Boita Lagila Asi Simhala Dvipare*, Lavanyavati, Canto-17, Verse 1. In the *Rasakallola* of Dinakrusna Das, there are also description of journey by ships. In a Bangali work entitled *Candimangala* of Mukundarama, there is description of Puri, where journey by sea begins. The eighteenth century Sanskrit work, *Garigabansanucharitam* mentions the oceanic voyage through the lake Chilika. Sea, Sahu, n. 37, Pp. 44-47.

39   K.P. Mohanty, *Bratakatha O Parvaparbanire Samudrajatrara Suchana*, in Behera, n. 25, Pp. 163-65.

40   A.P. Pattanaik, "Smruti O Bismrutira Ketoti Chhinnasutra" in Behera, n. 25, Pp. 107-11. The *Dalkhai usa* mentions

Memory of Orissa's oceanic voyages is to be found in the famous *Balijatra* festival that is celebrated on the foolmoon day in the month of *Kartika* (October-November). Miniature boats with burning lamp inside are floated. It is said that on this auspicious day, the *sadhabas* were going to Bali island[41]. The *Balijatra* is celebrated on the sands of river Mahanadi with thousands of people observing the ritual of floating miniature boats. In the innumerable folklore of Orissa the tradition of overseas trade is amply reflected. In the folk songs of the rural women, there is desire for the costly articles that were being brought earlier by the *sadhabas*. One folklore speaks about a woman's aspiration that her father-in-law would be king of village, mother-in-law the queen, her husband the emperor and she herself the chief queen[42]. In another song, the spinsters are said with satire that their future husbands are from *Javadvipa*[43]. The merchants were returning with lots of treasure and the relatives were

---

about ship building. Festival like *Satynarayan puja, Trinatha mela* and *Sanschara mela* etc also represent stories of *sadhabas* and their role in trade and commerce. See N.C. Panda, "Úsa bratare nau-banijya paramparara suchana", in Behera, n. 25, Pp. 156ff. In the *dipabali* festival also drawings of ships are made and *dipadana* is reminescent of paying homage to ancestors by the *sadhabas* see, Mohanty, n. 31, Pp. 166-167.

41   Mohanty, n. 39, Pp. 165-6.
42   Pathani Pattanaik, "Odissara lokakathare Samudrajatra" in Beheran, n. 25, P.75. The song goes like this. "Sasura hoibe ga rajana lo, sasu hoithibe rani... mo girastha heba kanak rajan, mun hebi patarani".
43   *Ibid.* "Achhi Achhi bara jhia jabadwipa ghare". In another, coastly ornaments like diamond, pearl etc are mentioned : "*Mesa chakshyu nila, brahmajati hira, tara mukuta kukuta dimba para*".

hopeful that they would receive golden toothbrush[44]. Thus, festivals and folklore point to Orissa's maritime activities in the past.

Ships

The ships were main forms of transport for trade of maritime kingdoms of Orissa. Close association of Orissa with ships and commerce finds place in numerous images on temple walls. The roof of Vaital temple itself resembles on overturned boat. On the *bhogamandapa* of Jagannatha temple at Puri, there is a sculptural representation of a boating scene having four females oaring the boat. A sculpture from Konarka depicts a boat with an elephant at bow and a royal person sitting near the centre. A frieze collected near Brahmesvara temple of Bhubaneswara depicts a large boat carrying an elephant and some humans and another slab depicts image of Mahisasuramardini with a boat below pedestal. On each portal of the roof of *jogamohana* of Konarka temple, the Ghantakarna Bhairavas are depicted dancing on a boat[45]. At Ratnagiri there are scenes of shipwreck on the relief carvings. The Goddesses Durga and Tara are invoked

---

44   J.B.. Mohanty, "Odia loka gitare nau-chalanara parampara" in Behera, n. 25, P. 117. The folksong goes like this : *Mo bhai asiba daria kati lo, hate suna dantakathi*. The sailors were going to distant lands after crossing seven seas for buying and selling : *Sata samudra arapare ho kariba kina bika*, Ibid. Even name of different commodities like textiles, salt, lime, spices, sandal wood used in trade are mentioned in the folklors : *Jahaji guaku lo ae gujurati, bohunka panakhia bada aniti... tankikia sadhi takara more, kali asiba baotia bhare*, Ibid, Pp. 117-8.

45   T.E. Donaldson, "Navigation and Maritime Goddesses of Orissa", in *Studies in History and Culture* Vol. 2, 1994 P. 3.

for safe journey on the seas. In the Ramacandi temple near Konarka, the image of Durga was worshipped for safety in navigation. The image of Tara of Ratnagiri dated to late eighth century has scenes of eight great perils carved on the back-slab. In the jalarnava-bhaya scene, three persons in a sinking ship invoke the Goddess to save them from drowning[46]. In the state museum of Orissa, there are four palm-leaf manuscripts depicting the pictures of boats. The prows of two boats are bird and elephant shaped. In the museum of department of History, Sambalpur University the palm leaf manuscript of the *Bhagavata Purana* written by Brajanatha Badajena (1730-99) contains the picture of a boat, where Raja Satyabrata was sitting with his family.

The *Arthasastra*[47] of Kautilya gives description of ship building activities in the Mauryan period. The superintendent of ships or *navadhyaksa* had department of navy under him. Kautilya had distinguished two types of ship; *pravahana* or ships meant for passengers and *samyati* or ocean going commercial ship. The ships were made of different kind of materials like bamboo, timber, inflated leather bags etc. Colandia type of ships of *author of the Periplus* was very large and meant for going to distant countries[48]. A fifth century C.E. work the *Silapadikaram* also mentions different type of boats and the eleventh century treatise *Yuktikalpataru* of Bhoja gives a detailed study of

---

46 *Ibid*, P. 18. In another image of Tara of late tenth or early eleventh century, the boat is no longer seen. In the third image of Astamahabhya -Tara in the Jalarnava-bhaya scene, the boat is also no longer visible. *Ibid*, Pp. 18-19.
47 R.P. Kangla, ed, *Arthasastra* (Bombay, 1969) Pp. 82ff.
48 Colandia is derived from Sanskrit *Kolantarapota*. The other kind of ships were Cotymba, Sangara, Trappaga etc. Schoff, n. 33, pp. 243-46.

ship-building industry in India[49]. There are many works dealing with art of shipbuilding like *Jalayana, Bahitra kirti Vaibhava* and *Visaka Nidesa* by writers from Orissa[50]. Some literary works in Bengali of fifteenth century C.E. like *Manasa Mangala* of Vamsi Dasa and *Candikavya* of Kavikankana Mukundadeva depict ships plying on the eastern coast of India[51]. The former has mentioned ships like Samkhachura, Chhatighati, Kajalarekhi, Durgabara, Manikya Merua, Rajavallabha, Hamsakhala, Udayagiri, Gangaprasad etc. *Candikavya* has mentioned trading centres like Puri, Banapura and Kalingapattanam and named seven kinds of ships, Madhukara, Gourekhi, Ranajaya, Ranabima, Mahakaya, Sarvadhana and Natasala. The ship building industries developed in seventeenth century, when ports like Harishpur, Pipli and Balasore developed and became centres of shipbuilding[52]. This might be due to the coming of European and availability of raw materials like timber.

The ships from the coasts of Orissa sailed with the help of monsoon winds. Taking advantage of pattern of monsoon and wind circulation, the sailors sailed in one monsoon and returned in another. As the monsoon blows from southwest from the month of *Asadha* to *Kartika* (June/July to October/November), the sailors started their journey at this time and returned in the month of October/November.

---

49   *Silappadikaram*, Canto XIII, II, and I.C. Sastri, ed, *Yuktikalpataru* (Calcutta, 1917), Pp. 223ff. The later work gives different kinds of woods used for building ships. It groups ships into two kinds, *samanya* and *visesa*.

50   C. Mohapatra, *Arnaba Vihara* referred in Pattanaik, n. 40, P. 86. But there is no trace of these works at present.

51   R.N. Das, *Odisare Arnaba Pota Nirmanara Parampara*, in Behera, n. 25,Pp.244-5.

52   K. Patra, *Ports in Orissa* (Bhubaneswar, 1988), P. 73.

The homecoming was celebrated on the *dipavali* night. From the month of *Kartika* to *Caitra* (October/November to March/April), the wind blows from the northeast. The morning hours of *Kartika Purnima* was considered the most auspicious day for starting the journey to southeast and southwest. To commemorate this tradition, *Baliyatra* is celebrated until today. The traders carry on the trade until the month of *Caitra* in Southeast Asia and their return home with ships full of imported materials was on the *Panasankranti* day in April[53]. At the time of journey, the ship had different kinds of persons performing varied tasks. The *Kaivarttas* were helmsman. For giving religious teachings as well as well as giving direction to the ship, the *brahmanas* were there, who were also known as *dalapati* or captain of the ship[54]. The *sadhabas* were the people who were owners of different commodities to be used for trading purpose. The *Patakaras* (carpenters) were incharge of repair of boats and *mallas* (musclemen) provided safety from pirates. The *nada jantra* was used to determine the speed of the boat, *pakshee jantra* to know the direction of the wind and *karma jantra* to determine the weather. Decorated with colorus, the prow of the ships were designed variously e.g., lion, tiger, elephant, duck and human head[55]. A large Kalingan ship used to carry about two hundred people[56] and would move about three hundred kilometres per day. The sailors for a safe journey in face of natural calamities and danger from pirates required a lot of expertise.

---

53   C.B. Patel, "Navigation and Maritime tradition of ancient Kaling", in *Chilika Boita Bandana Ustava* (Puri, 1992), P. 20.
54   Qanungo, n. 25, Pp. 211-12.
55   R.K. Mookherjee, *Indian Shipping* (Calcutta, 1912), P. 25.
56   R.C. Majumdar, *Hindu Colonies in the Far-East* (Calcutta, 1944), P. 8.

Items of Import and Export

As a maritime power, Orissa was exporting and importing various types of commodities. Items were brought from vast hinterland by land and water routes to different ports on the eastern coast. These ports like Palura, Tamralipti, Pithunda, Chelitalo also received goods through coastal routes from different parts of India. Palura was connected with South India through coastal route. The goods that were exported from Orissa are mentioned in works like Jataka, *Arthasastra* of Kautilya, *Mahabhasya* of Patanjali and *Indica* of Megasthenes. The fame of Kalinga as producer of fine textile continued from the time of Mauryas onwards. According to the *Mahabharata*, Kalinga was producing best type of cotton goods and their fame for weaving clothes was so much that the word 'Kalinga' in old Tamil meant cloth[57]. When a piece of very fine Kalinga linen was presented to the king of Ayodha, the princess appeared naked after putting it on[58]. The sculptures carved in the caves of Khandagiri and Udayagiri had excellent design of garments on them. This was also true of sculptural representation of excellent fabrics in the medieval temples of Orissa. *The Regions of the World* or *Hudud al Alam* mentions that Orissa was producing large quantities of cotton[59]. Textile export from Orissa continued unto late medieval period through ports like Pipli, Balasore and Hariharpur.

Diamond was another item of export. Both Kautilya and Ptolemy mentions about diamonds from Orissa and

---

57 A.C. Mittal, *An Early History of Kalinga* (Benaras, 962), P. 106.
58 K.S. Mishra, *History of Utkal* (Cuttack, 1951), P. 50.
59 V.Minorsky, ed *Hudud-al-Alam*, The Region of the World (London, 1937), P. 241. The Manasollasa (1127-38 A.D.) mentions about Orissan fabrics also.

much praise were lavished on diamonds obtained from Sambalpur region of Orissa in far away Rome[60]. According to *Brihat Samhita*, the finest quality of diamonds having lustre of *Sirisa* flower was found in the Kosala region[61]. Different sources like the *Mahabharata* and *Arthasastra* refer to best type of elephants of Kalinga. The ships were big enough to carry elephants. Hsuan-Tsang has mentioned that dark elephants of Kalinga were prized items in neighbouring countries and dark coloured elephants found in Kongoda mandala were capable long journey[62]. Therefore, it is not surprising that boats carrying elephants are represented on the sculptures of temples of Bhubaneswar and Konarka. Ivory also was another item of export as mentioned by the author of the *Periplus* and *Hudud-ul-Alam*. Orissa was exporting spices and semi-precious stones to Rome and pepper, ivory, elephants, betelnuts, drugs, diamonds and cotton textiles to China. Other items of export were aloes, rotang and conch-shells[63]. Rice was another important item of export. Orissa was in the rice route from Coromandel,

---

60 G.E. Gerini, *Researches on Potolemy's Geography of Eastern Asia* (New Delhi, 1974), Pp. 17, 71. Diamonds of Sambalpur were also sold in places like Greece, Iran and Egypt. There was presence of diamod mines of Hirakud of Sambalpur, where the present Hirakud dam is located. A professional class of people known as *Jharias* were collecting diamonds under state supervision. See S.P. Das, *Glories in Ancient India* (Sambalpur, 1964), P. 64.
61 V.S. Sastri and M.R. Bhat ed, *Brihat Samhita* (Bangalore, 1974), Chapter VIII.
62 Watters, n.10, Pp. 196-98.
63 Minorsky, n. 59, P. 87. Cereals, wheat, barley, salt, incense, timber, stone, iron-products etc. were also items of export. See A.P. Sah, *Life in Medieval Orissa* (Varanasi,1976), Pp. 110-11.

Bengal and Sumatra[64]. From Nubin, a port town of the Bhaumakaras, corn was being exported to Sumatra[65]. A traveller of sixteenth century Ralph Fitch has mentioned that ship from Malacca and Sumatra were coming to Hijli port of Orissa to take rice, cotton, cloth, sugar and butter[66]. From the ports of Pipli and Balasore, rice and muslin were exported to Pegu and Tenasserim in Myanmar (Burma).

Sandalwood was imported from Indonesian islands since the Mauryan period. Around first century B.C.E. ships from Rome and Greece were touching the port of Arikamedu and Palur and were going to the South East Asian countries. While returning, items like spices, aloeswood, sandalwood, resin, silk, copper and porcelain were brought. Orissa's involvement in Roman trade accelerated in first century C.E. and excavated sites of Sisupalgarh had yielded rouletted ware, iron callrops and foreign coins[67]. Tin, tortoise-shell, clove, silk, candy, and camphor were items of import from Southeast Asia. The *History of the Sung Dynasty* writes about the items like gold, silver, rhinoceros horn, elephants, pearls, camphor, sandalwood, pepper, silk etc brought from Java[68]. The glossy shell, *cowrie*, a medium of exchange in medieval Orissa was imported from the Maldives. Ceramics from China was an important item that was coming to Orissa as

---

64   G.Bouchon, "Sixteenth Century Malabar and The Indian Ocean" in A. Dasgupta and M.N. Pearson, ed, *India and the Indian Ocean* (Calcutta, 1987),P. 167.

65   Minorsky, n.59, P. 86.

66   R. Fitch, *Early Travels in India* (London, 1899), P. 26.

67   B. B. Lal, "Sisupalgarh" in *Orissa Historical Research Journal* (Bhubaneswar, 1967), Vol. XV, Pp. 54-55.

68   H.B. Sarkar, *Cultural Relations between India and South East Asian Countries* (New Delhi, 1983), P. 251.

evident from excavation at Khalakapatna near Konarka[69]. In the fifteenth and sixteenth century, the ports of Balasore and Pipli assumed much more importance. There was vigorous trade with place like Bantam, Pegu, Tenasserim, Achin and Malacca of Southeast Asia. The Portuguese were playing an important role in the commercial relations between Coromandel coast of Tamil country and Malacca[70]. Articles like brocade, brocatele, velvet, satin, taffeta etc were brought from Malacca, Sumatra and Borneo by Portuguese to Orissa and Bengal. Land and interestingly elephants were imported from Tenasserim in Myanmar. Thomas Bowery, a traveller records that merchants from Balasore and Pipli were going to Tenasserim to bring elephants[71].Thailand also had trading centres in Balasore, which were involved in trade of elephant and lead. Two large ships belonging to the Thai king brought elephants from Tenasserim[72].

Ports

Possessing a long coastline, Orissa had number of seaports through which Orissa had cultural and commercial intercourse with outside world. Places like Tamralipti, Pithunda, Palura, Kalinganagara, Che-li-to-lo became famous in international map. In late medieval period,

---

69   K.S. Behera, "Maritime Contacts of Orissa, Literary and Archaeological evidence" in *Utkal Historical Research Journal*, V, 1994, P.64.
70   S.J. Stephens, "Entreport of Malacca in the trading world of South East Asia and Portuguese networks of overseas commerce with the ports of Tamil country in South India" in *Journal of the Institute of Asian Studies* XII,pp. 16ff.
71   T. Bowrey, *A Geographical Account of Countries Round the Bay of Bengal, 1669 to 1679* (London, 1905), Pp. 179-80.
72   S. Master, *Draries of Streynsham Master 1675-1680 and other contemporary papers relating thereto* Vol. II (London, 1911), P. 236.

Pipli, Balasore, Hijli and Harishpur rose into prominence. Tamralipti or present Tamluk in Midnapore district of Bengal was an outlet for vast hinterland of eastern India and outlet to Southeast Asia and Sri Lanka. Midnapore was taken away from Orissa and incorporated in Bengal at the time of Mushid Quli Khan I (1714-1727 C.E.)[73]. According to the tradition of the *Mahabharata,* Bhima proceeded to Sumatra from Tamralipti[74]. The *Mahavmsa* and *Rajavalliya* refers to port of Tamralipti and mentions that prince Vijaya of Kalinga took seven days to reach Sri Lanka. Mahendra and Samghamitra travelled from Tamralipti to Sri Lanka with the Bodhi tree. The *Kathasaritasagara* mentions the importance of the port and an emporium centre during the period from fourth to twelfth century C.E. It also figures in the works of Pliny, Ptolemy, Fa-Hien, I-Tsing and Hsuan-Tsang[75]. The archaeological findings had unearthed copper coins, terracotta figures, rouletted wire and silver coins bearing Buddhist symbols[76].

Tamralipti was well connected with leading cities like Taxila, Mathura, Varanasi etc by land route and covered places of Orissa like Tosali, Lalitgiri, Jajpur and Soro. Tamralipti received good from all these places and afterwards ships made sea voyages to Myanmar, Malay, peninsula Indonesia and Indo-China. When the Murndas were ruling over Kalinga, there was export of horses from Tamralipti to Funan and Ko-Ying kingdom of

---

73 G.H. Salim, *Riyaz-us-Salatin,* trans by Maulavi Abdus Salem (Calcutta, 1902), P.255.

74 Referred in Sila Tripathy and S.R. Rao, "Tamralipti : The Ancient Port of India in *Studies in History and Culture,* II, 1994, P.34.

75 *Ibid*, P. 35.

76 *Ibid*, P. 34.

Java-Sumatra[77]. The trade between Tamralipti and other ports of Ganga Empire is proved by discovery of Ganga fanams from the port. Grains, earthenware, textile and glass were other items of export from this region. Spice was an important import item. The decline of the port started from around tenth century due to siltation in the river coarse, outside invasion and political anarchy.

The reference to Cheli-ta-lo appears in the account of Hsuan-Tsang during his visit to Odra kingdom in 638 C.E. Situated on the southeast of the kingdom and famous for rare and precious commodities, it was "a thoroughfare and resting place for seagoing traders and strangers"[78]. It was an important centre of Buddhism having five Buddhist vihars. The identification of this port with Charitra or modern Puri has been proved by number of scholars[79]. Recent archaeological findings have solved the problem of identification to an extent. The Khalkattapatna port situated near the mouth of river Kushabhadra could one of probable place but it had

---

77   P.P. Mishra, "Orissa's Cultural Contact with South-East Asia" in P.K. Mishra, ed, *Comprehensive History and Culture of Orissa*, Vol. I (New Delhi, 1997) In Print.
78   Wattern, n. 10, Pp. 193-94.
79   Cunningham identifies it with Puri presuming that it was one of five Buddhist *stupas* dedicated to Jagannatha. Cunningham, n.4, P. 430. N.K.Sahu argues that it stands for Sriksetra; Cheli standing for Sri and talo for tra and middle syllable kse being dropped. See, Sahu, n.2, P. 142. P.K. Roy suggests that it may be identified with Chitresvari situated at the confluence of Kadua river and the Bay of Bengal. P.K. Roy, "Karuma, An Ancient Buddhist Site" in *Orissa Historical Research Journal*, XXIV, 1981, P. 95. It has been identified with Manikpatna, See, A.K. Pattanayak, "Identification of the Port of Che-li-ta-lo : A Review" in *Utkal Historical Research Journal*, VI, 1995, P. 50.

proved to be a port of later period than Hsuan-Tsang's time. It could be identified with the recently excavated port of Manikpatna. Located on the bank of water channel connecting the Chilka lake with Bay of Bengal, it lies on the southeast of Odra as mentioned by the Chinese traveller. It was an ancient port as Puri-Kushana coins had been found in the region. Manikpatna was a fortified city also. So all evidences point to identification of Che-li-ta-lo with Manikpatna.

The port of Palur had enjoyed great reputation as a flourishing harbour and port-town from early Christian period. It is still in existence as a village named Paloor in the Chatrapur area of Ganjam. Sea voyages to Malay Peninsula were undertaken from here and the ships entered high seas from Palur after ceasing to follow the littoral line. The *Jatakas* mention it as ancient capital of Kalinga and the sacred tooth-relic of Buddha was said to have been taken to Sri Lanka from here. In the Nagarjunkonda inscription of third century C.E.[80]. Palur has been mentioned as an emporium. Ptolemy refers to the point of departure or apheterion for ships going to Myanmar immediately to south of Palura, which is Gopalpur-on-sea. The early Gangas made it their capital in 496 C.E. It has also been identified with the capital of Sailodbhavas. When they were driven out by the Bhaumakaras, the Sailodbhavas started their journey from Palur to the Suvarnadvipa and established a new dynasty know as Sailendras[81]. Suvakarasimha, a prince of Bhaumakara dynasty and renowned scholar

---

80   Sarkar, n. 68, P. 231. Nagarjunkonda was connected with Palura and Tosali, places of Buddhist importance.

81   S.C. Behera, *Rise and Fall of Sailodbhavas* (Calcutta, 1981), P. 197. This view is not accepted there days due to lack of sufficient proof.

went at the court of the Chinese emperor Hsuan Tsung and translated into the Chinese the *Mahavairochana Sutra*. He had embarked probably from the port of Palur in 715 C.E.[82] The tenth century Bateswara Mahadeva temple on the sea shore at Palur was said to have been worshipped by trading community before going to the high seas for a safe journey. Archaeological excavations of Palur had revealed potteries of Chinese origin belonging to twelfth century[83]. Therefore, probably Palur retained its trading link with outside world until that period. Acting as an emporium of Orissan commercial activity, Palur was exporting diamond, silver, pearl, and ivory, elephants, textiles etc and importing camphor, sandalwood, tin, copper and zinc from Southeast Asia[84].

From the time of Mahavira, Pithunda was a flourishing port as mentioned in the Jaina *Uttaradhyayana Sutra* and the Hathigumpha inscription of Kharavela has referred to its antiquity. Ptolemy positions it as equidistant between the mouths of Mahanadi and Godavari. Therefore, it may be located near Chicacole and Kalinga patnam to the south of Dantapur[85]. The people of Campa used to visit the port. Konarka at the mouth of old river Candrabhaga was

---

82 K.S. Behera, "Maritime trade in Ancient Orissa" in M.N. Das, ed, *Sidelights on History and Culture of Orissa* (Cuttack,1975), Pp. 119-20. Ibn Khurdadbin's geographical work mentions the itinerary along eastern coast. Kanja has been identified with Ganjam. Al-lava may be identified with Palur. See J.K. Pattanaik, "Palur Port Through the Ages" in *Studies in History and Culture* II, 1994, P. 28.
83 The excavations had also yielded Chinese celadonware, Roman rouletted wire, amphora piece etc. See Pattanaik, n. 82, P. 29.
84 *Ibid*, Pp. 29-30.
85 Sahu, n.2, P. 87.

a seaport. Such a gigantic temple of Konarka could never have been built without an outlet to water. Huge blocks of stones could not have been carried without the help of large boats. The sculptural representation of boats and a picture of giraffe add the plausibility of Konarka being a port. Dantapur as the capital of Kalinga had been referred in *Jatakas* and chronicles of Sri Lanka. It has been variously identified with Rajamahendri, Chicacole, Palura and Tekkali. Recently it has been identified with Radhanagar of Dharmasala in Jajpur district on the basis of accounts given in *Dhatavamsa* and archaeological excavation[86]. It was well connected by land and sea route to other areas in the country and abroad. Some of the medieval ports like Puri, Kalingapatanam and Banpur have been mentioned in Bengali literature[87]. The excavations conducted at Manikpatna near Chilka lake have yielded rouletted ware, amphora, Burmese ware etc proving the importance of it as an entrepot of indigenous and foreign merchants[88]. It has been mentioned earlier the importance of ports like Hijli, Balasore and Pipli in late medieval period. The medieval Arabic nautical sailing directories have mentioned about the Faradib or Paradip Port situated on the coastal route to Southeast Asia[89].

---

86   H. Prusty and others, "Dantapura, the Capital of ancient Kalinga : A Reappraisal in *Studies in History and Culture*, III, 1995, Pp.10ff.

87   S.K. Panda, *Medieval Orissa : A Socio-EconomicStudy* (New Delhi, 1991), P. 66. Banpur can be identified with modern Banpur on the bank of the river Salia near Chilka lake. Kalingapatnam is situated on bank of the river Vamsadhara.

88   Behera, n. 69, Pp. 62ff.

89   H.B. Sarkar, *Trade and Commercial Activities of Southern India in the Malayo-Indonesian world* (Calcutta, 1986), P. 245 Some believe that Paradip as a naval centre existed in an-

Cultural Milieu

The Orissan culture forming an essential part of cultural mainstream of India has retained its predominantly indigenous features providing a distinct identity. Developing itself within the syndrome of pan-Indian civilization, it has developed unique characteristics and thus enriched the Indian panorama. The reasons for developing the indigenous as well as Indian aspect were many.Acting as a bridge between northern and southern India, Orissa was open to cultural influence from all sides. The pre-historic and proto-historic migratory movements have made population of Orissa composed of diverse elements. River belts of Suvarnarekha, Vaitarani, Brahmani, Mahanadi and Rishikulya having diagonal directions made human contact easier. This cultural impact from all sides has been creatively synthesized to produce a unique Orissan culture. In its turn, Orissa disseminated this to neighbouring regions as well as Southeast Asia. The long coastline with its numerous ports facilitated the task. Southeast Asian region bear the evidences of Orissan culture in their tradition, place name, literature, rituals, art and architecture.

The general political stability was an added factor for the growth of Orissan culture. From pre-Christian centuries, there was rise and fall of powerful kingdoms until its decline in mid-sixteenth century. The dynasties like the Chedis, Matharas, Nalas, Sailodbhavas, Bhaumekaras, imperial Gangas and Gajapatis kept their kingdoms well-integrated politically and had left indelible impression on the cultural life of Orissa. Under royal patronage, artistic

---

cient times. A village near it, Boitakuda was a harbour for ships in ancient times. See H.B. Mohanty, "Development of a Port of Paradip" in *Orissa Review* XIV, 1957, P. 77ff.

and architectural wonders were created. The aesthetic sense and creative talent of people made Orissan culture acclaimed internationally. Architects of Orissa constructed grandiose monuments, sculptures designed exquisite icons and artists created famous *patta* paintings. It was Orissa, which produced Visnusarma and Jayadeva.

All the ramifications of Buddhism, Jainism and Hinduism were deep rooted on the soil of Orissa. The supreme faith of the deeply religious people of Orissa made the region stronghold of Jainism, Buddhism, Saivism and Vaisnavism. These kept on thriving in Orissa for a longer period after decline in their original place of prominence. The evergreen cult of Lord Jagannatha bringing under its fold right from animism to Vaisnavism has attracted pilgrims for centuries. Ranging from Vaisnavites of Bengal to international society for Krishna consciousness, the religious impact is clearly perceptible. The saints like Sankar, Chaitanya, Kabir and Nanak felt attracted towards Orissa. Here developed a liberal brand of Islam with the cult of *pir* worship. Orissa had a fine tradition of religious toleration. The proclamation of Kharavela in first century B.C.E. that he was 'worshiper of all religions and repairer of temples of all sects' could be applied to people of Orissa in general.

Archaeological endeavours in eighties and nineties have unearthed rich cultural heritage of Orissa in pre-history times. Proof of various stone age cultural sequence, metal age as a link between pre-history and early history, excavation of ports, discovery of rock arts etc have added new dimension to cultural heritage of Orissa. However, legendary accounts and literary sources are not that authentic like archaeological sources, they throw some light on early cultural history. From sixth century B.C.E.

onwards, cultural history is on firm footing. Both Jainism and Buddhism flourished in Orissa. From the Kalinga war of 261 B.C.E. begins the documented history of Orissa. Due to this cataclysmic event, Asoka became remorseful and turned his attention towards Buddhism.

Under Kharavela of first century B.C.E., eastern India and Deccan were under Kalingan suzerainty. Jainism flourished centring round Khandagiri and Udayagiri caves. The tradition of cave architecture reached its excellence. After a period of disunity, the Satavahanan and Murundas ruled over Kalinga. Under the domination of the Murundas from second to fourth century C.E., there was growth of Buddhism, Nagarjuna, the famous Buddhist philosopher was residing in the Gandhamardan hills of Orissa. Dantapur not only became a holy place for Buddhists as it was enshrining the sacred tooth relic of Buddha in a *stupa* but also it was an important port. Samudragupta's defeat of six rulers of Kalinga and South Kosala region resulted in popularity of classical texts and numerous architectural device and sculptural decorations. The Mathara (350-520 C.E.) rule was marked by rise of new urban centres like Simhapura, Pistapura, Devapura etc and some believed that Visnusarma wrote the famous *Panchatantra* during this period. In about 600 C.E. the eastern Gangas began their rule over Kalinga with their capital at Kalinganagar on present Mukhalingam near Srikakulum in Andhra Pradesh. The Sarvapuriyas and Nalas ruled over some parts of western Orissa in sixth and seventh century C.E. Over the Kongada region, the Sailodbhavas ruled from 610 C.E. to 750 C.E.In spite of rule by different dynasties, the cultural growth of Orissa was not impeded. The Kalinga style of architecture developed. The Gods and Goddesses adorned the outer walls of temples and decorative aspect of religious shrines developed. There was also the existence of Ratnagiri mahavihara in fifth and sixth century C.E. Hsuan Tsang's account gives a good deal of idea of places of Buddhist importance like Che-li-ta-lo, Po-lo-mo-lo-ki-li and Pu-sie-po-ki-li.

The rule of Bhaumakaras and Somavamsis is marked by cultural efflorescence in Orissa. Buddhism received new impetus under the Bhaumakaras and a ruler of this dynasty Sivakara. Unmattasimha sent an autographed copy the religious text *Gandavyuha* to his contemporary Chinese emperor Te-Tsong. From the Buddhist shrines of these periods icons of Dhyani-Buddhas, Avalokitesvara, Tara, Manjusri have been discovered. The Brahmanical cults also made rapid strides. Under the Bhaumakaras, Pasupata sect of Saivism made its ascendancy. The Shakta shrines like Vaitrala, Mohini and Uttaresvara temples came up. Kongoda, Utkala, Kosala and Kalinga regions were amalgamated into one political unit by the Somavamsis, under whose reign the famous temples of Lingaraja; Rajarani, Muktesvara etc were constructed at Bhubaneswar. From Kaunaj *brahmanas* came and settled here. There was also tremendous progress in education and literature. The internal and overseas trade continued to flourish. Orissa's cultural influence in Southeast Asia, Sri Lanka and China was another notable achievement in this period.

Under the imperial Gangas, Orissa had an extensive kingdom stretching from Ganga to Godavari. The monumental edifices like the Jagannatha temple at Puri and Sun temple at Konark were constructed. Carvings on the temples visualize a deep sensuous appreciation of human form and expressiveness giving an exquisite beauty of their own. Vaisnavism became popular due to Jayadeva the author of *Gitagovinda*. A clear picture of social, religious and economic life of Orissa could be gleaned from numerous epigraphs of the period. There was also development of Oriya language. The tradition of music, dance and drama had continued from ancient days. Dance and music was performed by the dancers or *devadasis* and musicians in the chambered porch or *nata mandapa* in the temples of Orissa. The surface of *natamandapa* of Konark temple is adorned with carvings of dancing girls and their musicians. Jayadeva inspired this classical Odissi by composing songs. The poses of Odissi are 'frozen fluidity' and these are preserved accurately in the form of temple carvings.

In 1434 C.E. the rule of Suryavamsi Gajapatis started when Kapilendradeva assumed power. This period is remarkable for development of Oriya language and literature. The *Madla Panji,* chronicle of temple Jagannatha was written during this period. It deals with various festivals of the temple and activities of the ruling dynasties. The *Mahabharata* of Sarala Dasa written in Oriya is a unique literary achievement. There also emerged a group of poets-cum religious reformers known as *Pancha-sakhas*, whose missionary activities made Vaisnavism popular. The great Vaisnava saint Chaitanya came to Orissa in 1510C.E. and galvanized the religious environment. There was synthesis of many religious strands in the cult of Jagannatha during this period. However, the glorious tradition of temple building was over under the Gajapatis. There was also a setback to flourishing trade and commerce of Orissa. Decline had already started. After the greatest and powerful expansion under Kapilendradeva and Purusottamadeva, Orissa witnessed repeated invasions from outside. Political anarchy followed Prataprudra's death. There were frequent internecine wars. Finally, Orissa was conquered by the Afghanss in 1568.

Religion

Throughout ancient and medieval period of Orissa, life has been closely interlinked with various religions and religious sects. The three great religions of India, namely, Jainism, Buddhism and Hinduism had great pull upon the Orissan culture, which was reflected in art, architecture, literature, politics and outlook towards life. Traditional account of Jain literature mentions that Jaina Tirthankaras were associated with Orissa. In the sixth century B.C.E. Mahavira is believed to have visited it. The Jain *Harivamsa Purana* has mentioned that Mahavira preached his gospel in Kalinga and the line fourteen of Hathigumpha inscription has stated that "the wheel of victory was well turned on the Kumari hill"[90]. Pithunda the famous port was an important centre of Jaina culture. Kharavela, the great patron of Jainism brought back the sacred image of Kalinga Jina, which had been taken away by the Magadhan king earlier. Jainism continued to be a living religion. The Murunda king Maharajadhiraja Dharmadamadhara was a Jain as revealed from the gold coin excavated at Sisupalgarh[91]. Hsuan Tsang had stated that Jainism was in a flourishing condition in the region[92]. Afterwards the religion could not maintain its dominant position. However, the kings of Orissa did not develop any antagonism towards it. Under the Somavamsi king Udyotakesari, Khandagiri became pivotal point of building activities of Jainas. Jainism lost its vigour under Gangas and Gajapatis, who patronized the brahmanical faith. It continued to remain as a minor religious sect. The construction of large number of caves, monasteries and images of Jaina Tirthankaras have added to the cultural

---

90   Sahu, n. 2, P. 354.
91   J. Pattanaik, "Jainism in Orissa" in Das, n. 82, 312.
92   Watters, n. 10, P.196.

heritage of Orissa. For the people all over India, the twin hillocks of Udayagiri and Khandagiri are still a place of attraction.

Buddhism made a notable progress in Orissa. Though there is no reference of Buddha preaching his sermons here, the *Dathavamsa* mentions the existence of Buddhism before Asoka and worshipping of tooth-relic of Buddha in the Kalingan capital Dantapura. It was the Kaling war of 261 B.C.E. that changed the mind of Asoka, who became a patron of Buddhism. Coming of his brother Tissa to Kalinga, sending daughter Sanghamitra to Sri Lanka, the Asokan pillar at Bhubaneswar, the elephant figure in the Dhauli hill containing a set of rock edicts etc are examples of Orissa's close association with Buddhism. It also played a prominent part in spread of Buddhism in Myanmar and Sri Lanka as monks and missionaries went to these places from Kalingan centres of Buddhism like Dantapur, Tosali and Puspagiri[93]. Orissa had contributed much to the rise of Mahayanism in about first century C.E. The *Astsahsrika Prajnaparamita* was composed here and the philosopher Nagarjuna wrote a commentary of it in second century C.E. The monastery of this philosopher was located at Po-lo-mo-li-ki-li or Parimalgiri, which has been identified with modern Gandhamardan hills of western Orissa[94]. Under the Bhaumakaras, Ratnagiri became a centre of Buddhist religion, *tantras* and *Yoga*. As has been mentioned earlier

---

93 K.C. Rath, "Buddhism in Orissa" in Das, n. 82, P. 322.
94 K.N. Mohapatra, "Po-lo-mo-lo-ki-li of Hsuan-Tsang's Account" in *New Aspects of History of Orissa* (Sambalpur, 1971), P. 68. Hsuan Tsang had mentioned that Buddhism was flourishing in Odra having one hundred viharas. He saw five Budhist vihars in Chelitalo and in Polomolikili he came across number of temples with golden statute of Buddha, See Watters, n. 10, P. 193, 194 and 201.

the Chinese emperor, Te-tsang received the autographed manuscript from Sivakara. In the Tibetan work, *Pag Sam Jon Zang*, there is reference that *Odivisa* (Orissa) is the land of origin of Tantric Buddhism[95]. A large number of *Siddhas* also flourished here. Indrabhuti, the king of Sambalpur wrote the Tantric work *Jnanasiddhi* and his sister Lakshminkara propounded the Sahajayana cult. The Mahayana Buddhism influenced life, religion philosophy, and literature of Orissa. But gradual decline of Buddhism started from around tenth century C.E. due to monastic abuses, internal division within Buddhism and lack of royal patronage from the Somavamsis and Gangas, who were champions of brahmanical faith. The resurgent Hinduism endeavoured to assimilate the Buddhist doctrines by projecting Buddhas as an incarnation of Visnu. An amalgamation of two strands of cultural development; pre-Aryan and Aryan, Saivism was a flourishing religion in Orissa since early times. Ascribed to fourth century C.E., the Asanpat stone inscription having a beautiful Nataraja image is the earliest epigraphic evidence[96]. It became one of the strongest religious movements of Hindus. The ruling dynasties like Nagas, Nalas and the eastern Gangas became ardent follower of this faith. The tutelary deity of the Gangas was Gokarnasvami Siva worshipped on the crest of mount Mahendra. The Sailodbhavas of Kongoda mandal were devotees of Siva and the early Siva temples of Bhubaneswar were constructed by them. Under the Bhaumakaras the Lakulisa-Pasupata sect gained ascendancy and the images

---

95 Sahu, n. 2 Pp. 446-47. The Orissan Buddhacharyas of 7th and 8th centuries like Luipa, Savaripa, Indrabhuti etc had composed many texts on *Tantra* see Das, n.93, P. 324.
96 N.K. Sahu, *Odiya Jatria Itihasa*, Oriya, (Bhubaneswar, 1977), Vol I, P. 336.

of Lakulisa are found in the Muktesvara temple in various *mudras*. Saivism reached its climax in tenth and eleventh centuries C.E. under the Somavamsis. The Lingaraja temple is the most notable Saiva shrine in Orissa. When the imperial Gangas turned towards Jagannatha, Saivism suffered a setback. There were attempts for a synthesis of Saivism with Vaisnavism. Even the *linga* of Lingaraja temple was regarded as Hari Hara. The temple of Harisankara built around fifteenth century was another example of this synthesis.

The worship of Sakti as the primordial female power originated from very early times under names like Chandika, Kalai and Durga. A large number of tribal deities were incorporated like Stambhesvari (Pillar Goddess), Jajpur became famous as Viraja *kshetra*. Mahisamardini Durga is found in large number of places like Jajpur, Somesvara, Banki etc. Sakti is worshipped in Orissa in various forms like Mangala, Samalesvari, Varahi, Carcika, Kali, Vimala etc till-to-day. The Sakta-tantric cult also became popular in medieval Orissa. The Vaital temple, a Sakta shrine has sculptures showing an amalgamation of Saktism, Saivism and Mahayana Buddhism. Sakta-tantric worship had a great influence on the religious cults of Orissa. Several images of Vajrayana order of Buddhism appeared on Hindu temples. Even Jagannatha was conceived as Bhairava. The influence of Sakta-tantric cult resulted in the primordial deity of Buddhist pantheon Tara absorbing within herself a number of divinities. Sakta-tantric cult was a powerful rising movement in Orissa and its ascendancy was supported by rulers from the eighth to eleventh centuries.

Vaisnavism came to Orissa around fourth century C.E. at the time of Matharas focussing on the worship of paramabhagabata. The Saravapuriyas of western Orissa also embraced Vaisnavism. At the time of Chodagangadeva, Sri Ramanujacharya visited Orissa and impressed upon the ruler. Chodagangadeva, a devotee of Siva was converted to Vaisnavism along with his contemporary Jayabhanja Dev[97]. A Visnu image was installed in the Madhukesvara temple at Mukhallingam[98] and later on the king constructed a huge temple at Puri, the most important centre of Vaisnavism in Orissa in twelfth century for Purusottama and Laksmi Jayadeva in his *Gita Govinda* stressed the worship of Radha along with Krsna. The synthesis of Vaisnavism and Saivism also started and the cult of Jagannatha assimilated in its fold different creeds. Prataprudra's reign marks the climax of Vaisnavism. *Bhakti* movement was gathering momentum. The missionary activities of *Panchasakhas* with their emphasis on *prema-bhakti*, on vernacular language, casteless society etc had popularized Vaisnavism. The advent of Chaitnya exalted the Radha Krsna cult and made popular the concept of Jagannatha's identity with Krsna. His teachings became widespread. Vaisnavism had far-reaching consequences in the socio-religious life of Orissa.

Religious life of Orissa has been dominated by the cult of Purusottama-Jagannatha, an outstanding contribution of the region in the field of religion. Nilamadhba, the tribal deity of *savaras* was installed in the shape of Jagannatha. The Jagannatha iconography appears to be of a tribal look and the special group of priests in the temple known as *daitapatis* are supposed to be descendants of original tribal priests. Jagannatha has been referred in literary and epigraphic records as Purusottama and the term

---

97 *Epigraphia Indica*, Vol. XIX, P. 43.

98 H.V. Stietncorn, "The advent of Visnuism in Orissa" in Eschmann, n. 19, P. 23.

Jagannatha became popular in thirteenth century[99]. Puri also has been termed as Srikshetra after Purusottama and Laksmi. Codagangadeva had built the great temple for both. It is also known as Cakratirtha after the installation of Sudarsana *cakra* (disc), the important weapon of Visnu. The Puri Sudarsana does not have any disc but a wooden pole wrapped in cloth. Therefore, Puri Sudarsana was originally movable idol or *calanti pratima* of Jagannatha as in other Hinduized cults like Samalai of Sonepur and Bhagvati of Banpur[100]. It is carried around the city on certain occasions. Puri has another name as *Sankha ksetra* as the location of city looks like conch or *sankha*. Under the imperial Gangas and Gajapatis Jagannatha became the imperial cult and their main source of legitimization. As has been pointed earlier the cult of Jagannatha became synthesis of many religions. One sculpture carved on the *Bhogamandapa* on northern side is that of Durga Madhava, where Jagannatha is seen along with Durga and Siva. Customs and traditions of different sects and communities were taken together and coalesced into one religious cult for universal appeal. Puri is one of the four Hindu places of pilgrimage and an integrating factor in the cultural life of Orissa.

Art and Architecture

Orissa occupies a unique place in the art history of India due to its magnificent monuments and exquisite sculptures. When the Orisons went to neighboring countries, this distinctive style influenced great deal the art

---

[99] G.C. Tripathi, "On the concept of Purusottama in the Agamas" in Eschmann, n. 19, Pp. 36ff.

[100] Anncharlott. Eschmann, "Hinduization of Tribal Deities in Orissa : the Sakta and Saiva typology" in Eschmann, n. 19, Pp. 90-91.

tradition of those regions. The standardized architectural text, *Bhuvanapradipa* mentions three major categories of temples: *Rekha deula, pidha deula* and *khakhara deula*[101]. The first two generally form two components of a single shrine, former having curvilinear spire and the latter pyramidal roof. Barrel-vaulted towers characterize the third type. The general pattern of early Orissan temple was that of a square or rectangular shrine called *vimana* of *rekha* order having the icon of worship preceded by a porch of *pidha* order known as *mukhasala*[102]. Both *mukhasala* and *vimana* are interlinked and the former is lower in height than the latter. Afterwards *natamandapa* (dancing hall) and *bhogamandapa* (refectory hall) were added to the *mukhasala* or *jagamohan*. Depending upon the vertical projections of the body or *bada*, the *vimana* may be *tri-ratha, pancha-ratha* and *sapta-ratha*. The *vimana, jagamohana, natamandapa* and *bhogamandapa* comprise of *pistha* (pedestal), *bada* (peripendicular wall), *gandi* (curvilinear spire) and *mastaka* (crowning element). The *bada* moulding of Orissan temple is generally *tri-ratha* in plan. Whereas the *gandi* of main shrine has a curvilinear outline, the hall in front is pyramidal. *Anga sikharas* or miniature temples adorn the later day curvilinear spire of *vimana*. Facing to the east, the Siva and Visnu temples were square in design while in the Devi shrine it was rectangular. The three ancillary units of temples are Laksmi dvara, torana and navagraha features. The front walls of the shrine

---

101   K.V.S. Rajan, *Early Kaling Art and Architecture* (New Delhi, 1984), P. 31 Another text is *Silpa Prakasa* dealing with construction of *mukhasala* or hall in front of a shrine, *vimana* or main shrine and *sikhara* or tower.

102   Vidya Deheija, *Early Stone Temples of Orissa* (New Delhi, 1974), P. 122.

are heavily carved as mentioned by the *Silpa prakasha*[103].

One of the peculiarities of the Orissan temple is shape and decoration of the *sikhara*. It goes upwards in the form of a pyramid forming a solid block on the hollow interior above cells or *garbha-griha*. Over the lintel, there is a corbelled arch. The crowning element comprises of recessed cylindrical part, ribbed disc and cranium structure resembling flattened bell *Pancha-ratha* in plan, *sikhara* has five vertical segments. The central portion or *raha paga* comprises of moulding decorated with triple *caitya* medallions[104]. A figure or bust of deity is there in the centre of these medallions. The front portion above the doorway is sculptured with icons. Horizontal divisions or *bhumi* of the spire is decorated with erotic sculptures and different motifs. The niches are embellished with erotic motifs or brahmanical deities. At the top of *sikhara*, four lions are placed. In a Siva temple there is a kalasa at the top of *amalaka* and in a Visnu, there is *cakra*.

Based on style, motifs and iconography temple architecture could be divided into early, middle and later periods. The earliest group of *rekha* temples is short with flat roof over cubical sanctum. Bhubaneswar has important early temples like Bharatesvara and Satrughnesvara belonging to sixth century C.E. The seventh century C.E. temples are Parsuramesvara, Svarnajalesvara, Simhanatha etc. Sisiresvara, Kanakesvara, Markandesvara etc belong to the Bhaumakaras from eight to tenth centuries C.E. The *Khakra* temple of Vaitala belongs to eighth century C.E. Under the patronage of Somavamsis, temple architecture

---

103 A.R. Boner and S.R. Sharma eds, *Silpa Prakasa*, (Leiden, 1966), II, P.111.
104 These are ornamental motif like the window of a rock-cut *caitya* hall in the shape of a horse-shoe.

further progressed with *sikhara* possessing a soaring height, *jagamohan* becoming an integral part and carvings more ornamental. The examples one Kosalesvara, Panchupandava, Muktesvara, Rajarani and Lingaraj temples. In architectural activity, the Ganga period was marked by grand temple of Jagannatha at Puri and Sun temple of Konarka. As regards sculpture, it could be divided into two categories, cult images and decorative motifs. The first include icons of Gods and Goddesses and the second contains a variety of objects like erotic figures, semi-divine beings, *caitya* arches, lotus medallions, fables, *kirtimukha* (face of a lion with strands of pearls dripping from its mouth), *makara* (crocodile-type aquatic animal), male and female figures. Some of the finest temple sculptures are found in Muktesvara, Rajarani, Lingaraja and Konarka temples.

Orissa also possesses an extremely rich cultural heritage of Jaina and Buddhist monuments. Khandagiri and Udayagiri, the prominent Jaina centres represent Orissan cave architecture. There is pillared *verandah* on the front of the cell of the cave doorways having pilasters with animal figures and arches over them decorated with flowers, creepers, animal motifs etc. The important caves are Ranigumpha, Hathigumpha, Manchapurigumpha, Alakapurigumpha etc. All the caves have sculptured friezes and decorative patterns. The Buddhist remains are scattered over Orissa in places like Dhauli, Lalitgiri, Udayagiri, Ratnagiri, Bhubaneswar, Baud, Ganiapali etc. The rock cut elephant at Dhauli hills is the earliest specimen of Buddhist art. Images of Boddhisattva found in Lalitagiri are some of the most beautiful figures produced anywhere. Other noteworthy sculptures of the place are figures of Padmapani, Tara, Aparajita, Manjusri etc. The Ratnagiri mahavihars were important centres of learning.

Ornamented doorway of monastery number one is a class by itself. A gigantic image of Buddha in *bhumisparsa mudra* is there in the shrine chamber. The brick *stupa* of Udayagiri contains fine images of Buddha. In Boudh, there is a colossal image of Buddha in *bhumisparsa mudra Muchalinda* Buddha image found in Ganiapali is one of the rarest kind of its type in India. Thus, Orissa played a very significant part in development of Buddhist art.

The pre-historic paintings are found in places like Ulapgarh, Manikmeda, Ushakothi, Yogimatha, Gudahrdi of western Orissa. In the historic period, paintings on the walls of Khandagiri and Uudayagiri have vanished but the *Ravana Chhaya* painting at Sitabhanji depicting a royal procession is of high order. The stories of Rama, Krsna, Siva, Sakti etc are subject matter of paintings adorning the temple walls and *mathas* of Puri. In the *Jagamohana* of Puri temple paintings like scenes from *dasavatar* are found. Outside walls of Biranchi Narayana temple at Buguda are covered with mural paintings. The illustrated palm leaf manuscripts possess a special charm and originality of their own with themes drawn from works like the *Gita Govinda* and *Bhagavat Purana*. Orissa has also a fine tradition of *patta* paintings executed on cloth. It is also noted for 'tie and dye' weaving best represented in Sambalpuri saris. The subject matter is confined to religious theme. Paintings on earthen pot, toy making out of clay, paintings of pictures on the courtyards on festive occasions are also examples of traditional folk art.

Archaeological Perspective

Archaeological excavations in various parts of Orissa have not only placed the region in pre-historic map of India but also have corroborated in an authentic manner literary and epigraphic evidences of Orissa's interaction with

Southeast Asia. Since V. Ball brought to light paleolithic artifacts in the last century, many pre-historic sites like Kuliana, Kuchai, Baidyapur, Golbai, Kuchinda, Sulabhdihi etc have given the idea of palaeolithic, mesolithic, neolithic, chalcolithic and iron age culture of Orissa[105]. Excavation of historic sites like Sisupalgarh, Ratnagiri, Lalitgiri, Udayagiri, Asurgarh, Manumunda, Khalkatapatna, Manikpatna, Barbati etc have thrown light on ancient society and culture of Orissa.

There was a land route between Orissa and Southeast Asia through northeast India. The *savaras* speaking a mundary language belonging to the Austric family of languages found in Southeast Asia is an evidence of Orissa's link with the region. There might be also some racial links as there are some folk customs of Southeast Asia like monument to the dead by erecting stone menhirs being practised by the Austric-speaking tribes of south Orissa. The distribution of pre-historic shouldered adzes in both the regions corroborates the evidence of cultural interaction. R. Von Heine-Geldern had argued that these were brought to Orissa from Southeast Asia through land route in northeast India during 2500-1500 B.C.E.[106]. Shouldered adzes from neolithic sites of Kuchai and Baidyapur are techno-typologically alike that of Southeast Asia[107]. The excavations at Sulabhdihi in Sundergarh had yielded chisels resembling closely pick-adzes of Southeast Asia[108].

---

105   For details see, K.K. Basa, *Problems and Perspectives in Archaeology of Orissa, India*, Occasional Paper 4 (Bhubaneswar, 1994), Pp. 2ff.

106   K.K. Basa, "Cultural Relations between Orissa and Southteast Asia : an archaeological perspective", in P.K. Mishra, n. 77, (in print).

107   Behera, n. 69, P. 59.

108   P.K. Behera, 'Sulabhdihi : A Neolithic celt Manufacturing

The problem of dating of these adzes in northeast India and Orissa have created problem about date of Orissa's contact with Southeast Asia. Beginning of interaction cannot be earlier than second millennium B.C.E. as neolithic culture emerged in Southeast Asia around fourth to second and in eastern India during second millennium B.C.E.[109]. However, evidences pertaining to later period are available regarding overseas trade of Orissa through archaeological evidences.

Excavations conducted at Golbai in Khurda district have provided sequence of culture from neolithic age to iron age[110]. In the neolithic phase (1600 B.C.E.) hand made pottery in dull red and gray ware have been found. The next phase is chalcholithic (1400-900 B.C.E.) and large number of tools on stone; bone and copper have been recovered. A beautiful shouldered celt also has been found. The copper specimens were bangle, ring and chisel. In the next phase (900-800 B.C.E.) evidence of iron is there. Earlier iron artifacts were recovered from Sisupalgarh and Jaugarh pertaining to a later period. In the centuries before Christ, Orissa witnessed remarkable change with the use of iron, development in agriculture and growth of trade centres. The

---

    centre in Orissa", *Puratattva*, 1992, XXII, P. 129. Some earlier type of adzes such as oblong type indicate indigenous origin but others have similarities with finds from northeast India and Southeast Asia. See, R.N. Das, "Orissan Neoliths : A Typo-Technoloical Study" in *Orissa Historical Research Journal*, XXXV, No.3 and 4, Pp. 109-110. The shouldered adzes have been found from Kuchai, Rairangpur, Sitabanjhi, Sankarjung, Jajpur, Sisupalgarh and Golbai. See, Basa, n. 106, P.2.

109   Basa, n. 106, P. 3.
110   B.K. Sinha, "Discovery of The 'Missing Link' in the Proto-History of Orissa" in *Studies in History and Culture*, 1994, II, Pp. 27-32.

excavation at Sisupalgarh gives proof of an early historical city between third century B.C.E. to fourth century C.E. and its relics point to Orissa's overseas trade. An iron age burial site in Thailand, Ban Don Ta Phet receiving items from India by trade is dated to fourth century B.C.E.[111]. Rouletted ware, knobbed vessels, glass beads, semi-precious beads, ivory etc are evidences of cultural contact between the two regions. Knobbed ware pottery, semi-precious stones and ivory were items available in Orissa[112]. Don Ta Phet has yielded these items also. So, there are possibilities of a strong link between the two regions. So, Orissa's trade relationship with Southeast Asia may be traced to third century B.C.E. The Roman objects found from Sisupalgarh like fine variety of rouletted ware, clay bullae etc show contact between Orissa and Rome.

The excavation at Khalkattapatna[113] in Puri district showed its importance as a port between twelfth and fourteenth centuries having contact with Southeast Asia and China. It has yielded Chinese celadon ware, porcelain and copper coins. Contact with Arab merchants was also there as evident from discovery of Arabian glazed pottery and ware. The discovery of potsherd from both peninsular Thailand and Khalkattapatna bear testimony to Orissa's contact with Southeast Asia. Excavations from

---

111   Basa, n. 106, P. 7.
112   Coarser variety of rouletted ware numbering 20 have been found from Sisupalgarh. It has also yielded semi precious stone beads (180) like onyx, agate, chalcedong, amethyst etc. Western Orissa also had rich deposits of these like diamond, garnet, saphire, rubby, topaz etc.
113   B.K. Sinha, "Khalkattapatna : A small port on the coast of Orissa" in B.U. Nayak and S.C. Ghosh ed, *New Trends in Indian Art and Archaeology*, (New Delhi, 1992), Vol. II, Pp. 423-28. See also Behera, n. 69, P.64 and 66.

Manikapatna,[114] which is situated on the left bank of the water channel connecting the Chilka lake with the Bay of Bengal have established its importance as a port town of medieval Orissa. As mentioned earlier it has been identified by some with Che-li-ta-lo of Hsuan Tsang[115]. It was an important port in sixteenth and seventeenth century also. Serving as entrance to Orissa from the south, deposits from early historical period were two neolithic celts, two sherds of Indian rouletted ware, fragments of amphora, sherd with Kharoshti inscriptions and Puri-Kusana coins - all pointer to Orissa's cultural contact with outside world. Deposits from the next phase, separated from earlier by sand layer have yielded celadon ware, Chinese copper coins, coins of Shasamalla and brown glazed ware. The last item known as Maratuan ware, after the name of the place in Myanmar was proof of trade link with Myanmar. Link with China is established through discovery of coloured celadon and a copper coin[116]. Celadon of poor quality has also been found, which suggests that they may have been imported from Thailand or Myanmar. Monochrome glass beads have been found from Manikpatna. Excavations conducted in Sembiran of Indonesia and pre-historic sites of Thailand have yielded such beads. Unlike Southeast Asia, India was having many important manufacturing units of glass beads. Therefore,

---

114   Behera, n. 69, Pp. 64ff.
115   Pattanayak, n. 79 VI, P. 50.
116   The fragmentary copper coin with characteristic square hole came from China by sea-trade. Wang Tu-Yuan (1330-1349) mentions that each of Orissa's silver coin is equivalent to ten tacels of Chung-tung Ch'ao. Exchanging for 11,520 *cowries* (medium of exchange in Orissa. *Cowries* were imported from Maldive island), each coin can buy 45 baskets of rice. See, Behera, n. 69, Pp.65-66.

these were imported from India[117]. Discovery of terracotta animal fabrics of Indonesia and potsherd with Kharosthi inscription also bear testimony of Orissa's overseas contact.

The yielding of rouletted ware from Manikpatna, and Sisupalgarh as well as from Sri Lanka and Indonesia is a testimony of maritime network linking these regions. Excavations in archaeological sites of Sri Lanka like Mantai, Kantarodai, Anuradhapura citadel have yielded Indian rouletted ware pertaining to the period two hundred B.C.E. to one hundred C.E.[118]. The northern black polished ware point to north Indian contact, whereas the rouletted ware had primarily east and south Indian contacts. This had distribution focussing around the Bay of Bengal but extending upto the coasts of Java and Bali[119]. Other trade objects like shell bangles, intaglio seals, Roman wins, lapis lazulli and ivory carvings have been discovered from these sites. The last item was of Orissan origin as there was brick trade of ivory in Orissa. When one takes into consideration Buddhist remains of Orissa and the excavated sites of Sri Lanka like monasteries in Anuradhapur, Abhayagiri Vihar and Jetavanaramaya; the Orissa-Sri Lanka contact assumes importance. The Kalingan faction of the royal house of Sri Lanka was able to put Shahasa Malla on the throne in 1200 C.E. The discovery of his coins from the Polonnaruva, the port town of Sri Lanka and Manikapatna suggest close link between two regions.

So Orissa was an important zone of trade and com-

---

117   Basa, n. 105, P. 9.
118   Martha Prickett, "Sri Lanka's Foreign Trade Before A.D. 600. Archaeological Evidence" in K.M. de Silva and others ed, *Asian Panorama : Essays in Asian History, Past and Present* (New Delhi, 1990), P. 161.
119   *Ibid*, Pp. 169-170.

merce from about third century B.C.E. The archaeological excavations are strong pointers to the role of Orissan commerce in maritime network of South and Southeast Asia. Gradually there was cultural interaction between the two regions. As with other parts of India, many facets of culture of this region influenced Southeast Asia.

CHAPTER-11

Cultural Profile Of Southeast Asia

The term Southeast Asia came to be used at during the Second World War, when the region was placed under Lord Louis Mountbatten's Southeast Asia command. Most of the scholars use the designation to include the area to the east of Indian subcontinent and to the south of China comprising countries like Brunei, Cambodia, Laos, Malaysia, Myanmar (Burma), Thailand, Vietnam, Singapore and the Philippines. A region of ethnic, cultural, linguistic and historical diversity; Southeast Asia has nourished many cultural expressions since very early times. In spite of external influences like Indian, Chinese, Islamic and European civilizations leaving imprints on the indigenous culture, Southeast Asia has retained its own identity.

Land and People of Southeast Asia

In a geographical sense, Southeast Asia comprises of two broad groups: mainland comprising Myanmar, Thailand, Laos, Cambodia and Vietnam and island consisting of Indonesia, Malaysia, Singapore, Brunei and the Philippines. To the northeast of the whole region lies the Pacific Ocean and to the southeast the Indian Ocean. The absence of a common focal point in the region is due to innumerable mountains, rivers and valleys. Rivers like the Irrawaddy, Chindwin, Chao Phraya, Song Koi, Song Bo, Mekong flow in the same north-south direction. The mountain ranges like Arakan, Tenasserim, Annam etc also run in a north-south direction. Therefore, commercial and population movements were not in east-west direction but north south.

Human settlement in Southeast Asia started about one million years ago.[120] From Java and Vietnam, remains of early human of the specie *Hormo erectus* have been found. The Java man or *Pithecanthropus erectus* was found in 1891 in deposits on the banks of the Solo river in central Java. From the same area skulls of *Homo sapiens* or human beings, belonging to the old stone age has been discovered. The racial groups inhabiting Southeast Asia before historic times were the Austroloid, Negrito and Melanesian, who constitute the indigenous population.[121] Migration to Southeast Asia was not uniform. The southern Mongoloid constituting the great majority of inhabitants gradually replaced the indigenous Australo-Melanesian population. Originally moving from southern China, their movement was due to demographic advantages provided by agricultural economy and mobility arising out of advanced seagoing and

---

120 Peter Bellwood, "Southeast Asia before History" in N. Tarling, ed, *The Cambridge History of Southeast Asia* Vol. I (Singapore, 1992), P. 51.

121 Some of the races of India like the Negritos, the proto-Australoids and the Mongloids figure among Southeast Asian people. The dwarfish Negroid inhabit in southern India, Assam, Andaman and the Malay Peninsula. See H.B. Sarkar, *Cultural Relations between India and Southeast Asian Countries* (New Delhi, 1985) Pp.92-93.

navigational skills.[122] The elements of neolithic culture were brought by the proto-Malays in about 2500 B.C.E.E. and the deutero - Malays coming around 300 B.C.E.E. introduced bronze and iron. The former was pushed into the interior by the later, who dominated the coastal districts. Before the beginning of Christian era, Myanmar received the Mons from northeastern India and southwestern China and the Karens from eastern Tibet. The Khmers, who were closely related in language and race to the Mons, migrated from southwestern China and northeastern Asia around 2500 B.C.E.E. The Tai or Thai migration began from southern China covering the period between eighth to thirteenth centuries of the Christian era. Thus, Southeast Asia is a region of anthropological complexity.

The two important language families of South Asia; Austroasiatic and Austronesian represent the agricultural population, which had displaced the foraging, groups.[123] Tibeto-Burman and Tai-Kadai were two other languages, which were found in large areas due to conquests and state formation. The Austroasiatic language family having one hundred and fifty language has two subgroups; Mon-Khmer of Southeast Asia and Munda of India. Mon, Khmer, Vietnamese, Khasi, Aslian languages of Malay and Nicobarese belong to the Mon-Khmer grouping. The Munda or Kol languages of Orissa, Bihar and West Bengal are widespread. The Austroasiatic language were spoken in far-flung region stretching from eastern India, Nicobars and mainland Southeast Asia. Knowledge of rice in proto-Austroasiatic languages is also in accordance with neolithic archaeology from northeastern India across to south

---

122 Bellowood, n.1, P. 74.
123 *Ibid*, P. 109.

China and North Vietnam.[124] The principal languages of Austronesian are Malay, Javanese, Balinese, Melanesian dialects and Polynesian dialects. The Austonesians dominate the island of Southeast Asia.

Pre-historic Culture

Apart from domain of language and linguistics, important source for study of pre-historic culture of Southeast Asia is archaeology. The skeletal remains of early man found in the region have been referred earlier. They belong to pleistocene or ice age. There have been discoveries of chopping tools belonging to middle pleistocene period from middle Irrawaddy, Nui Do, Kota Tampan, and Walanae valley area. The archaeological records of places like Tingkayu in north Borneo, Niah, caves in Sarawak and Lang Rongrien cave in south Thailand point to tools of flaked stone and a foraging lifestyle.There appeared microlithic and blade technologies in the Holocene period. The dominant industry from about thirteen thousand years ago until the arrival of agriculture in mainland Southeast Asia is known as Hoabinhian after discovery in the former Hoa Binh (presently Ha Son Binh) province of Vietnam.[125]Similar types of culture have been found from Luang Prabang in Laos, Chiengrai in Thailand, Perak in Malaysia etc.All these type of finds are commonly known as Hoabinhian culture. The Hoabinhian traits were frequent use of rock shelters

---

124 *Ibid.*
125 For details see, *Vietnam Studies* (Hanoi), 48, 1978; C.F. Gorman, "Hoabinhian : a Pebble tool complex with early plant association in Southeast Asia", *Science* 1969, CLXIII, Pp. 671ff. and N.K. Vien, *Traditional Vietnam : Some Historical Stages* (Hanoi, n.d.), Pp. 10ff.

and a distinctive pattern of food remains. This foraging community was replaced or assimilated to an extent by the speakers of Austroasiatic languages.

Later there was rise and expansion of agricultural communities in Southeast Asia. Remains of houses, pottery, elaborate burial practices, bones of domesticated animals and plant remains associated with agriculture were some of the evidences in this regard. From the finds of Spirit cave in north and Non Nok Tha in northeast Thailand, the primacy of Southeast Asia in plant domestication and rice culture can be established.[126] Remains from Spirit cave point to the use of nuts, pepper, cucumber and beans in between 7000 B.C.E.E. to 10,000 B.C.E.E. Rise (Orzya sativa) cultivation began around 5000 B.C.E.E. as excavations at Non Nok Tha had yielded rice chaff. Apart from rice, the agricultural economy of Southeast Asia focussed on cultivation of wheat, barley and maize.

The neolithic mode of technology appeared in lowland and coastal regions of Southeast Asia between approximately 4000 and 1000 B.C.E.E. The discoveries of artifacts and metallurgical objects have pushed back the cultural history of the region. People with varied agricultural economics had settled in large parts of Southeast Asia around third millennium B.C.E.E. The metal tools industry was very much necessary for sedentary agriculture. Apart from technological improvement, bronze became associated with idea of status. Weapons, vessels and ornaments of bronze might have been used for trading purposes in these societies. At Non Nok Tha in Thailand, piecemoulds for bronze casting of local sandstone, crucibles and bronze

---

126   I.W. Mabbett, "The 'Indianization' of Southeast Asia : Reflections on the Prehistoric Sources" in *Journal of Southeast Asian Studies*, VIII, No. 1, 1977, Pp.5ff

artifacts have been found and the date for metal industry in the area has been suggested to be 2700 B.C.E.E.[127] The bronze finds at Hang Gon in Vietnam is dated to about the end of the third millennium B.C.E.E. Round axe and the quadrangular adze were two important elements of neolithic culture of Southeast Asia. Pottery with rounded or pointed bases, shouldered stone adzes, flexed burials etc have been discovered from the coastal regions of Vietnam. The upper layer of Spirit cave of Thailand had yielded pottery with cord-marked decoration, untanged stone adzes and slate knives. In the mainland Southeast Asia, the bronze age continued until the coming of iron, whereas in island Southeast Asia, bronze and iron came into existence from five hundred B.C.E.E. onwards.

Iron made its appearance in Thailand in three hundred B.C.E.E. as evident from yielding of artifacts made of iron; neck rings, spearheads, bracelets and knives from sites like Ban Chiang and Ban Na Di. The excavations at Dongson in Thanh Hoa province of Vietnam had provided the level attained by Southeast Asia before impact of Chinese and Indian cultures. Splendid bronze drums discovered from the region marks the indigenous achievement in metallurgy. The Dongsonian culture arrived in Vietnam around 600 B.C.E.E. and in the archipelago about 300 B.C.E.E. These drums numbering two hundred have been found throughout Southeast Asia. The range of Dongson bronze goods includes bowls and situlae, miniature drums and bells, bracelets, belt locks and knives with hilts resembling human figures in the round.[128] In between 500 and 200 B.C.E.E. bronze and iron made their appearances simultaneously in the island Southeast Asia. Apart from

---

127   Ibid, Pp. 6-7.
128   Bellowood, n.1, P.123.

the knowledge of metallurgy, the Dongson people had their farming based on irrigation cultivation. Their art demonstrated the practice of ancestor worship and animism. Temples were constructed on hills and the ashes of the dead were buried in jars or megalithic dolmens. The culture of Southeast Asia was already developed before they were exposed to China and India.

Apart from the knowledge of metallurgy, rice and plant domestication; the people of Southeast Asia were quite acquainted with navigation. The bronze drums of Ngoc Lu in north Vietnam show picture of boats carrying warriors and drums. There is evidence of early connection between the archipelago and coasts of the Indian ocean. The traders from Southeast Asia were playing an important role in the Indian ocean as the outrigger canoe was invented on the Indochinese coast by four hundred B.C.E.E.[129] The Dongson people were excellent sea-farers guiding the navigational movement with knowledge of astronomy. Another cultural heritage of people of Southeast Asia was their ability to build megaliths; north Sumatra, Nias, the Nusa Tenggara islands and interior of Suluwesi and Borneo were examples of it. The most important Indonesian complex of prehistoric large stone monuments are there on the Pasemah plateau of south Sumatra. In the slab-lined underground burial chambers, there were interior decoration of humans and buffaloes with polychrome paintings. The burial site at Viet Khe included more than one hundred bronzes. Laos has splendid monuments in the Plain of Jars. Along with practice of ancestor worship and animism, the Dongsonian related their Gods to agriculture. There was also cosmologically oriented mythology in which the theme was dualistic

---

129   W.G. Solheim, "New Light on a Forgotten Past" in *National Geographic*, 1971 CXXXIX, Pp. 330ff.

elements of mountain and sea, winged race and aquatic race, and men of mountains and men of coast. The Javanese had developed before they came into contact with Indians, many aspects of Indonesian cultural life: *wayang* or puppet shadow theatre, *garmelan* orchestra, *batik* work in textiles, a monetary system, knowledge of navigation and rice cultivation.

Chinese Influence on Southeast Asia

It is on an indigenous substructure that later cultural superstructure based on Chinese and Indian influences were developed in Southeast Asia. As the region has been on the crossroads on the Asian map, it is exposed to external influences. As a meeting ground of culture, commerce and civilization, cultural context became the vital theme in the history of Southeast Asia. The northern Vietnam was influenced by China politically from the mid-third century B.C.E.E. onwards and ultimately became a Chinese protectorate in 111 B.C.E.E. There was predominance of Chinese cultural influence in the cultural zone consisting of Tonking, Annam and Cochin China; whereas Indian influence was greater in 'outer India' or *L' Inde exterieure*. In fact, the Annam range marks the line of demarcation of Sino-Indian cultural influence: to the north and east of the range is culturally based on China and to the west and south is based on India.[130] The Chinese writings had identified the region as little China or *Nan Yang*. Under Han rule, most of Vietnam came under the Chinese influence. In spite of that, the Vietnamese developed a cultural identity of their own. There was a period of territorial expansion under the Chin Empire that brought coastal region of Southeast

---

130 R.L. May *The Culture of Southeast Asia* (New Delhi, 1972), P. 9.

Asia under the Chinese control. The Chinese contact was intensified under emperor Wu-Ti of western Han. The cultural interaction between the Chinese and Vietnamese was there in third century B.C.E.E. as pottery from Dongson sites had close parallel with geometric-paddle impressed pottery of south China. Specimens of Han pottery had been discovered in Indonesia from first century B.C.E.E., which proves commercial relations between the two regions. The Sangeang drums of Indonesia show figures in Chinese costumes and a drum of Kai islands near New Guinea has inscriptions in Chinese characters.

Towards the end of third century B.C.E.E., the historical record of Southeast Asia began with the coming of Chinese soldiers and officials on the shores of South China Sea. The Han Chinese conquered north Vietnam in the first century C.E. and by the end of third century C.E. there was stable provincial administration due to endeavour of Chinese frontier administrators. The territorial expansion of middle kingdom was achieved at the cost of the non Chinese, who were pushed beyond what came to be the new boundaries of China. Sending of periodic tribute was there as a mark of subordination. China required its vasals to send tributes to the Emperor, whose paramount position was ensured. The period of political stability in China coincided with active interference and domination of Southeast Asia.[131] There was also brisk commercial activities through the seas by the Chinese. In the first century C.E., trade connection to India was from upper Yangtse basin through the Mekong and Salween rivers to the Irrawaddy valley in Myanmar and then to the coast of Bay of Bengal.[132] After seventh

---

131   D.R. Sardesai, *Southeast Asia : Past and Present* (New Delhi, 1981) P. 15.

132   J.F. Cady, *Southeast Asia : Its Historical Development* (New

century, C.E., the Chinese influence on Southeast Asia was intensified under the T' ang dynasty. The T'ang rulers did not undertake any conquest but were satisfied with the tribute system. Southeast Asia did not appropriate the Confucianist mandavrinate system. As it was already acquainted with Indian cultural more, Southeast Asia turned towards India.

Indian Cultural Influence on Southeast Asia

From prehistoric days, India had trade and cultural relations with West Asia, Rome, China and Southeast Asia. Indian traders went to the cites of Mesopotamia, where their seals belonging to the period between 2400 and 1700 B.C.E.E. have been found. India also sent its missionaries, conquerors and traders to the neighbouring countries where they founded settlements.[133] During Darius the Great, Greece and India had earliest contact in about 510 B.C.E.E. Before the beginning of the Christian era, there was a large volume of sea borne trade between India and Western countries as far as Africa. After the discovery of monsoon by Hippalus in first Century C.E., it was possible for the Roman vessels to play directly across the Indian ocean. Palura on the eastern coast of India had an important role. The ships came here from Arrkamedu, crossed the Bay of Bengal and went to the delta of Irrawaddy, from where they proceeded to the Malay Peninsula.[134] Demand for oriental goods had the effect of stimulating Indian trading with Malay Peninsula. It is not surprising that Roman coins, pottery, amphora etc have been found from Sisupalgarh

---

    Delhi, 1976), P.22.
133 R.S. Sharma, *Ancient India* (New Delhi, 1981), P. 164.
134 F.G. Morehead, *A History of Malay and Her Neighbours* (Hong Kong, 1965), P. 14.

and Manikpatna. Indo-Roman contact declined during third and fourth centuries C.E. But India's relationship with Southeast Asia continued.

One of the significant factors in spreading of Indian cultural influence in Southeast Asia is geographical proximity between two regions. Most of the trading activities were carried on from the ports lying on the large seacoasts of India. There was also a land route to Myanmar through northeast India. The wealth of Southeast Asia was an attraction for the Indians. The type of names given to different regions of Southeast Asia is recognition of this desire for economic gain. The *Ramayana* the Pali *Nidesa*, the *Jatakas* and many other works refer to *Suvarnabhumi* (land of gold), *Suvarnadvipa* (island of gold), *Narikeladvipa* (island of coconuts), *Karpuradvipa* (island of camphor), *Yavodvipa* (island of barley) etc.[135] Fabulous wealth of Southeast Asia attracted the Indians for many centuries. In respect of kingdom of P'an-p'an it has been said that the numerous *brahmans* of that kingdom came from India in search of wealth. Inscriptions had attested the arrival of Indian brahmans to Cambodia and settling there after marrying in royal families. The missionary activities of Buddhists also resulted in large number of Indians settling in the region. Another cause of exodus of Indians was military activities of the Kusanas in the first century C.E. and the Guptas in fourth century, C.E. This is a mere hypothesis and not supported by facts. It might be possible that due to wars, some members of royal families would have looked to distant lands.

The relationship between India and Southeast Asia goes back to prehistoric times. As has been pointed earlier

---

135   P. Wheatley, *Golden Khersonese* (Kuala Lumpur, 1961), P. 49.

there was racial and linguistic affinity. The archaeological excavations are also a testimony of the interaction between the two regions. In the Korat plateau of Thailand, glass and stone beads have been found, which is an indicator of trade contact with India?[136] Ban Chiang in Thailand had yielded bimetallic spearheads belonging to first millennium B.C.E.E. The same types of artifacts have been reported from places like Mahurijhari in Madhya Pradesh, Gilmanuk in Bali, Prajekan in Java and Dongson in Vietnam. The Buni complex in Java had yielded Indian rouletted ware of the first and second centuries C.E.. Sembrian in Bali is another site, whose finds include sherds of pottery of types paralleled at Arikadmedu, an important Indo-Roman trading centre. Indian type of gold foil funerary eye cover had been recovered from the site of Gilimanuk. In Oc Eo in Vietnam, which was an entreport from second centuryC. E. onwards, finds were beads, intaglios and seals with Sanskrit inscriptions. Therefore, the early centuries of Christian era saw greater impetus in the direction of Indo- Southeast Asian relations. This was there in prehistoric times and became brisker in pre-Christian centuries. Hinduized kingdom of Funan and Campa had already came into existence.

Sea Routes

In the spread of Indian culture, sea had played an important role. There was intensification of sea-borne commerce in the early centuries of Christian era. Along with traders; missionaries, priests, literati, adventurers and fortune seekers went to Southeast Asia. The ancient port of Tamralipti at the mouth of Ganga was one of the earliest places of embarkation. From there, the ships proceeded

---

136   Bellwood, n.1, P. 121.

to Malay Peninsula either along the coasts of Bengal and Myanmar or through the Bay of Bengal. The Chinese texts of third century C.E. attest to this fact.[137] A trader from western India reached Funan in the second century C.E. and the Funanese king Fan Chen, after learning from the trader about India, sent one of his relations to it. The later embarked at Teu-ki-li, reached the mouth of Ganga and proceeded further. Ships from the Mediterranean were visiting this port of Tamralipti, which was situated at the extremity of Orissa's domain. The vessels were then sailing to Southeast Asia and China. After the decline of Indo-Roman trade, the route from India to China through Southeast Asia did not cease. The port of Palura had been referred by Ptolemy as an apheterion, where the ships ceased to follow littoral and entered the high seas. Palura was the port of departure for Roman ships before sailing to Southeast Asia and afterwards to China.[138] The ships were reaching Aden from Egypt and arrived at the coast of India. From Arikamedu the ships sailed to Palura and reached Arakan through Bay of Bengal. They went south along the coast to the delta of Irrawaddy and then turned into the gulf of Martaban. The ships reached the port of Oceo after passing through Takkola, Klang and Pattani. Final destination was the port of Kattigara. The traders avoided the risky sea route round the coast of Malay Peninsula. They went to Thailand through Kedah and took the land route to Canpa after crossing Laos and Cambodia.[139]

During the early centuries of Christian era, trade with China through Southeast Asia followed two routes. The first

---

137 R.C. Majumdar, *Ancient Indian Colonisation in Southeast Asia* (Baroda, 1955), P.18.
138 For details see, Morehead, n. 15, Pp. 12ff.
139 K. Nag, *India and the Pcific World* (Calcutta, 1941), P. 96.

was from the Telengana and Kalingan coast, from where the ships went to Irrawaddy valley of Myanmar after crossing the Bay of Bengal. From the valley, the traders went to the upper Yangtse basin through Salween and Mekong rivers. The second route started from Tamralipti, reached Sri Lanka and sailed directly through the Nicobar islands either to the Sunda straits or straits of Malacca. From places like lower end of Sumatra or western end of Java, it was easy to go up the Malay coast past Pattani, Singora and Ligor to the port of Oceo. The voyage then covered the coast past Campa to Chio-Chi port in Vietnam or on to Canton. After reaching the ports of Malay, the Indian sailors were either going through the pirate-infested straits of Malacca or safer land route to the east coast. Across the narrow isthmus of Kra, from Takupa on the western side to Chaiya on the eastern; there was a short cut. Another route was from Tavoy over the three pagodas pass and then by Kanburi river to the valley of Menam. Still there was another passage connecting the Menam region to the Mekong by way of the Korat plateau via Sr. Tep and the Mon valley. It is not surprising that some of the places mentioned above are archaeological sites and places of Indian influence. The monsoon wind was playing a major role in determining the maritime operations on the Bay of Bengal. As the southwest monsoon during April to October caused adverse weather conditions in the straits, sailors preferred northeast monsoon at the time of October to April for starting their journey from India. The ships sailing from China would come to the straits on the northeast monsoon and up the straits in time for the next northeast monsoon to sail to India.

Apart from Palura and Tamralipti, there were other ports on the eastern coast of India: Arikamedu, Masulipatnam (Machhlipatna), Kamana (Kalapattana),

Poduke (Pondicherry), Supatana (Cheenai) and Puhar (Kaveripattanam). On the west following the nomenclature of Periplus, there were, on the mouth of Narmada, Barygaza (Broach), Suppara (Sopara), Calliena (Kalyan), Semylla (Chaul), Naura (Cannanore) etc.[140] Another work *Milindapanha* of first century C.E. refers to the name of places of India and Southeast Asia and mentions the name of important ports like Sovira (lower Indus valley), Suratta (Gujrat), Cola Pattana (Coromandel coast), Vanga (Bengal) and Suvarnabhumi (lower Myanmar).[141] The ports were also playing an important role as diffusion centre for Indian art elements to Southeast Asia. The port of Amaravati at the lower reaches of Krsna river was not far from Palura. Sailing from the ports of Palura-apheterion complex, the early Buddhist missionaries and migrants carried with them the sculptures of Amaravati school of art.[142] The images of this school had been found from various places in Southeast Asia: Palembang, east Java, West Celebes, Korat and Dong Duong. Spots from where these sculptures have been found are situated on the sea-route taken by Su-wu in the middle of the third century C.E.[143].

Trade and Commerce of Southeast Asia

It has been mentioned earlier how Southeast Asia was playing an important role in maritime trade involving the Mediterranean, India and China. The Southeast Asians pioneered some of the significant features of maritime technology. These traders were playing a major role in

---

140   B.Sahai, *The Ports of India* (New Delhi : 1986) P. 13.
141   *Milindapanha* tr. T.W. Rhys Davids. *Sacred book of the East*, Vol. 35, 36, P.269.
142   Sarkar, n. 2, P. 213.
143   Wheatlay, n. 16, P. 24.

the Indian ocean by 2500 B.C.E. The yielding of beads of different varieties, sherds of Indian rouletted ware, drums, fine pottery, shell bracelets and other artifacts from different sites of Southeast Asia hint strongly the role of the region in international trade and commerce. From prehistoric times, the people of the region sailed thousands of kilometres from their homes; from Madagascar on the African coast to Easter Island in the Pacific. These Malayo-Polynesian people were nomads of the southern ocean and prime movers in the links between trading centres.[144] They were residing on the coast of Malagasy at the time of Roman Empire.

The Chinese were acquainted with the Malay sailors by the third century B.C.E. Pliny, the Roman historian described cinnamon traders between Africa and Asia. This commodity reached the markets of India, West Asia and the Mediterranean through the Malays trading in east Africa. They also traded in bananas, which reached Africa through India and spread across the continent.[145] The musical instrument xylophone also began its journey from Southeast Asia and reached Africa. The mariners of Southeast Asia came into the Indian ocean through the straits of Malacca and Sunda. Their contact with India might have started in centuries proceeding Christian era. The steppe nomads cut off India's supply of gold from central Asia after the downfall of the Mauryas. The merchants of India turned towards *Suvarnadvipa* or island of gold.[146]

---

144   K.R. Hall, "Economic History of Early Southeast Asia", in Tarling, ed, n.1,PP. 185-86.

145   *Ibid.* P. 186.

146   P. Wheatley, *Nagara and Commandery : Origins of the Southeast Asian Urban Traditions* (Chicago, 1983), PP. 119ff. Golden Khersonese corresponds to the *Suvarnadvipa* of the *Ramayana*. The Buddhist *Jatakas* also refer to the island of gold.

Trade and commerce increased along the Asian sea route during the first two centuries of Christian era. Ptolemy's geography and atlas of the known world gave impetus to the trading world. The port of Oc eo in South Vietnam near the Cambodian border was situated at a junction of canals linking the Gulf of Siam with the main channels of the Mekong. This important entrepot from second century C.E. onwards had yielded beads, gold medallions, seals with Sanskrit inscriptions etc. The particular location of the port offered the sailors protection from the troubled seas and they had to stay in Oc eo for considerable time for shifting of winds blowing towards the continent. Therefore, cultural interaction between local people and sailors coming from India must have developed. The ports in the Sunda strait region had also assumed importance and sailors from these ports were going to India for direct trade. Third-century visitors from China had mentioned import of horses from India by the king of Zhiaying on the southeastern coast of Sumatra.[147] The ports of west coast of Borneo were also engaged in trade with India. All these ports also introduced Southeast Asian products in international markets. Sumatran pine resins and benzoin were introduced in the beginning. Camphor of Barus, a port on Sumatra's north west coast, aromic woods, cloves and spices of Maluku were important commodities that sailors of Indonesian archipelago traded. The old coastal was neglected and by six century an all-sea route developed via the straits of Malacca. Consequently, Oc eo lost its primacy. Textiles, horses, Chinese silk, reconditioned bushy tail of Yak, frankincense, myrrh were some of the

---

147 O.W. Wolters, *Early Indonesian Commerce : A Study of the Origins of Sri Vijaya* (Ithaca, 1967), P. 62.

items being exported to Southeast Asia. Articles of import from the region were finest spices, pepper aromatic wood and resins, salt, sandal, rubber, tin, nutmeg etc. Merchants would sail into unknown seas to find 'spice islands'. Southeast Asia was the spice capital of the world.

Religion

By the beginning of Christian era, Southeast Asia had already reached a high level of civilization. This resulted in people choosing the forms of Indian religion that were consistent with or could be adapted to their beliefs. The elite assimilated important elements of Indian religion and gradually it percolated to common people. Religion became an important force in the life of people and it was reflected in bas-reliefs of temple walls, in the stories of the *Ramayana*, oral tradition and popular beliefs. All religious sects existed side by side in mutual toleration. Hinduism was a religious accumulation derived from long periods and it could be transferred in a selective way. The Southeast Asians did not appropriate the philosophical implications of brahmanism and caste system. As in India, Hinduism accommodated pre-Aryan cults, so also in Southeast Asia on easy *rapprochement* was made with animistic worship. In Campa, Siva was moulded to the tradition of earth God identified with territory inhabited by particular groups. The worship of mountains as dwelling place of Gods and mount Mahameru developed into important cult in Indonesia. Volcanoes were considered as living mountains: Siva becoming the Lord of the mountain and Brahma came to be identified with fire. Mountain symbolism was adopted in architecture of Cambodia. The *Naga* cult in Southeast Asia was a blending of Indian and indigenous elements.

The *brahmans* greatly influenced the court culture of

Southeast Asia. They were employed as priests teachers and counsellors. The rulers found it convenient to legitimize their rule through the services of the *purohitas*, the chief priest with official and ritual functions. Inscriptions of the king Mulavarman of Kutai in east Kalimantan mention precious gifts like thousands of cattle and gold to the *brahmans*.[148] Kaundinya I, a *brahamana* of India founded the Funan Empire in first century C.E.He got married to the local *naga* princess, Soma or Lin-yeh. As he had violated the law of Manu by this marriage, their issue was to be a Vyadha or hunter. Hence, the first capital of Funan became Vyadhapura. Apart from performing royal consecration and funerary rites, the influence of brahmanism also resulted in some people choosing the life of a hermit in the *ashramas*. In the Dieng plateau in central Java, there was a community of monks and ascetics from early times with titles like *pitamahas* and *devagurus*[149] The influence of the *brahmans* could be gauged from the fact that they performed ceremonies in the court of Buddhist courts of Pagan in Myanmar and Sukothai in Thailand.

Vaisnavism existed in the early times and numerous inscriptions of the region attest this. The prince Gunavrman's inscription indicates devotion to Visnu, for whom an image of his footprints was built and a temple of Chakratirthasvami was erected at Thap-moi. Visnupura was the name of one of the early cities of Pyu people and Sriksetra had a place for images of Visnu and Laksmi. In Java, there was even a *Vaisnava* community as had been

---

148   J.G. de Casparis and I.W. Mabbett, "Religion and Popular Beliefs of Southeast Asia before c. 1500", in Tarling, ed, n. 1, P. 305.

149   *Ibid*, P. 308.

mentioned by the *Nagarakertagama*[150] and statues of the God with his emblem like *conch* or *sankha*, disc or *cakra*, mace or *gada* and lotus or *padma* were common in Java. The rulers of Angkor were great patrons of Visnu and the most famous monument of Angkor that was built by Suryavarman II (1130-50 C.E.) had ritual and cosmological symbol devoted to Visnu worship. The *Pancaratra* sect worshipped Visnu through devotion or *bhakti* and it existed in Angkor in seventh to tenth centuries Visnu in his incarnations as Krsna and Rama became very popular. Krsna saga was very much appreciated in Laos and Thailand. The Rama legend was prevalent in Southeast Asia with local variations. In the process of adoption, the stories of *Ramayana* have been transformed. Campa has even Valmiki temple, which is very rare in India. The *Ramayana* tradition affected the life, custom, belief, geography and history of Southeast Asia. Performing arts like shadow play and puppet shows had continuous interaction with Rama story. In bas-relief of temples, there are representations from the *Ramayana stories*.[151] The balustrade of *Candi* Lora Jongran is adorned with panels depicting stories of the *Ramayana*. In ancient kingdom of Campa and Cambodia the cult of Siva was prevalent. In the royal capital of Campa at Mison, Siva was known as Bhadresvara and was principal object of worship. Monuments of Cambodia had Siva *lingas* in their cental shrine. Most of the Siva images in Java are represented in Mahadeva form as well as in Bhairava form. The Arrakan region of Myanmar was a stronghold of *Saivism* and coins bearing Saivite symbols have been discovered from the

---

150 *Ibid*, P. 314.
151 For detils see, K. Deva, "The Rama Legend as depicted in India and in Indonesia" in *Man and Environment* 1996, Vol. XXI, Pp. 1ff.

region. From the middle of thirteenth century to fifteenth century, *Saivism* was popular in Singhasari and Pantataran. One of the Saivite sects, Pasupata cult was popular in Cambodia.[152] The devotional aspect of Siva worship made him not a possession of royalty alone put a personal God. The Gods and Goddesses of Hindu pantheon like Ganesa; Durga, Sita, Hanumana, Surya etc. also find place in the religious life of people. Presently also people worship Brahma at Eravan in Bangkok and Laksmi is worshipped as N. Pohaci Sangyang Sri in West Java.[153]

Brahmanism and Buddhism existed side by side in Southeast Asia. Though Buddhism has all but disappeared from India, in mainland Southeast Asia, Theravada Buddhism is established religion; whereas in Vietnam, Mahayana Buddhism predominates. In Bali, Hindu-Buddhist religion still prevails. Asoka sent Sona and Uttara to preach Buddhism to *Suvarnabhumi* in third century B.C.E. According to the local tradition preserved in *Ourangkhanittan* chronicle of Laos, at the time of Asoka, five Buddhist monks brought the relics of Buddha from Rajgir[154]. Sailors and merchants of India brought the message of Buddha to the region. The monastery of Nalanda attracted large number of pilgrims for Indonesia. Sri Lanka played an important role in propagating Buddhism as Theravada Buddhism originating from there flourished in Myanmar and Thailand. As a faith repudiating caste and race, the missionaries of India and pilgrims of Southeast

---

152   O.W. Wolters, "Khmer 'Hinduism' in the seventh century" in R.B. Smith & W.Watson eds, *Early Southeast Asia : Essays in Archaeology, History and Historical Geography* (London, 1979), P. 43.
153   Personal observation of the author.
154   Virachith. Keomanichanh, *India and Laos* (New Delhi, 1981), P. 58.

Asia transmitted Buddhism. As a religion of the traders, Buddhism became acceptable to many. The Mahayana concept of Boddhisattva status of near divinity to merciful rulers appealed to the royalty and the ambitious kings claimed this status. Buddhism was strongly patronized by the Sailendra rulers of Java, which was reflected in art, and architecture of the period and the greatest of these monuments is Borobudur. The *candi* Sewu and Plaosan are inspired by Mahayana faith with emphasis on worship of Bodhisattvas. King Kertanagara of Singhasari (1268-92 C.E.) was known as Siva Buddha and his inscriptions point towards practice of Tanrtric Buddhist sect, Vajrayana.[155] The images representing Buddhist tantric pantheon of *candi* Jago in east Java have inscriptions in the script akin to the type prevalent in Orissa at that time. This assumes significance considering the fact that Mahayana used to flourish in Ratnagiri and Lalitgiri. In the mainland Southeast Asia, the Chinese travellers like Hsuan-Tsang and I Ching had given valuable account of Buddhism. When Jayavaman I was the ruler of Kambuja, Buddhism was flourishing in the seventh century. Archaeological excavations in Hmawza of Myanmar had yielded number of Buddhist sculptures and terracotta. In the eleventh century, at the time of Anawrata of Pagan, Buddhims was the state religion. The discovery of Buddhist inscriptions at Noen Sa Bua in east Thailand dated 761 C.E. attests to the expansion of Buddhism in Thailand. In Southeast Asia, Buddhism co-existed with Saivism and their close relations reached high watermark in the reign of Kertanagara who was known as Siva-Buddha. The Manjusri image inscription of 782 C.E. in central Java expressed that the Boddhisattva embodies Brahma, Visnu, Mahesvar and Indra. Equating of the highest Boddhisattva stages with

---

155   Casparis and Mabbet, n. 29, P.320.

Hindu Gods by the Mahayana text, *Dasabhumikasutra* is another example of religious toleration.

At the time of decline of the Indianized kingdoms of Southeast Asia, Islam began to penetrate the region.[156] The Arab traders played an active role in bringing the region under spell of Islam. They purchased pepper from Sumatra and spices of Moluccas and Bandas. After the advent of Turks to India, Islamization of Southeast Asia began. The conquest of north India by the Turks was an event of far reaching consequences for Southeast Asia. From India, Islam went to Southeast Asia. The spice-and pepper trade to the Mediterranean by the Gujrati traders resulted in establishment of Muslim settlements in Southeast Asia. From Gujrat and Coromandel coast, where contact with Southeast Asia was there from earlier times, the traders visited the region and helped in spreading Islam. As the Indian Muslims brought the religion, Islam in Southeast Asia was not like orthodox Islam of Arabia. The Indian traders were themselves newly converted, so the religion that they brought was not completely alien. For the Southeast Asians, they preserved some Hindu-Buddhist characteristics long acquired by their contact with India. Javanese tradition attributed the coming of Islam to nine preachers or *wali-sanga*. A trader from Gujrat named Malik Ibrahim was the first one and his tomb at Gressik near Surabaya is dated 1419 C.E.[157] As described by Marco Polo, the northern point of Sumatra saw the stronghold of Islam for the first time. On his homeward journey, he came to the port of Perlak in 1292. He mentioned that inhabitants

---

156 P.P. Mishra, "Islm in Southeast Asia : A Case Study of Southern Thailand" in *Asian Studies* 1987, V, P.1.
157 Casparis and Mabbet, n. 29, P. 331.

of the city had been converted to Islam.[158] The ports like Samundra and Achen became Islamized subsequently. By the end of fourteenth century, northern Sumatra accepted Islam. The tombstone of the Sultan Malik al-Saleh of Pasai is dated 1297 and the stone was supplied from Cambay in Gujrat. However, the progress of Islam became rapid after rise of Malacca. The earliest evidence of Islamic presence in the Malaya Peninsula was a stone inscription found at Trengganu.[159] It says that the local people have accepted Islam. Paramesvara, a rebel refugee from Majpahit founded Malacaca and converted himself to Islam taking the name of Iskandar Shah in 1414. Malacca soon became prominent politically as well as commercially. The Malaccan Empire included Kedah, Trengganu, Jahore and Pahang. It also became an emporium. The spice trade route was from Moluccas to India through Malacca. This port attracted many traders from neighbouring areas as well as India and many of the traders were Muslims. The Gujratis, Parsis, Arabs, Bengalis, Kalingans etc. constituted the trading communities. The Tamils were also involved in politics and rose to high position. These *Marakkayars* from the Coromandel were playing major part in politics as well as trade.[160] Malacca was also becoming the main diffusion centre of Islam in Southeast Asia. By 1459 Pehang, Jahore, Benkalin, Bintang etc. had become Islamized and Pattani kingdom of southern Thailand in 1498. Brunei accepted

---

158 Aa. Ricci, trans, *The Travels of Marco Polo* (1931) P. 282.
159 G. Coedes, *The Indianized States of Southeast Asia* (Honolulu, 1965), P. 231.
160 For details see, S.J. Stephen, "Entrepot of Malacca in the trading world of Southeast Asia and Portuguese networks of overseas commerce with the ports of Tamil country in South India" in *Journal of the Institute of Asian Studies*, XII, No.2, PP. 16-28.

Islam through trade from Malacca and sultanate of Brunei was set up in 1440. On the eve of Portuguese conquest of Malacca in 1511, Islam was firmly entrenched in west Malaysia, northeast Java and important centres in north Sumatra. After coming of Islam, there was no clear break with the pre-Muslim past. In Java, the influence of pre-Islamic doctrines was retained. It absorbed certain elements of Islam but earlier Hindu and Buddhist practices continued. Even the tradition of *ashramas* continued until the middle of seventeenth century. As late as early nineteenth century, people in Java did not take Islam seriously and even some observed the Hindu taboo on beef eating.[161] Fundamental unity of old and new religions was specified and one of the ancestors of Mataram dynasty stated, "there is no difference between Buddhism (which included other religions of Indian origin) and Islam: they are two in form, but only one in essence (literally: name)".[162] Ancient traditions were retained in many rituals and a spirit of compromise was there. In Malaysia, Indra's thunderbolt symbol was there on the armlets worn by the Sultan and capital of Pahang was called Indrapura. It took some more time for Islam to be entrenched fully. Process of Islamization is still going on and in places like Bali indigenous belief still predominates.

A Critique of Indianization Theory

Indianization is the term generally used for Indian cultural influence upon Southeast Asia. The Indian cultural penetration was by peaceful and non-political methods.[163]

---

161 Cady, n. 13, P. 170.
162 Quoted in Casparis and Mabbett, n. 29, Pp. 332-33.
163 P.P. Mishra, Contact between Orissa and South East Asia in Ancient Times" in*The Journal of Orissan History* , 1980, Vo.I, no. 2, P. 16.

Earlier tendency of the scholars had been to regard the process of Indianization as an Indian initiative. Southeast Asia was at the receiving end and playing a passive role. Nationalist historian of India as 'colonies' of India described the region. In 1926, the 'Greater India Society' was established to enlighten the role of India in Southeast Asia. The region was regarded as colony of India. Its members referred to Indian adventurers going in ships and setting up kingdoms after kingdoms.[164] Indigenous population was characterized as passive recipients of Indian culture. This type of misconception still lingers on in certain quarters. The earlier view of large scale Indian migration colonizing Southeast Asia no longer holds good. Arrival of large number of Indians would have made significant demographic changes. The people of Southeast Asia did not adopt even dietary habits of the Indians like curry powder or milk products. Politically also none of the supposed Southeast Asia 'colonies' showed any allegiance to India. Economically speaking, the states of Southeast Asia were not colonies as there was no scope of economic exploitation. India also did not enjoy monopoly in the field of foreign trade.[165] However, the role of the nationalist historiography

---

164　For details see, R.K. Mookerji, *Indian Shipping* (Calcutta, 1957). Some of the titles of the books of earlier scholars is also suggestive. R.C. Majumdar and P.N. Bose named their books as *Ancient Colonies in the Far East* and *The Indian colony of Siam* respectively. Majumdar even writes in a biased way. "The Hindu Colonists brought with them the whole framework of their culture and civilization and this was transplanted in its entirety among the people *who had not yet emerged from barbarism*, emphasis added. See R.C.Majumdar, *Greater India* (Bombay, 1948), P. 21.

165　V.R. Thakur and B.K. Singh, "Studying Indian Cultural Influence in South East Asia in Manjushree Rao and oth-

should not be undervalued. It had a role to play under the colonial rule of the British, by projecting past glory of ancient India. The nationalist historians were also erudite scholars. Moreover, influence of Indian culture should be put in proper perspective and should not be minimized. N. Tarling's edited work. *The Cambridge History of Southeast Asia*, Volume I has not done sufficient justice to the Indian influence in the region. The role of Kaundinya in Funan had been neglected (p. 193) and part played by Indian Muslim in Southeast Asia had not received adequate attention (pp. 330-33). Even in the 'Bibliographic Essay some of the works of Indian scholars have not been mentioned. J.C. van Leur has stated that various forms of 'foreign culture' and 'world religions' had not brought "any fundamental change in any part of Indonesian social and political order."[166] This is far from true. W.G. Solheim has also in his writings not given due justice to Indian cultural elements.

Absence of concrete evidences regarding Indian cultural expansion has resulted in postulating various theories regarding motives and process of Indianization. Even the use of term 'Indianization' has been criticized because "it may suggest a conscious effort on the part of Indians to spread their culture over major parts of Southeast Asia".[167] Some western scholars have preferred the term 'classical' and the terms like 'Indic' and 'Indianization' had been discarded. One author went to the extent of saying that his objection to the term 'Indianization' was "the modern prejudice against Indians in twentieth-century

---

ers ed, *India's Cultural Relations with SouthEast Asia* (Delhi, 1996), P. 21.

166   J.C. van Leur, *Indonesian Trade and Soceity* (The Hague, 1955), P. 95.

167   Casparis and Mabbett, n. 29, P. 281.

Burma, where because of many Indians were of a lower socio-economic status, we concluded that they surely could not have influenced Burma in the past."[168] In spite of objection in certain quarters, regarding the use of the term 'Indianization', the author for study of Indian cultural influence has retained it. It has been used in a broader context with due emphasis on Southeast Asian initiative or *indigenization*. Regional bias also complicates the matter, different regions of India claiming credit for their role in cultural expansion. However, consensus is that process of Indianization was accomplished by peaceful means and it was non-political in character.

The polemics is about the factors, process and extent of Indian influence in Southeast Asia. Various theories have been propounded in spite of the fact that they are not entirely exclusive of one another. There is first the *ksatriya* (warrior class) theory, which presupposes that the Indian cultural expansion was due to the seminal influence of the Indian warriors and conquerors, who migrated in large numbers to Southeast Asia. The adventurous *ksatriya* immigrants established 'colonies' after 'colonies' in Southeast Asia. They got married into local ruling families and afterwards enlisted the service of *brahmans* for buttressing their political authority. Due to disturbed political condition in India, large number refugees migrated to seek new places across the ocean. There is no proof of large-scale migration after Asoka's conquest of Kalinga in 261 B.C.E.; rather the war made remorseful Asoka turning towards Buddhism. Neither Kusana invasions of first century C.E. nor Samudragupta's campaign resulted an exodus of people. The propounder of

---

168 M. Aung Thwin, "The Classical Southeast Asia : The Present in the Past" in *Journal of Southeast Asian Studies*. 1995, XXVI, P. 81, f.n. 22.

this *ksatriya* hypothesis C.C.Berg visualized introducing of Indian culture because of the activities of Indian warriors playing the role of robber barons, marrying locally and producing a society of mixed blood.[169] R.C. Majumdar, another proponent of this hypothesis puts forth the view that Indian influence can be explained by colonization due to the warriors[170]. All the above postulations are speculative and there is no real evidence for it. Indian immigration was not so massive otherwise; there might have been demographic changes among the inhabitants. There is no doubt that persons of Indian origin are residing in some pockets of Thailand as in Nakhon Sri. Thammarat and Bangkok. It is not known in what circumstances they came. The argument that overseas empires were colonized and administered from Indian centres can be dismissed due to absence of evidences. In the inscriptions of Southeast Asia, one does not find any reference to the ancestry of these warriors or the reasons for their coming to distant lands. However, it is plausible that sons passed over in the succession might have gone to far off places to seek glory and power, which they considered their due.[171] This is a mere suggestion only and not supported by any fact.

The *vaisya* (merchant class) theory postulates that Indian cultural penetration began with traders, who intermarried with local women and impressed the indigenous population with their goods and culture.

---

169   D.G.E. Hall, *A History of Southeast Asia* (New York, 1964), P. 19.
170   R.C. Majumdar, *Ancient Indian Colonies in Far East*, Vol II, (Dacca, 1937), pp.138-47.
171   I.W. Mabbett, "The 'Indianization of Southeast Asia : Reflections on the Historical Sources" in *Journal of Southeast Asian Studies*, 1977, VIII, No. 2, P.156.

From the trading establishments of the Indians, the Indian culture was diffused. The traders were thus transmitters of the culture to the Indianized elite. Apart from N.J. Krom,[172] G. Coedes has stated that commerce was the prime factor behind the Indian expansion in first century C.E.[173] He says that Indian traders in search of spice and gold came to Southeast Asia, married into the local families and an Indian imposing himself as chief over local population or a local chief becoming Indianized established Indian style kingdoms.[174] The services of the *brahmans* were enlisted, who merged the Hindu religious system with local cults and made the rulers as *avataras* (incarnations) of God and eventually transmitted legal codes. Coedes had not supported the idea of mass migration and had recognized the local initiative as well as vitality of its culture. The *Vaisya* hypothesis may be criticized on following point: i) merchants were not enlightened enough to transmit a higher culture or to have contact with royalty[175] ii) they were versed in vernacular language only and not Sanskrit[176] iii) the scholastic character of Indian culture in Southeast Asia had been learned by the people and not brought by Indians[177] iv) if the traders had played a major role in spreading Indian culture, the early centres of Indian civilization would have been found in the coastal regions, whereas the centres were in the interior of Java and royal abodes, were also not in coastal regions v) commercial contacts were not enough for

---

172   *Ibid*, P. 144.
173   Coedes, n. 40, p. 19.
174   *Ibid, Pp. 21-26*.
175   n. 47, P. 107.
176   F.D.K. Bosch, *Selected Studies in Indonesian Archaeology* (The Hague, 1961),PP. 1f.
177   W.F. Stutterheim, *Indian influence in the Land of the Pacific* (Weltevreden, 1930), pp. 4ff.

transmission of civilization.[178] In spite of serious objections to the *vase* theory, it contains elements of truth. It would be wrong to assume that merchants were not competent to transmit elements of culture. In spite of the caste system in India, there was social mobility among different castes. The *brahmans* were performing functions other than besides being priests. If they could travel overseas despite sastric injunctions, they could take vocations like trade. The *ksatriyas* were not warriors only and there are numerous instances of kings and princes well versed in literature. Therefore, it would be wrong to say that the *vaisyas* were not acquainted with Sanskrit and were well versed in vernacular literature only. It is also not convincing to say that character of Indian culture was scholastic; whether the people who had learned elements of Indian culture were locals or Indians who had come to Southeast Asia.[179] It is also not correct to say that only interior areas were centres of Indian influence. Oc eo, Palembang, Trang and Kedah were ports, which had traces of Indian influence. They were not only centres of commercial activities but places of cultural interaction. Oc eo was one such place, where archaeological excavations had proved Indo- Southeast Asian contact. Sanskrit inscriptions of earlier period had been found from Kedah. The find spots of Amaravati sculptures were on the sea-route joining Kedah, Polembang, coast of east Java and west Celebes. Among the merchant groups, Buddhism also was stronger. Removal of caste barriers and restrictions on maritime voyages resulted in coming of sailors. The *Jataka* stories had dealt with maritime activities of the traders. Influence of Buddhism on maritime commerce was on increase. The Buddha images of Amaravati school had been

---

178   Bush, n. 57, Pp. 8-10.
179   Mabbebt, n. 52, P. 157.

found in Southeast Asia. The sailors were devotees of Dipankara Buddha, 'Calmer of Waters' and evidences of Indianization are these Buddha images.[180] The activities of Buddhist missionaries gave impetus further as they were coming to the royal courts of Indonesia converting the ruler and establishing new order of monks.[181] Therefore, overall, in spite of criticism against the *vaisya* theory, it contains certain degree of historical truth and through trading centres, elements of Hindu and Buddhist culture spread.

The third theory, commonly known as *brahmana* theory accorded primacy to local initiative: indigenous port patricians and rulers enlisted the service of *brahmans* to buttress their political authority through Hindu ceremonies and rituals. This view of J.C. Van Leur propounded in 1930s opened new perspective by not only rejecting the earlier two theories but also giving importance to local initiative. He wrote, "The Indian priesthood was called east-wards certainly because of its wide renown for the magical, sacral, legitimacy of dynastic interest and the domestication of subjects, and probably for the organization of the ruler's territory into a state[182]". Emanating from the court, the Indian cultural influence was focussed on consecration formulas, royal proclamations; which were in the sacerdotal language of the *brahmans*. The priests became counsellors in the affairs of the courts and provided political support to the rulers by giving them a sort of investiture and genealogical list, which elevated their position. Thus, the *brahmana* theory made Indianization process an initiative

---

180 Coedes, n. 40, P. 21 and P. 23.
181 Hall, n. 50, p. 20.
182 Van Leur, n. 47, P. 103.

of elite of Southeast Asia. Though the local elite had awareness of their own traditions; this does not 'proclaim a total victory for the *brahmana* theory[183]'. Van Leur has also contradicted his own views sometimes. In one place he says that there was no fundamental change in social and political order of Indonesia but in another place writes, "Alongside the priesthood, Indian artifice came to the royal courts and the architectural activities of the rulers and the official activities of these overseas states alike show the unmistakable imprint of Indian civilization on Ceylon, Indonesia, Farther India, and Southern Indo-China[184]." Even if one agrees to the view propounded by the *brahmana* theory that it was local aristocracy who took the initiative, nevertheless the Indian elements like Sanskrit language, the Hindu-Buddhist cults, *Dharmasastras*, concept of royalty etc. became essential features of the early states of Southeast Asia. Although a small population of the region was affected by Indian culture, this aristocracy had bequeathed to their people cultural heritage in the form of literature, monuments and icons. It is also difficult to agree with the proposition that Indian influence was confined to royalty and court. The common people were influenced by it. As it has been rightly said,"... to understand religious history in its social reality, we need to step outside the monastery or temple library and look at the didactic bas-reliefs on

---

183 Mabbett, n. 52, P. 157. Mabbett further argues, "Purely local myths, rites and styles may have acquired membership in the library of an originally Indian great tradition, or put on Indian style dress in order to qualify, but whether the library was begun by adventurers, traders, priests in the employment of traders, priests in the employment of locals or educated locals remain an entirely open question". *ibid.*
184 Van Leur, n. 47, P. 95 and P. 103.

the temple walls... at the stories told to children of the spirits of heroes who lived long ago..."[185].

Therefore, all the three hypotheses narrated above contain some amount of historical truth. The whole process of Indianization was outcome of endeavours of warriors, traders and priests along with the indigenous initiative. Most probably all the three categories of people were involved in the process. Quite often, the three types of people; *ksatriya, vaisya* and *brahmana* were not distinct in the Southeast Asian context. A *ksatriya* might be a trader or a *vaisya* might indulge in power struggle of the court. All these classes of people also might seek local help to serve their interests and the latter in turn would have desired assistance from the influential Indians.

Another approach towards studying Indian cultural influence is in the context of indigenization and the subscribers to this view went to the extent of replacing the term 'Indic' with classical.[186] The attempt to give importance to greater role of Indians or purely indigenous initiative may result into a 'semantic' one. Rather the interaction between Indian and local cultures should be emphasized. Southeast Asia had already reached a high level of civilization which made it to choose those elements of Indian culture which were either consistent with or could be moulded to its own beliefs. Visnu's concert Laksmi became Goddess promoting fertility in rice fields in west Java. Siva was transformed to the tradition of cult of earth God in Campa. In the site of Ba Phanom of Cambodia, the Goddess receiving sacrificial rituals was an amalgamation of earlier *Me Sa* (white mother)

---

185   Casparis and Mabbett, n. 29, P. 282.
186   Aaung-Thwin, n. 49, P. 79. The term 'classical' period in Southeast Asian history means the period between the ninth and fourteenth centuries A.D.

with the Indian Goddess Mahisasuramardini. The stories of *Ramayana* were changed in the Thai, Lao or Indonesian versions. In the *devaraja* cult, there was blending of Hindu concept with Southeast Asian mountain cult. These type of example, are numerous and will be dealt with in subsequent chapters. The Southeast Asian peoples absorbed into their indigenous cultural patterns the Indian elements after adapting it to their own necessities.

It would be not, out of place to discuss how the 'Indian culture', which is not one organic unit but composed of different traditions spread in India itself. If 'Indianization' of Southeast Asia was an extension of 'Aryanization' within India,[187] there might be some similarities between the way Indian culture spread in Southeast Asia with the same process it advanced in different parts of India. The two way process between Sanskrit culture and the outlying group involving initial contact as well as permeation of that culture resulted in upward social mobility. The idea of Sanskritization is associated with M.N. Srinivas, who defines it as a "process by which a low Hindu caste, or tribal or other group, changes its customs, ritual, ideology, and way of life in the direction of a a high, and frequently, 'twice-born' caste",[188] Sanskritization was not only confined to Hindu castes but also to the tribals undergoing this process. Even before Srinivas, other scholars had studied this aspect of Indian society. A.C.Lyall,[189] has stated that

---

187 Coedes, n. 40, P. 15 & 25. Coedes writes that the Indianization of Southeast Asia is the "Continuation overseas of a 'Brahmanization' that had its earliest focus in Northwest India and the process began before Buddha and is continuing in Bengal and South India". *Ibid*. P. 15.

188 M.N. Srinivas, *Social Change in Modern India* (New Delhi, 1972), P. 6.

189 A.C.Lyall, *Asiatic Studies* (Lodon, 1882), Pp. 102-3.

among the aboriginal or non-Aryan communities social change is going on for centuries. The upward mobility results from discovery of a Hindu lineage by the *Brahmans*. H.H. Riley[190] has pointed out the process by which tribals underwent the process of brahmanization: tribal chief being allied to a recognized caste as the ruling families of Chotanagpur claiming to be Rajputs, a whole tribe accepting brahmanical rites and some getting converted to Hinduism without discarding tribal designation or their deities.

Max Weber[191] in his study of religions of India has presented the scenario of Hinduism spreading to different parts of India, from the core region of Aaryavarta under the Guptas. The ruling groups of the tribes were initiated to particular Hindu customs through extensive Hinduization of tribal areas. The *brahmans* gave the tribal rulers testimony that they were of *kshatriya* blood. By this process of legitimization, the rulers were integrated into Hindu society as the legitimate Raja and became the master of subject classes. The 'intensive' Hinduization of Weber referred to the process in the areas already under Hindu domination, where people of lower strata rose to higher position. Srinivas dealt with the 'extensive' and 'intensive' Hinduization half a century afterwards. The concept of Sanskritrization became the most influential instrument in studying the social change in Indian society. Srinivas later added *ksatriya, vaisya* and *sudra* models to the brahmnical model, which had stressed the adoption of brahmanic way of life by lower caste. Whereas the brahmanical model is more or less akin to Weber's 'intensive' Hinduiztion, the

---

190 H.H. Risley, *Tribes and Castes of Bengal* (Calcutta, 1892), XVI.
191 H. Gerth and D. Martindale, trans, Max weber's *The Religion of India* (Glencoe, 1958), pp. 10-11.

ksatriya model like his 'extensive' Hinduization resulted in tribal chiefs becoming *ksatriyas*.[192] They improved their status by claiming Rajput origin and thus legitimized their new position. The Sailodbhavas of Orissa had tribal origin[193] and there are numerous examples like tribals of central India claiming to be Rajputs. Thus, the 'ksatriyaziation' of tribal rulers and their surroundings resulted in Hinduization of tribal areas.[194] The prestige and rank of *brahmans, ksatriyas* and *vasyas* varied from locality to locality and the lifestyles of traders and peasants were taken as role models in the areas, where they were predominant. Sanskritization became a major process of cultural change throughout Indian history.

The process by which the dominant theme of Indian culture spread to different parts of India has been applied in spreading of Indian culture in Southeast Asia also. Influence of Weber's concept of Hinduization had taken place in the field of Southeast Asian Studies[195]. Van Leur makes comparison of spread of north Indian culture to south India

---

192 S. Sinha, "State Formation and Rajput Myth in Central India" in *Man in India*, 1962, XXXII, pp. 35ff. This model is also known as Rajputization. D.F. Pocock has also mentioned the *Ksatriya* model and M. Singer talks of three models see Srinivas, n. 69, Pp. 7-8.

193 H.Kulke, *Kings and Cults State Formation and Legitimation in India and Southeast Asia* (New Delhi, 1993), p. 273.

194 H. Kulke, "Max Weber's Contribution to the Study of Hinduization in India and 'Indianization' in Southeast Asia" in D. Kantowsky ed, *Recent Researches on Max Weber's Studies of Hinduism* (London, 1984), P. 104.

195 *Ibid*, P. 108, See also Coedes, n. 40, p. 15 & 25. S. Levi and L. de la Vaillee Poussin also makes comprarsion see Mabbett, n. 52, P. 158, f.n. 121.

with explanation of India's influence in Southeast Asia[196]. He says that the *brahmans* were instrumental in making south India Hinduized. Indonesia and south India had contact through trade. The Indonesian aristocratic groups invited the *brahmans* for legitimizing their interest. Like Weber, Van Leur had highlighted the importance of *brahmans* in organizing the ruler's territory into state[197]. Indian culture consists of plurality of traditions, which evolved out of interaction between Sanskrit culture and vernacular lore of dominant groups. It spread to Southeast Asia also because of interaction between indigenous and imported cultures.

Indian culture was diffused through the autochthonous societies of Southeast Asia, whose material base was of such a standard that it could assimilate elements of that culture. The people of Southeast Asia had knowledge of metal industry, long-established contact with outside world, acquaintance with marine technology and a developed agriculture. An attempt to assign greater role either to India or to Southeast Asia would be futile. Moreover, giving importance to terminology like Indic, Indianization, Classical or Indigenization would result into semantic controversy. The whole process of Indian cultural influence was interaction between culture of India and Southeast Asia.

---

196 Van Leur, n. 47, Pp. 97-103
197 Kulke, n. 95, P. 10. Kulke writes, "In regard to his (Van Leur's) refutation of the concept of 'Indianization' of Southeast Asia, Van Leur's thesis in essentially a 'transplantation' of Weber's Hinduization theory to Indonesia", *Ibid*, P. 111.

CAHPTER-111

Orissa's Relations with Myanmar and Thailand

(A) MYANMAR

Political and Cultural Development

The constituent geographical parts of present Myanmar is the history of several peoples like the Mons, Pyus, Shans, Karens and Burmans interacting and fighting for supremacy for many centuries. The Burmese got the upperhand eventually and the area is known as Burma. Afterwards the name was changed to Myanmar. The whole area may be regarded as tropical. In the north, the boundary between Myanmar and China has not been clearly demarcated. Rugged Arakan mountains separate northwestern Mynamar from states of Assam and Manipur in northeastern India. This part of Southeast Asia is adjacent to India and a land route existed since pre-historic times, when there was migration of different races between northeast India and Myanmar. On the west, most of Indian influence had reached through Bay of Bengal. The gulf of Martaban is on the southwest. On the eastern side, the frontier touches Thailand and Laos and the Pakchan river forms the southern boundary. Situated between two major powers India and China, Myanmar is influenced by culture of both.

The region is referred as *Suvarnabhumi* or golden land in the Buddhist *Jatakas*[198]. Geographically closet to India, Myanmar was a vital link between India and Southeast Asia. According to legends, people from eastern coast of India were going towards eastern region. Local traditions speak of Indian immigrants establishing political authority all over the region. However, there are no evidences to it. One of the popular legends mentions that a prince of Sakya clan of Kapilavastu of Nepal, Abhiraja migrated to upper Myanmar and founded the city of Sankissa (Tagaung) on the upper Irrawaddy valley[199]. He declared himself the ruler of the region and after his death, his two generations became the rulers of Arakan and Sankissa. Kings of Ganga valley occupied the latter and after sixteen generations, foreign invaders occupied Sankissa.

The earliest people to come and in contact with India were the Mons living in lower Myanmar and to the east of Solween river in Thailand. Before Christian era, they were living in central Myanmar and later they migrated to south. They were also known as Peguans or Talaings. The belief that they migrated from Telengana region of Andhra Pradesh and their identification with *Kirats* of ancient Indian literature does not have any historical basis[200]. The Mon

---

198 V. Fausball, ed., *The Jatakas*, Vol. VI (London, 1897), P. 22.
199 R.C. Majumdar, *India and Southeast Asia* (New Delhi, 1979), P. 161.
200 That *Kirats* were messangers of Indian culture and tradition in Myanmar does not have any basis. See N.K. Sahu, *Oriya Jatira Itihas* in Oriya (Bhubaneswar, 1977), P. 384.

settlements were known as Ramanna-desa and their capital was at Hansavati, the name of modern Prome[201]. They were linguistically and in physical appearances akin to the Khmers and their having migrated from India is without any base. The Mons were expert in the art of navigation and they had contact with the Coromandel coast, interior Telengana and Orissa[202]. On the eastern side of Tenasserim, the first Mon state was located and it was known as Dvaravati. The people were having cultural and commercial intercourse with the India. Theravada Buddhism spread throughout mainland Southeast Asia from ancient Mon countries of lower Irrawaddy and Menam valley.

The Pyus were a significant ethnic people, who migrated southward from southwest China into the Irrawaddy basin. Corresponding roughly with Irrawaddy basin, they set up an Indianized kingdom in third century C.E., which was called Piao by the Chinese[203]. The kingdom centred round the present town of Prome and was known as Sriksetra around 638 C.E., which was founded by the Vikram dynasty[204]. Buddhism flourished in the region as evident from yielding of fragmented Pali texts going back to sixth century C.E. According to the Chinese sources, the people were extremely peace loving and even extraction of silk was avoided as it involved killing of silk worms[205].

---

201 Ibid.
202 J.F. Cady, *Southeast Asia : Its Historical Development* (New York, 1976), P. 15 and P. 113.
203 G. Coedes, *The Indianized States of Southeast Asia* (Honolulu, 1965), P. 62.
204 Cady, n. 5, P. 112. In Hsuan Tsang's account it is known as She-li-cha-ta-lo and in Burmese, Thayekhettaya, See Coedes, n. 6, P. 77.
205 D.R. Sardesai, *Southeast Asia, Past and Present* (New Delhi, 1983), P. 34.

A gigantic statue of white elephant served as oracle for purpose of justice. There was an overland trade between China and India through this kingdom. One of the important contributions of the Pyus was the Vikram era, which was named after the ruling dynasty. Starting from 638 C.E., this era having Indian origin spread to Thailand and Cambodia and is still used in Myanmar and Thailand[206]. After the attack by powerful Nan Chao kingdom of Thais in 832 C.E., the Pyus were finished politically. In Arakan region, there was another Indianized kingdom having two branches of ruling family with capitals at Tarupattana and Vaisali. The ruins of the royal family known as Dharmarajanuraja Vamsa had a list of nine kings and some of the monuments show the Gupta influence.

After the collapse of the Pyu state, the Mrammas (Sanskritized Brahma) or Burmans founded their chief city, Pagan (Arimarddanapura or city where enemies were exterminated) around 849 C.E. They had been pushed back by the ethnic Chinese around second millennium B.C.E. from north-west China to eastern Tibet, from whose they moved to Myanmar over several centuries. The first Burman centre developed in the rice-growing Kyawkse plain at the confluence of Irrawaddy and Chindwin rivers. After defeating the Pyus, they dominated the northern part of Irrawaddy valley. According to the local chronicles, Pagan began as a group of nineteen villages, each having its *nat* or local spirit and later the *nats* were fused into the cult of common spirit for all the inhabitants to worship[207]. The nearby mountain Poppa became the place for setting up a pair of spirits. Thus, religious and territorial

---

206   *Ibid.*
207   Coedes, n. 6, P. 106.

unification was achieved[208]. Deriving divine royal authority from sacred mountains was alike the Khmer beliefs. The Burmese legends speak of intrigue and bloodshed in the early Pagan history until the emergence of king Anawratha or Aniruddha (1044-77 C.E.).

Aniruddha conquered the Mon country of Thaton in 1057 C.E. resulting in infusion of Mon culture into Pagan. He maintained friendly contact with the king of Sri Lanka Vijayabahu. The Cola ruler Kulottunga I was threatening the latter[209]. Vijayabahu asked for help to the Pagan king, who sent military supplies. Sri Lanka's king sent Aniruddha the tooth relic of Buddha, which was enshrined, in the Shwezigon pagoda. Both the kingdoms were maintaining friendly relations. Pagan was brought into the maritime trading network linking the eastern coast of India. Along with the Mon monk and scholar, Shin Arhan, Aniruddha was responsible for spreading Hinayana Buddhism among his people. This quickly spread all over Myanmar and eventually to mainland Southeast Asia. Aniruddha also is credited with constructing a large number of Pagodas including the Shwezigon Pagoda. He even visited the Bengal region and got married to an Indian princess[210]. Aniruddha developed the small principality of Pagan into an extensive kingdom and a distinct Burmese civilization

---

208   *Ibid*. The pair of spirits were that of a brother and sister, who had been killed by a neighbouring king. The brother was *Min Mahagiri* (Master of the great mountain) and sister's name in Burmese carried similar meaning, i.e., *Taunggyi Shin ibid*.

209   K.K. Pillay,*South India and Sri Lanka* (Madras, 1975), Pp. 76 n and Ranvir Chakrabarti, "Rulers and Ports" in K.S. Mathew, ed. *Mariners, Merchants and Ocean* (New Delhi,1995), Pp. 65ff.

210   Majumdar, n. 2, P. 486.

started to grow based on Mon literature, script, art and architecture.

The second prominent king of Pagan was Thileuin Man (Kyanzittha), who ruled from 1084 to 1112 C.E. He crushed the Mon uprising that had claimed the life of earlier king's son and successor, Man Lulan and made peace with rival Thaton faction of the Mons by matrimonial alliances. In accordance with the brahmanical ritual, he had the coronation ceremony elevating the Burmese kingship to a higher level. The Thervada monkhood flourished under his patronage. Even he fed eight Indian monks with his own hands daily for three months and heard about Buddhist monuments like the famous Ananta temple in the Udayagiri hills of Orissa. He constructed the magnificent Ananda temple in imitation of the above cave temple and it was designed in Indian style.[211] He completed the Shwezigon pagoda. Kyanzittha also visited Bodhgaya and helped in repairing the Buddhist shrines[212]. He tried to bring assimilation of different cultural traditions prevalent in Myanmar and the Myazedi pillar of 1113 C.E. had identical inscriptions in four languages, Burmese, Pali, Pyuand Mon. He sent a mission to China, which recognized the sovereignty of Pagan.

The transition from Mon to Burman culture occurred during the rule of the grandson of Kyanzittha, Alaungsithu (Cansu I), who had a long reign from 1112 C.E. to 1165 C.E. He undertook punitive expeditions to Arakan and Tenasserim. Relations with Sri Lanka deteriorated over interference with trade between Angkor and Sri Lanka. Alaungsithu nurtured Buddhism and completed the

---

211 W.S. Desai, *A Pageant of Burmese History* (Calcutta, 1961), P. 19.

212 Cady, n. 5, P. 118.

imposing Thatpinnyu temple in 1144 C.E. He also asked the king of Arakan to repair the Buddhist shrine in Bodhgaya. The last of important kings of Myanmar was Narapatisithu (Cansu II, 1174-1211 C.E.) who ended the Mon influence in the Pagan court and the Burman idiom was reflected in the temples and monuments. He built the Gawdawpawlin temple. Relations with Sri Lanka improved, resulting in end of friendship of Burmans with Colas and promise of non-interference by Pagan in Sri Lanka's trade over isthmus region[213]. The king also introduced reforms in monkhood.[214] However, his successors were unsuccessful and gradual deterioration started in the Pagan kingdom. The shrinking of central authority resulted in Arakan and Pegu becoming independent. The Tai people known as Shans began to enter Pagan. There was also subsequent Mongol expeditions against the kingdom. The last king of the dynasty Narasimhapati (Cansu IV) was a boastful ruler and his subjects murdered him for his flight at the time of Mongal invasion. Under the leadership of the Shans, the Mongols were evaluated and the kings of Pagan were forced into a ceremonial role only[215]. Further, there was fragmentation of Pagan polity. The problem of Myanmar had been to hold together different ethnic groups and this was faced by the Toungoot dynasty of sixteenth century and Konbaung dynasty (1792-1885 C.E.).

---

213   *Ibid.* 124.
214   M. Aung Thwin, *Pagan : the origins of modern Burma* (Honolulu, 1985), Pp.169ff.

215   K.W. Taylor, "The Early Kingdom" in N. Tarling, ed. *The Cambridge History of Southeast Asia* Vol I (Cambridge, 1992), P. 167.

Indian Influence

The prevalence of Sanskritized names and commercial relations point to the close link between Indian and Myanmar. The region was geographically nearest to India among the Southeast Asian countries and there were land and sea routes through which cultural relations developed. From very early times, the Indians proceeded through these routes to Southeast Asia. Cultural intercourse between the two regions grew probably through traders and Buddhist missionaries reaching lower Myanmar. The Indianized kingdoms were set up. Compared to evidences of Indian cultural influence in Funan and Campa, the evidences in Myanmar belong to a later period. This might be due to circumstances causing the disappearance or delayed discoveries of older sites[216]. The Pyu people set up the kingdom of P'iao in the third Century C.E. They followed Hinduism and Buddhism. The Mons had extensive contact with the Telengana region. The theories of kingship, religion, art and architecture were some of the elements that influenced Myanmar. In the adoption of Indian practices, people exercised discretion like giving a women high place in society and rejecting the caste system.

Though Buddhism dominated in the life of people, Brahmanism was mingled with it. The *brahmans* conducted the ceremonies like royal consecration. Derivation of divine royal authority from sacred mountain like Poppa mount had already been described. The outside influence form India was closely interwoven with ancient beliefs of local people. At the place, where king Kyanzittha's place was to be built, *naga* spirits were propitiated and services of *brahmans* were required[217]. The king was proclaimed as an

---

216   Coedes, n. 6, P. 62.
217   J.G. De Casparis and I.W. Mabbett, "Religion and Popular

avatar (incarnation) of Visnu after his death. The name of one of the early cities of Pyu people was Visnupura (modern Beikthano) and it was a centre of Visnuite influence. In Sriksetra, there was a place for images of Visnu and Laksmi. In the Kagyun cave site, there is a relief of recumbent Visnu and in Myanmar only, there are statues of Visnu standing on his mount Garuda[218]. The image of Brahmanical Gods like Visnu, Brahma and Siva are found in different places of Myanmar. Images of Garuda and Hanumana have been found from Mergui, Surya, Durga and Visnu from Arakan and remains of a Siva *linga* from Kalagangon[219]. Whereas in Indian tradition, Buddha is an incarnation of Visnu, the reverse is true of Myanmar. Visnu is a *rsi* or sage, who built the city of Sriksetra.

Compared to Brahmanism, the sway of Buddhism in Myanmar was greater. In the Buddhist *Jatakas,* there are frequent references to sea voyage to *Suvarnabhumi* or golden land, which has been identified with Myanmar. It has been mentioned earlier the way Theravada Buddhism came to the region. The missionary activities of Asoka, commercial contact with eastern India, relationship with Sri Lanka, visit to Buddhist centres in India royal patronage-all these factors contributed to spread of Buddhism in Myanmar. The Mon countries in the lower Irrawaddy and Menam valley were vital link for spreading Theravada Buddhism throughout mainland Southeast Asia. The archaeological excavation in Visnupura has yielded Buddhist monuments

---

     Beliefs of Southeast Asia before C. 1500" in N. Tarling, n. 18, P. 286.
218   *Ibid*, P. 290.
219   U. Thakur, "A Historic Survey of the elements of Hindu Culture in Burma" in *Imprints of Indian Thoughts and Culture Abroad* (Madras, 1980), P. 147.

with square bases and drum-shaped superstructure of second century C.E.[220]. Inscriptions on gold plates found in Maungun reflect the Pali tradition. There were evidences of Mahayana Buddhism also in the art of Pyu, which included images of Boddhisattvas and Buddhe Dipankara. The Pyu people were aware of a Sanskrit Buddhist canon coming from northeastern India[221]. The Chinese travellers like Hsuan tsang and I Ching attest that Sriksetra was a Buddhist kingdom. In the Mon kingdoms, according to traditions, Buddhism came in fifth century C.E. with the advent of great scholar, Buddhaghosa. Kanci of south India was another place from where Buddhist traditions might have come to Myanmar. The kings like Aniruddha and Kyanzittha were patrons of Buddhism and due to their endeavour, the religion took firm roots in Myanmar. Mahayana Buddhism of Bengal and Orissa influenced the tantric Buddhism prevalent in Myanmar. There was also the example of Atisa (982-1054 C.E.) of Bengal, who spent twelve years in *Suvarnabhumi* and went to Tibet to bring about reforms in the tantric tradition[222]. The practices of Ari sect, images of Hayagriva and inscriptions of Minnanthu temple describing the heterodox practices of Samantakuttaka monks are examples of the tantric practices prevalent in Myanmar. There was also impact of ancient Indian texts. Dhammasenapati, a monk living in the monastery of Ananda temple composed *Karika* marking the beginning of Pali literature[223]. The influence of *Manusmriti* on legal

---

220 Casparis and Mabbett, n. 20, P. 293. These are like stupas of eastern India. See *Report on the Excavations in Beikthano* (Rangon, 1968), referred in, *ibid*.
221 *Ibid*.
222 *Ibid*.
223 Thakur, n. 22, P. 150.

treatise like *Dhammavilasa* is remarkable. The Buddhist *Jataka* stories known as *nibhatkhin* were very popular and stories from it were enacted in dramas[224].

Orissa's Cultural Impact

The geographical proximity of Orissa and Myanmar had resulted in commercial and cultural relations from early times. In Chapter-I, it has been mentioned that there was some affinity of Mon-Khmers with the Munda speaking tribes of Orissa. From the prosperous Orissan ports like Palura and Che-li-ta-lo, sea voyages were undertaken to Southeast Asia through Menam valley of Myanmar. Through the Bay of Bengal separating eastern India from Myanmar, close relations developed between two regions. The legends of the country speak of people coming by sea to lower Myanmar region. According to these, trade relations between the two regions were there at the time of Buddha. Pali became the medium of cultural exchange. The *Dharmasastras* of Manu, Narada and Yajnavalkya formed the basis of treatise on law. Tapussa and Bhallik, the two merchant brothers of Utkala became the first lay disciples of Buddha, while the latter was having the bliss of emancipation at Rajagriha[225]. They were going to Majjhima-desa region with five hundred cartloads of merchandise. The legends of Myanmar mention that two brothers were

---

224 Anupa Pande, "The Jatakas and the Origins of Burmese Drama" in Manjushree Rao and others ed, *India's Cultural Relations with Southeast Asia* (Delhi, 1996), Pp. 163-7. The origin of drama is traced to the *Jatakas*, which also helped in growth of it. *Ibid*, P. 166.

225 N.K. Sahu, *Buddhism in Orissa* (Cuttack, 1958), P. 9. See also Fausball, n.1, pp. 22ff. *The Mahavagga* of the *Vinayapitaka* also confirms this. See J. Eggeling, *Satapatha Brahmana*, XIII, Pp. 81-84.

coming from Okalaba (a variant form of Utkala) to the delta of Irrawaddy. Tapussa and Bhallika received eight handfuls of hair from Buddha and these were enshrined in Asitanjana in a *Chaitya* in Sri Lanka.

Buddhism made progress in Orissa after the Kalinga war of 261 B.C.E. The rock edict XIII of Asoka mentions that both *brahmans* and *sramans* endured war. The war became a turning point in the life of Asoka. Buddhism received stimulus under his patronage. After the third Buddhist council, missionaries were deputed to propagate the religion. Sona and Uttara went to Myanmar and son of Asoka; Mahendra went to Sri Lanka. The monks and missionaries sailed from Kalinga to distant lands for propagation of *dhamma*. Due to efforts of Sona and Uttara, who had been asked by Theravada *sangha* in 250 B.C.E. to proceed to *Suvarnabhumi*. Buddhism spread in Irrawaddy and Menam valley and this became a vital link in spreading Theravada Buddhism in other parts of Southeast Asia. The Pali tradition became important as evident from inscriptions on gold plates found in Maungun[226]. A number of Buddhist teachers were going to the Pyu capital Sriksetra from eastern shores of India for imparting education in Pali[227]. Two gold plates discovered near Prome were having inscriptions written in Pali[228]. The style and language were akin to some of the inscription of Matharas and eastern Gangas of Kalinga. Few of the hymns of Theravada Buddhism discovered in Sriksetra (modern Hmaw-za near Prome) also have similar characteristics. The Buddhist structures of second century C.E. excavated from Visnupura are similar to *stupas* of

---

226   Casparis and Mabbet, n. 20, P. 293.
227   Sahu, n. 23, P. 385.
228   K.P. Jayaswal and R.D. Banerjea, ed, *Epigraphia India* (Calcutta), Vol. V, Pp. 101-102.

eastern India[229]. Influence from Orissa and Bengal could be seen in Mahayana Buddhism and tantric practices that developed in Myanmar. Hsuan tsang, who visited Orissa in 638 C.E., had attested to the fact that *Wu-cha* or *Odra* country was a flourishing centre of Mahayana Buddhism[230]. In seventh and eighth centuries, tantric Buddhism had become a dominant force in Orissa. The Tibetan text *Pag-Sam-Jon-Zang* refers to Odiyan as land of origin of Tantric Buddhism[231]. Lama Taranath had given a list of *siddhas*, who flourished from middle of tenth century to thirteen century C.E. Mahayana Buddhism with its variant forms like *Vajrayana, Sahajayana* and *Kalacakrayana* was popular in Orissa. As has been referred earlier, Mahayana Buddhism was prevalent in Myanmar. Boddhisattvas were popular before the rise of Pagan and thirteenth century images associated with tantric practices were found. The heretic arannyavasi (forest dwelling) and Ari sects was in existence in Myanmar[232]. Tantric works of *mahakalacakra* variety were

---

229   Cassparis and Mobbet, n. 20, P. 293. Archaeological excavation in both the regions will definetely throw more light. Excavations in Manikpatna had yielded a brown glazed ware. This is known as Maratuan ware from the name of the place located in Myanmar. See, K.S. Behera, "Maritime Contacts of Orissa : Literary and archaeological Evidences" in *Utkal Historical Research Journal*, 1994, V. P.66.

230   T.Watters, *On Yuan Chwang's Travels in India* in, Vol. II (London, 1908), P.193.

231   Sahu, n. 28 Pp. 58ff.

232   The forest-dwelling sect headed by Mahakassapa was prevalent in thirteenth century. Two centuries before, the Ari sect was in existence as testified by the official Burmese tradition, *Glass Palace Chronicle*. Probably, the tantric *siddhas* of Orissa and Bengal who had gone to Myanmar introduced this. See, N. Dutt, Hinduism and Buddhism in Southeast Asia" in *Journal of Indian History*, V, P. 121.

also there. It is not unlikely that this form of Buddhism came from Orissa as well as Bengal. They had long tradition of cultural and commercial relations. The monks from these regions were going to Myanmar. Orissa, the birthplace of tantric Buddhism must have been the disseminator of this to Myanmar.

The names of ancient places resembling Orissan geographical places suggest the influence of this region. The old name for Pegu was Ussa (Odra, i.e., Orissa)[233] and it was known as Kalingaratha in old chronicles.[234] Ukkala or Utkala was the northwestern part of the region. The name Sri ksetra suggests familiarity with the sacred place of Puri. Puri was named as Sriksetra after advent of Goddess Laksmi (or Sri). She was worshipped inside the area of Jagannatha temple before the construction of main temple.[235] Codagangadeva did not construct a separate temple for Laksmi. Puri as a Visnuite *ksetra* (place) is referred in the *Visnu Purana* of fifth century C.E. If the chronicles of Myanmar were to be believed, Visnu laid the foundation of the city. The Mons, who were also known as Talaingas had their capital at Trilingan, which had been linked with Trikalinga region of Orissa. However, this argument is not

---

233   Codes, n. 6, P. 33.
234   G.E. Gerini, *Researches on Ptolemy's Geography of Eastern Asia* (New Delhi, 1974), P. 32.
235   G.C. Tripathy, "Concept of Purusottama in the Agamas" in AnncharlottEschmann and others ed, *The Cult of Jagannatha and Regional Traditions of Orissa* (New Delhi, 1986), P. 42. The Goddess Vimala, whose shrine exists withint he Puri temple is known as *Pithesvari* and *Sriksetradhisvai*. The sorrounding area was sacred even before the construction of the main temple. See H.V. Stietncorn, "The Advent of Visnuism in Orissa" in Eschmann, *Ibid*, P. 26.

at all convincing. G. Coedes[236] has mentioned that in lower Myanmar region there were 'colonies' set up by people of Orissa, the principal one being Thaton or Sudhammapura. However, he has given no evidence in support of this.

The languages like Sanskrit and Pali had influenced the language and script of Myanmar. Some of the scripts of Southeast Asia are derived from the *Siddhamatrka* script used in eastern India.[237] Most of the inscriptions of early rulers of Arakan are written in the late Brahmi and *Siddhamatrka* script. The Pali language had contributed to the evolution of the vernacular literature along with important canonical literature and commentaries written in that language. There is a view that Pali originated from Kalinga-Andhrka region[238]. The basis of the argument is derived from the cultural link between the region and Sri Lanka and the language of the first century B.C.E. Hatigumpha inscription of Kharavela. The gold plates found in Maungun had scripts similar to the scripts used by Matharas and eastern Gangas. Some of the coins belonging to eighth century had symbols of Nandi and Trisul, which had close resemblance to the Ganga kings of Kalinga[239].

The art and architecture of different schools of India influenced the Southeast Asian countries. Some of the concepts were India, but in choice of pattern and other details, indigenous touch is there. The different schools of Indian art like Amaravati, Gupta, Pallava, eastern school (Pala and Sena) etc had influenced in varying degree art and architecture of Southeast Asia. The Pyu people had left beautiful monuments at Prome belonging to eighth

---

236   Coedes, n. 6, P. 63.
237   D.C. Sircar, *Indian Epigraphy* (Calcutta, 1939), Pp. 202-203.
238   Sahu, n. 28, P. 35.
239   *Ibid*, P. 385.

century. The cylindrical type of *stupas* with hemispherical or pointed dome had its origin in northeast India and coastal Orissa[240]. Another form characteristics of Pyu kingdom was a monument with an inner chamber supporting the superstructure or *sikhara* of cylindro-conic shape, which is similar to some of the Bhubaneswar temples of Orissa[241]. The five characteristics Pagodas of Pagan architecture are Shwezigon, Ananda, Thatpinnyu, Gawdawpawlin and Mingalazedi. The first one at Thaton was started by king Aniruddha and completed by Kyanzittha in 1112 C.E. The Pagoda is famous for housing the Buddha tooth replica form Sri Lanka. A pyramidal edifice, it has square lower stages and circular upper levels culminating in a *stupa* spire in the form of a bell. The passageways are lined with sculptures. Hairstyle and dressing of some are of Orissan variety and the bas-reliefs of the Pagoda show affinity with early medieval art of Orissa[242]. Resemblance of a 'Siva image seated with Parvati with Hara-Parvati icon on the outer walls of Vaital temple of Bhubaneswar is striking.

King Kyanzittha constructed the famous Ananda temple with its receding terraces surmounted by a sikhara, stone-sculptures and terracota bas-reliefs. Borrowing heavily from Mon standards of architecture, the temple was built in the period between 1082 to 1090 C.E. The legends speak that the king had heard from eight Buddhist monks about the Ananta cave temple in the Udayagiri hills of Orissa and this encouraged him to construct a similar

---

240   Coedes, n. 6, P. 87.
241   P.V. Bapat, "Cultural Migration from India to countries in Southeast Asia", in *Studies in Asian History*, Proceedings of Asian History Congress (New Delhi, 1961), P. 176. See also Coedes, n. 6, P. 87 and Sardesai, n.8, Pp.34-35.
242   N.R. Roy, *Brahmanical Gods in Burma* (Calcutta, 1932), P. 57.

structure[243]. A solid core in the centre bore the weight of the central spire, the design of which has been influenced by mouldings in the towers of Orissan temples. The shape of the terminal *stupa* having vertical ribs and horizontal planes are also akin to the temples of Orissa[244]. The temple of Ananda along with Thatpinnyu and Nanpaya had terraces, spires and latticed windows of Orissan variety. In the ancient site of Sriksetra, King Taung Thugyi built a Visnu temple known as Nat Hlaung Kyaung in the tenth century C.E. The brick temple is square at the base, the walls of which are adorned with statues of the divinities placed in ornamental niches. The dome is surmounted by a *sikhara* having decorative panels and recessed corners. On the outer walls of the temples the ten *avatars* of Visnu are represented by sandstone sculptures placed in niches, which bear the impression of influence from Orissa and Bengal.

Trade and Commerce in Seventeenth and Eighteenth Centuries

The period of imperial Gangas (1035-1435 C.E.) had marked the continuation of overseas trade of Southeast Asia. The cultural contact of the earlier period also went on. Orissa left imprints of its culture in Myanmar. With the accession of Gajapati monarchs (1435-1533 C.E.), this process received a setback. The rulers were busy in internal trouble and foreign aggression. Source material of Gajapati monarchs also does not speak about overseas trade. The narrative of foreign travellers gives sketchy references to the maritime trade. Caesare Frederick visiting in later

---

243 G.E. Harvey, *Outline of Burmese History* (Bombay, 1926), P. 31.
244 A. Bhattacharjee, *Greater India* (New Delhi, 1981), P. 65.

half of sixteenth century mentioned that foreign traders were coming to the kingdom of Mukundadeva (1559-1568 C.E.)[245]. At the time of Afghan rule (1568-1591 C.E.), the indifference of rulers to overseas trade resulted in further deterioration of Orissa's maritime trade. Even at the time of Mughals, the provincial governors controlled the coastal areas for aggrandizement of Mughal Empire. The European powers established their trading centres and ports like Balasore, Pipli and Harishpur rose into prominence. It was the Portuguese, Danes, Dutch and British, who took the leading part. Even the political boundaries of Orissa were subjected to changes and districts of the region came to be controlled by Bengal and Madras. In the south, area from Ganjam to Godavari was regarded as a part of Golconda and came to be known as Gingelly coast, a name it derived from oil seed Gingelly. The Europeans had their factories in Balasore, Pipli and Hariharpur under the chief of Bengal Council. In seventeenth and eighteenth centuries, northern Orissa, i.e. from Puri to Hijli coast was treated as part of Bengal and the coastal belt Ganjam and further south up to river Godavari was regarded as part of Coromandel region. Though Orissa role in trade network of Indian ocean was not that important compared to earlier period, still it was playing its part in a reduced scale.

A number of ports like Baluster, Pip and Harishpur prospered in seventeenth and eighteenth centuries attracting European and Asian merchants. The Dutch and English were firmly established in Orissan ports by mid-seventeenth century. Among the local merchants, the Mughal administrators were prominent. There were also

---

245 P. Mukherjee, *The History of Gajapati kings of Orissa* 2nd ed. (Calcutta, 1981), P. 20. The ships from Malacca and Sumatra were also coming to Orissan ports.

merchants from Orissa proper, who played an important role in the second half of the seventeenth century. Khemchand and Chintaman Shah, the two Balasore merchants were acting as brokers to the English Company[246]. The traders of Hindu and Muslim communities were also carrying trade activities[247]. In the Gingelly coast, the important mercantile community was *Kommatties*[248]. All these merchants were carrying extensive trade from ports of Orissa with countries of Southeast Asia, Sri Lanka and Maldives. The Orissan ships were going to different parts of Myanmar like Pegu, Arakan and Tensserim apart from trading with places like Kedah, Achin, Gale and Jaffna[249]. The commercial importance of Balasore could be attested from the fact that number of ships recorded for Balasore was in preponderance[250]. The import to Tenasserim and Achin were woolen cloth, butter, rice and textile and export from these ports were elephants, tin, spices and non-precious metals[251]. Thomas Bowery's travel accounts mention that traders of Hugli, Pipli and

---

246 S. Chaudhuri, *Trade and Commercial Organization in Bengal, 1650-1720* (Calcutta, 1975), P. 62.

247 *English Factories in India, 1670-1684*, New Series, I, ed by C. Fawcett, Oxford, 1936-53, P. 250.

248 S. Arasaratnam, *Merchants, Companies and Commerce in the Coromandel Coast*, 1650-70, (Delhi : 1986), P. 11. This community still survives in Orissa as *Kumuti* caste indulging in business activities.

249 Om Prakash, "The European Trading Companies and the Merchants of Bengal", in *Indian Economic and Social History Review*, 1964, 1(3), Pp. 40-43.

250 *Ibid*, Pp. 40-42. The Dutch shipping list recorded the departure and arrival of ships in the name of Balasore from and for various ports of Southeast Asia. Between 1680-81 and 1717-18, number is 32 out of 53.

251 Om Prakash, *Dutch-East India Company and the Economy of Bengal, 1630-1720* (Princeton, 1985), P. 28.

Balasore had twenty ships sailing annually for Tenasserim, Sri Lanka and Maldives.[252] There was setback to the trade at Balasore in the middle of the eighteenth century because of Maratha invasions. However, the two Gingelly ports of Ganjam and Vizagpatam showed signs of prosperity. In the eighteenth century, from these ports textiles were being exported to Southeast Asia.

Orissa maintained its position as exporter of foodstuff in the Indian ocean area. Rice as an item of export continued until nineteenth century from Balasore to the ports like Tenasserim, Achin, Kedah and Parah[253]. Overall in the beginning of eighteenth century, Orissan trade was confined to foodstuffs and coarser variety of textiles. Elephants, tin, copper, porcelain, spelter and spices were main items of import from Southeast Asia. From 1680-81 to 1687-88, the number of ships coming to Balasore is known[254]. Khemchand and Chintaman, two Balasore traders imported elephants from Tenasserim in between 1680 and 1684 and from Cochin-China (South Vietnam) elephants, cowries and cloves in 1684[255].

---

252 T. Bowrey, *A Geographical Account of the Countries Round the Bay of Bengal*, 1669 to 1676, ed by R.C. Temple (London, 1905), P. 179.

253 In 1681-82, 200 maunds of ghee and 100 maunds of oil was sent to Tenasserim by Khemchand, a trader from Balasore. In 1683-84, he sent 9000 maunds of rice, 8000 maunds of sugar, 250 maunds of oil and 300 maunds of butter to Achen. See Prakash, n. 52, P. 40.

254 Om Prakash, "Dutch East India Company in Bengal; Trade Privileges and Problems", 1633-1712 in *Indian Economic and Social History Review*, 9(3), 1972, P. 40. The figure is : 10 from Tenasserim, 2 from Malacca, 1 from Achin, 2 from Pegu and 1 from Arakan.

255 K.N. Sethi, "Merchants and Commercial Organisation in

In the above period, Orissa's contact with countries of Southeast Asia was through trade only. From very early times, cultural interaction as well as commercial relations marked Orissa's relationship with the region. This phase continued upto fourteenth and fifteenth centuries. Afterwards cultural interaction became minimized. Upto eighteenth century, Orissa could take part in trading activity involving European and Asian nations. Even the trade relationship suffered under the colonial rule of the British. Moreover, the political dismemberment of the state led to its reduced role in Indo- Southeast Asian relations. When the colonial powers began to extend their domination over Southeast Asian countries, there was shortage of labour and to fill this gap Indians went there. The migrants going from Orissa went to Myanmar particularly and they hailed from Ganjam district. Thus, until the middle of this century, Orissa's role was that of supplying labourers to the region.

(B) THAILAND
Political Development

Thailand formerly known as Siam had rich pre-historical heritage as mentioned earlier. The excavations conducted in places like Ban-kao, Don Ta Phet, Non Nok Tha, Ban Chiang, Spirit cave etc have pushed back the history and culture of Thailand. Though the exact origin of the Mon Kingdom of Dvaravati is obscure, Buddhism of it is well attested. The oldest known Mon-Buddhist inscription near Nakhon Pathom is probably not much earlier than six century C.E. The Buddhist sites like Phra

---

Coastal Orissa in the seventeenth and eighteenth centuries", M.Phil. dissertation, Jawaharlal Nehru University, 1994, Pp. 114-15.

Pathom and Phong Tuk were part of Dvaravati kingdom[256]. This kingdom with strong Buddhist influence stretched to northern Thailand on one side and into Malay Peninsula on the other. During eleventh century, the kingdom started to decline and most of its parts were absorbed into the advancing Khmers. Dvaravati had a developed technology and its art and architecture influenced the region after the end of the kingdom. Before the Tai people came to Thailand in large numbers by the beginning of thirteenth century, different areas of Thailand were under Funan and Sri-Vijaya kingdoms. The neighbouring Khmers also had established authority in central Thailand. Due to pressure from the Mongols, the Tais were compelled to leave Nan Chao in Yunan. The migration process towards south was slow earlier but the conquest of Nan Chao by the Mongols speeded up the process. The decline of Khmer power facilitated their task.

The Tais declared themselves as independent after challenging Khmer suzerainty and thus the first Tai state was set up by Rama Khamhaeng in 1279 C.E. Operating from Sukhothai, he emerged as the strongest personality. He annexed the entire Menam valley and northern part of Malay Peninsula. He also claimed suzerainty over Luang Prabarg, Vientiane and Pegu regions. The central part of Indo-Chinese Peninsula, which was under the Khmer control henceforth saw the Thai domination. It was done

---

256 Coedes, n. 6, P. 63. The discovery of an ivory comb having engraved Buddhist motif from Chansen may be dated to first or second century A.D. See Casparis and Mabbett, n. 20, P. 294. The Buddha icons of Amaravati school dating from second to fourth centuries also have been discovered. These are pointer to Indian influences before sixth century A.D.

at the expense of other races. The Mons specially suffered and their last kingdom, Haripunjaya in the northern Thailand was occupied by the Thais. The accomplishment of Rama Khamhaeng and his successors was in the cultural plane also : achievements in language, script and religion became a distinctive part of Thai culture for centuries to come.

In the middle of fourteenth century, the Thai political power shifted from Menam basin to further south in Ayuthia. The kingdom established by Ramadhipati lasted for the next four centuries. Ruling over much of the former Angkorean empire, the kingdom became the most powerful political entity of the Peninsula. By the end of Ramadhipati's reign in 1369 C.E., the territorial extent of the kingdom covered entire Menam valley, part of Mon country and Malay Peninsula. Rebellions in the north involving Sukhothai and Chieng Mai claimed the attention of Ayuthia. In 1438 C.E. Sukhothai was finally annexed but the problem of Chieng Mai continued. The capture of Khmer capital by the Thais brought new territory and influx of Khmer bureaucrats, artisans and *brahmans* to Ayuthia. Under king Trailok's reign (1448-1488 C.E.), there was efficient system of administration. He brought all the Thai principalities together under the centralized control and divided the kingdom into number of provinces, each headed by a governor.

The second half of sixteenth century was notable for disastrous war with Myanmar. Ayuthia was kept as a vassal state for fifteen years until the Thais defeated the Burmans in 1584. In the seventeenth century, there was peace between them. But the Thai- Burmese conflict was soon revived. During the second half of eighteenth century, the four-century-old beautiful city of Ayuthia was sacked resulting in the end of the kingdom. It was not rebuilt and after the expulsion of Burmans, the Thai capital was established in Bangkok. The new period in Thai history known as Bangkok period began with the establishment of a new dynasty by Rama I in 1782. This Cakri dynasty is still reigning in Thailand.

Indiana Cultural Influence

Thailand had been influenced by external influences from Cambodia, Myanmar, China, Sri Lanka and India. The latter's contact with Thailand could be dated from fourth century B.C.E. as evident from the excavations in the iron age burial site of Ban Don Ta Phet, where bronze bowls have been found. The late pre-historic sites such as Ban Chieng, Ban Na Di, Non Muang, Ban Tha Kae etc have yielded glass beads. These are tangible indicators of contact of Thailand with outside world. The region was technologically developed at the time of India's contact. In the Chapter II it has been mentioned that these excavations bear testimony to cultural interaction between the two regions. Evidences of Buddhism coming to Thailand could be found from discovery of ivory comb having Buddhist motif and icons of Amaravati school of art. The oldest known Mon-Buddhist inscription near Nakhon Pathom is probably not earlier than sixth century C.E.[257]. The Mon kingdom of Dvaravati had Buddhist sites like Phra Pathom and Phong Tuk. One of the special feature of Buddhist art is the representation of Buddha descending from heaven with Indra and Brahma. From Phra Pathom, the aniconic representation of Buddha such as *dharmacakra* with crouching dear point to the strong influence of Buddhism in this kingdom. The Tai conquest of thirteenth century gave further impetus. Rama Khamheng

---

257   Casparis and Mabbett, n. 20, P. 293.

was an ardent follower of Buddhism and made the capital Sukhothai a place of Buddhist centre with monasteries and images of Buddha. In the *Jataka* engravings of Wat Si Jum, influence from Sri Lanka is obvious[258]. The Hinayan form of Buddhism came to Thailand from Myanmar and Sri Lanka. In the development of Buddhism in Thailand, influences from India, Sri Lanka, Cambodia and Myanmar were quite discernible.

Along with Buddhism, the brahmanical faith also had influenced the cultural life of people. The imges of Visnu have been found from the Si Thep (Sri Deva) area in Menam basin datable to the end of sixth century C.E. A Visnu temple wes in existence in eighth or ninth century as evident from inscription of Takupa[259]. The Visnu images are found with Laksmi or with his mount Garuda. There are place names associated with *Nurai* (Visnu) such as village of Visnu (Ban Phra Narai) and mountain of Visnu (Khao Narai). The inscription of Sri Suryavamsa Rama of 1361 C.E. speaks of installation of images of Siva, Visnu and Buddha[260]. There were also large bronze status of Siva and Visnu erected at Kampen Phet[261]. In Thailand Buddhism and brahmanism were often fused together and there was no differentiation. The king of Kampen Phet Dharmasoka held high brahmanical beliefs. Originally a brahmanical

---

258   A.K. Coomaraswamy, *History of India and Indonesian Art* (New Delhi, 1972), P.177.

259   D. Daweewarn, *Brahmanism in Southeast Asia* (New Delhi, 1982), P. 103. H.G.Q. Wales discovered a Visnu temple and Vaisnava image at Sri Deva in 1835. *annual Bibliography of Indian Archaeology* (1935), P. 111.

260   C.B. Pandey, "Indian Influence in Siam" in *Imprints of Indian Thought and Culture Abroad* (Madras, 1980), P. 135.

261   Coomaraswamy, n. 61, P. 177.

monument, the shrine of Phra Prang Sam Yot was later on turned into Buddhist use[262]. In Sukhothai, Wat Pra Pai Luang and Wat Sisawai were built for brahmanical worship as evident from sculptures of Hindu Gods and Goddesses[263]. The icons of Parvati, Hanumana, Ganesa, Indra, Brahma etc adorn Wats in Thailand. Ganesa images are installed in newly constructed buildings sometimes and the image of Brahma at Eravan in Bangkok, where people worship till today are pointers of India's influence. Even the kings of Thailand had attributes of Hindu Gods. He is the incarnation of God. The *brahmans* were conducting the royal consecration in Buddhist Sukhotai kingdom. They perform the rituals connected with this till today : preparing for *homa* (fire sacrifice), ceremonial bath, making of consecrated water and an ointment. The chief *brahmana* hands over to the king great crown and royal regalia and he is the first to offer homage to the king[264]. The *brahmans* also officiate ceremonies like ploughing (*Piti Raek-Na-Kuan*), tonsure and swing ceremony. In the ploughing festival, the minister of agriculture is chosen as Lord of the festival (*Phya Raek Nah*) by the king. This national festival is conducted by the *brahmans* in the month of May, who foretell the years best crop. The tonsure ceremony is an old one and exists in Thailand among royal princes between eleven and thirteen years of age. A mixture of Buddhist and brahmanical rites, it represents the re-birth of a child.

262 Daweewarn, n. 62, P. 144.

263 The author's own observation. The temple of Kampheng Luang at Ratchaburi also was originally a Hindu temple. There are icons of Visnu on his mount Garuda and dvarapalas.

264 G.N. Jha, "Indo-Thai Relations. Problems and Prospects" in *International Studies*, XVI, 3, P. 333.

The royal prince's head is shaved a mound is erected in imitation of Siva's abode, Mount Kailasa and the *brahman* invoke Siva and Visnu[265]. The swing ceremony or *Loh Chingecha* is celebrated each year during the second lunar month, the date falling between December and January. Image of Visnu is carried by the *brahmans* and placed on a swing. The *Songkran* festival is like the colour or *holi* festival of India. It is the astrological New Year for Thailand and falls on 13 April, the date for Sun's entry into Aries. The themes of Thai classical dance and drama are derived from Indian classics like the *Ramayana* and *Mahabharata*.

Some of the ancient place names of Thailand like Sukhothai, Ayuthia, Haripunjaya, Lopburi, Dvaravati, Sajjanalaya etc had origin from Sanskrit. The influence of India is clearly marked on the names of the kings also : Indraditya, Rama, Ananda, Suryavamsa Mahadharmarajadhiraja, Cakrapat, Trailok etc. There are also innumerable words in Thai language originating from Sanskrit : Akas (*Akas*), Maha (*Maha*), Sthani (*Sthan*), Racha (*Raja*), Sabadi (*Svasti*), Pratehet (*Prades*), Narai (*Narayana*), Isaun (*Isvara*), Samkha (*Samgha*), Jatura (*Catura*), Radu (*Rtu*), Tepa (*Deva*), Thatu (*Dhatu*), Phram (*Brahmana*), Nakhon (*Nagara*), Sakhon (*Sagara*), Pinai (*Vinaya*) etc. The Indian classical literature also has influenced Thai literature. All these suggest strong affinity between the two regions. There were four important brahmanical works in the Ayuthia period : Oath to the king, Tosarat teaching Rama, Palee teaching his brother and Aniruddha[266]. The stories from *Sakuntala, Madanabodha, Savitri* and *Ilorat* became part of Thai literature.

The Indian culture also was diffused in Thailand through the *Ramayana*. One of the Rama legends relates

---

265   For details see, Daweewarn, n. 62, Pp. 242-44.
266   *Ibid*, P. 227.

to Lopburi (Sanskrit Lavapuri). Rama created Lopburi and rewarded it to Hanumana[267]. The city of Ayuthia (Ajodhya) was named after Rama's capital in India. Many kings of Thailand assumed the title of Rama. The version of *Ramayana* written by king Rama I was main source of *Ramayana* literature in Thailand and became basis for Thai painting, dance and drama. The Thai version known as *Ramakien* differs in many ways from the *Ramayana* of Valmiki : Hanumana is a romantic person falling in love with ladies, Ravana's daughter Vinayaki assumes the form of Sita, Dasaratha and Ravana are cousins etc. The Rama and Sita temple in Ayuthia dating back to fourteenth century is in ruins. The scenes of *Ramayana* also are found in temples of Thailand. On the bas-relief of Phimai temple, there are scenes depicting Rama's war with Ravana. The paintings on the outer gallery of Wat Phra Keo in Bangkok depict scenes from the *Ramayana* like remorseful Sita in Lanka and Rama-Ravana battle. The classical dance of Thailand takes many episodes from the *Ramayana*. In the shadow-plays known as *nang*, stories of Rama and Sita are enacted. Thus the *Ramayana* has left deep imprint on the cultural life of the Thai people.

Orissa and Thailand

Orissa like other region of India has influenced the culture of Thailand. The archaeological excavations conducted in the last two decades had pushed back the period of cultural contact between the two regions to pre-historic era. Ban Non Nok Tha (3rd to 2nd Century B.C.E.) lying on the western side of Korat plateau in Thailand contained burrials covering neolithic and early metallic

---

267 P.A. Rajdhon, *Life and Ritual in Old Siam*, trans by W.J.Gedney, (New Haven, 1961), Pp. 70-71.

phases and has yielded untonged adzes, shell beads and cord-marked and rare painted potterry [268]. Another site Ban Chiang (mid-second millenium B.C.E.) situated about 120 kilometres to the north-east has yielded glass beads, pottery with fairly elaborate cord-marked, incised and burnished decoration[269]. Bronze bowls (knobbed ware) and beads have been excavated from Ban Do Ta Phet (4th century B.C.E.)[270]. In general, the glass and precious stone beads found in Korat plateau in dated after 200 B.C.E.[271]. From archaeological sites of Orissa similar items have been unearthed. As has been mentioned in Chapter I, yielding of items like krobbed ware, semi-precious stones, beads of different varieties, pot-sherds etc from Sisuspalgarh, Jaugarh, Khalkattapatna, Manikpatna, Manumunda and Khambesvarapali are pointer to contact between Orissa and Thailand. So, it can be inferred that maritime contact between the two regions commenced before Christian era.

The Mon kingdom of Dvaravati in lower Menam valley had received elements of Indian culture. From lower Irrawaddy and Menam valley Theravada Buddhism spreaded throughout mainland Southeast Asia. The Mons had extensive contact with eastern coast of India. There was direct communication between India and southern Thailand. In eighth and ninth centuries, cultural influence from Bengal and Kalinga penetrated the region[272]. The

---

268 P. Bellwood, "Southeast Asia before History" in Tarling, n. 20, P. 97.
269 *Ibid*, P. 98.
270 H.P. Ray, "Early Maritime Contacts Between South and Southeast Asia" in *Journal of Southeast Asian Studies*, 1989, XX, 1, Pp. 48-51.
271 Bellwood, n. 71, P. 121.
272 B.N. Puri, "India and Thailand", in *Our Social Fabric : India and South-East Asia, a study in Cultural Relations* (New

art and architecture of Thailand was greatly influenced by Indian styles. The temple (*Wat* or *Vat*) stupa (P'*ra*), monastery (Vihara) and hall (Bot) are examples of Buddhist structures of Thailand. Monuments of Sri Deva, Visnulok, Svargalok, Vajrapuri, Lopburi, Sukhothai, Ayuthia and Bangok are marked by Indian influence. Certain similarities with Orissan style could be marked. The development of *sikhara* or curvilinear spire in temple architecture of Orissa was remarkable. There is resemblance between the *sikharas* of temples at Bhubaneswar and Maha Tat temple of Svargalok[273]. The twelfth century *wat* Mahadhatu shows affinity to the Bhubaneswar temples in detailed treatment. *Mandapa* is after the Orissan style. The walls of the *wat* had been painted with pictures depicting episodes from the *Ramayana* like the temples of Phimai and *wat* Phia Keo.

From the Chansen area in central Thailand an ivory comb had been found withh *Srivatsa* motif, which is similar in design obtained from Hathigumpha inscription of Kharavela[274]. There is similarity between clay ear plugs of Tha Kae with Khandagiri and Uudayagiri in Orissa[275]. The images of Visnu, Brahma, Siva, Ganesa have been found in Thailand. They follow the rules of Indian *silpasastras*.

Delhi, 1979), P. 49.

273 P. Brown, *Indian Architecture : Buddhist and Hindu Period* (Bombay, 1959), P. 187.
274 K.S. Behera, "Maritime Contacts of Orissa : Literary and Archaeological Evidence", in *Utkal Historical Research Journal*, 1994, V., P. 63.
275 K.K. Basa, "Cultural Relations Between Orissa and Southeast Asia : An Archaeological Perspective", in P.K. Mishra, ed, *Comprehensive History and Culture of Orissa*, Vol I (New Delhi, 1997), In Print.

Unlike Myanmar, evidences of tantricism are less. A four armed Vatuka Bhairava image representing the terrific form of Siva have been found in Weing Sa. Bhairava is generally associated with tantric cult in India. The sculptural representations of Bhairava are there in Sakta temples of Bhubaneswar and Prachi Valley[276].

In some of the Thai festivals, one finds close affinity with their conterparts in Orissa. They are performed according to brahmanic rites. The royal ploughing ceremony of Thailand is very much akin to the *Aksya Trutiya* festival of Orissa[277]. Cultivation for the year starts after the Lord of the Festival (*Phya Raek Nah*) tills the land with the help of officating *brahmanas*. Another festival known as festival of lights (*Loi Krathing*) celebrated in the month of November was introduced by Napamas, the daughter of a *brahmana* priest and astrologer of king Rama Khamheng[278]. The floating of small boats made of lotus leaf or plantain bark with a burning candle inside, is similar to *Boita Bandana* festival of Orissa.

---

276   P.K. Mishra, "Influence of Brahmnism in Early Siamese Art", in *Art and Archaeology International Conference on Thai Studies*, august 1984 (Bangkok), P. 10 and f.n. 33.

277   A. P. Pattanaik, "Daksina Purva Asiare Sanskrutika Upanivesa" in *Utkala Prasanga*, XXXII, 1986, P. 132.

278   Daweewarn, n. 62, P. 227. She composed a Thai literary text known as *Tao Sri Chulalak*, where the brahmanic origin of the festival in early period has been mentioned. The names of Goddess of Rice (*Mae Bhosop*) and Goddess of water (*Mae Kongkha*) are invoked also. The latter has nothing to do with deity, pillar Goddess or (Khambesvari) of Orissa as has been pointed by some historians.

CHAPTER- IV

Orissa and Indo-China

The Indo-Chinese region comprising the former French possession of Cochin-China, the Tonking, Cambodia and Laos are presently independent states of Vietnam, Cambodia and Laos. Here flourished powerful kingdom of Campa, Funan, Chenla, Angkor and Lan Xang. Before the Christian era, penetration by Indian and Chinese cultures began in the region. The mountain range of Aannam was the dividing line between two cultures : the Chinese influence was predominant to the north and east of the region, whereas Indian cultural influence was to the west and south. To the north of Indo-China there is Chinese province of Yunan and Kwangsi, South China sea on the east and south and to the west Thailand and Myanmar are situated. The Vietnames, Khmer and Lao (a branch of Tai) inhabit the region apart from tribal groups like the Moi, Kha, Muong and Meo.

(A) VIETNAM
Historical Development of Vietnam

Vietnam has a rich pre-historical cultural heritage. In the former Hoa Binh (presently Ha Son Binh) province, archaeological discoveries in the 1920s have made famous the Hoabinhian culture that covered the mainland Southeast Asia from Myanmar and southern China southwards to Malaysia. The main traits of foraging community were frequent use of rock shelters and a distinctive pattern of food remains. In Hang Goan, the bronze finds is dated to about the end of the third millenium B.C.E. The excavations at Dong-son in Thanh Hoa province has given the level of culture attended by Vietnam before the impact of Sino-Indian influences. The Dong-sonian culture arrived in Vietnam around 600 B.C.E. Apart from the Dongson, the sites at Viet Khe, Lang Ca and Lang Vac have yielded bronze implements like miniature drums and bells, bowl and situlae, braclets, belt looks and daggers with hilts resembling human figures in the round[279]. The Dongsonian people were also excellent navigators. Cultural interaction between China and Vietnam was there in third century B.C.E. as pottery from Dongson sites had close parallel with geometric paddle-impressed pottery of South China. In southern part of China, among the non-Chinese people that inhabit the region were Yue or Viet, who were ancestors of the Vietnamese. They gradually moved southwards to the Hong (Red) river delta, which became the focal point of Vietnamese civilization.

The Au Lac kingdom of third century B.C.E. had a predecessor in the Van Lang kingdom, which might have existed as early as seventh century B.C.E.[280]. Under Han rule most of Vietnam came under Chinese influence. The Chinese emperor Wu-ti conquered the region in 111

---

279   P. Bellwood, "Southeast Asia before History" in N. Tarling, ed, *The Cambridge History of Southeast Asia*, Vol I, (Singapore, 1992), P. 123.
280   *Ibid*, 125.

B.C.E. With this Vietnam entered the historical era and the Chinese accounts mention about Vietnam regularly. By the end of third century C.E. there was stable provincial administration by the Chinese, which required its vassals to send tributes to the Emperor. Vietnam under the Chinese domination included northern portion of Vietnam. While the northern Viet tribes were greatly influenced by the Chinese, the southern Viets remained ethnically and culturally distinct from their occupiers. The Vietnamese people never acquiesced to the Chinese rule and there were constant uprisings. The gaining of independence after nearly one thousand years of Chinese rule came in 939 C.E. Ngo became the first independent king. Dai Viet gradually became a strong and well organized country. The Vietnamese began to expand southwards by putting pressure on Campa.

The people of Campa known as Chams are ethno-linguistically Malay. Speaking Austronesian language, they inhabit the eastern coast of central and southern Vietnam. At its maximum territorial extent, it covered the central coast from Hoanh Son in the north to Phan Thiet in the south. The Chams resisted the Vietnamese advance to the south and were ultimately absorbed by them. The state of Campa or Lin-Yi came into existence in 192 C.E. by Sri Mara, whose territory corresponded with Quang Binh, Quang Tri and Thua Thien provinces. The loss of control of southern border by the Han empire gave Campa an opportunity to extend southwards. Diplomatic missions were being sent to the Chinese governor of Tonking region. In the middle of fourth century C.E., the Funanese province of Panduranga was annexed. The Chams were greatly influenced by Indian culture and its king Bhadravarman built a Siva temple at Misson. Their move northwards against Chinese controlled

Tonking region failed and the Chams looked southward. In the middle of sixth century C.E., they occupied the lower Annamese coast. One of the features of Campa's history was invasion by the Chinese, Khmers and Vietnamese. In 910 C.E. there was a Khmer invasion. The Vietnamese sacked the Cham capital Vijaya twice in eleventh century C.E. Finally in 1471, a Vietnamese army seized the capital Vijaya and incorporated the area north to the southern boundary of Binh Dinh province[281]. The southernmost Cham principalities became vassal states of the Vietnamese and the Cham kings ruled in the Panduranga region in the province of Thuan Hai till 1832. The Vietnamese in their march to the south (*nam tien*) against the Chams absorbed several elements of Cham culture like music, dance and sculpture.

Indian Cultural Influence

The discovery of items like shouldered adzes, knobbed ware, glass beads etc. from different sites in India and Vietnam point to the relations between the two regions in pre-historic times. There was also commercial relationship between India and Vietnam in early times. Along the Asian sea route, trade and commerce increased during the first two centuries of Christian era. One of the trade routes between India and China passed through the coasts of central and southern Vietnam. The Indian traders arriving on the Malay coast were crossing the Gulf of Siam to reach the port of Oc eo in South Vietnam near the Cambodian border. The voyage then covered the coast post Campa to Chio-Chii port in Vietnam or on to Canton in China. Situated at a junction of canals linking the Gulf of Siam with the main channels of Mekong, the port of Oc

---

281   K.W. Taylor, "The Early Kingdoms" in Tarling, n.1, P. 155.

eo was an entrepot from second to sixth centuries C.E.[282]. The particular location of the port was suitable for sailors offering protection from troubled sea and they had to stay for sometimes to wait for shifting of winds blowing towards the continent. So, cultural interaction between local people and sailors coming from India must have developed. Oc eo has yielded beads, seals with Sanskrit inscriptions, gold medallions and rare piece of statuary. A standardized metal currency in the region was being used by sixth century AC.E. and *srivatsa* coin became the prototype for coins of mainland Southeast Asia for a period of more than five hundred years[283]. The Chams were actively participating in the maritime trade and their items of export were camphor, sandalwood, procelain ware, lead and tin.

The northern Vietnam under Chinese rule became a centre of Buddhist learning as it was a convenient halting place for pilgrims and missionaries on their journey between India and China. There was coming of Buddhist monks to Tonking region. At the end of third century, Marajivaka went from India to Tonking. In the seventh century, the Vietnamese monks such as Moksadeva, Khuy Sung and Hue Diem went on pilgrimages to different places[284]. There were twelve Vietnamese names in the list of Buddhist scholars prepared by the Chinese traveler I. Ching[285]. One

---

282   *Ibid*, P. 158.
283   H.P. Ray, "Early Maritime Contacts Between South and Southeast Asia" in *Journal of Southeast Asian Studies*, XX, 1989, P. 52. The *srivatsa* motif appeared for the first time in the Hathigumpha inscription of Kharavela.
284   J.G. De Casparis and I.W. Mabbett, "Religion and Popular Beliefs of Southeast Asia before c 1500" in Tarling, n. 1, P. 293.
285   J.F. Cady, *Southeast Asia : Its Historical Development* (New Dellhi, 1976), P. 104.

of the important aspects of Vietnamese Buddhism was that there was no attempt to integrate Hindu Gods and it has been associated with Confucianist and Taoist traditions. In the southern kingdom of Campa, there was prevalence of the closely related Theravadinns sect, *aryasammitiyanikaya* as has been noted by I. Ching[286]. Buddhas images of Amaravati style pertaining to early centuries of Christian era have been found from Dong-duong near Danang in central Vietnam. Aan inscription of the same region describes the installation of a Buddha image in 875 C.E. and construction of a Buddhist temple and monastery by Indravarman II[287].

There was a remarkable degree of brahmanical influence in Campa, which is reflected in art and architecture, literature and social life. The social, cultural and religious institutions of different political centres like Vijaya (Binhdinh), Kauthara (Nha-trang) and Panduranga (Phanrang), were deeply affected by elements of Indian culture. The Hindu trinity was well known in Campa but added emphasis was on *Siva linga* and in the aspect of Bhadresvara *linga* of the royalty, it was quite well known[288]. Ninety two inscriptions have been dedicated to Siva out of one hundred and thirty epigraphs discovered in Campa[289]. Siva was known by his

---

286   H.A. Giles, ed, *A Record of Buddhist Kingdoms* (London, 1962), P. XXIV.
287   *Ibid*, P. XXIV.
288   The Siva cult was interpreted sometimes as a way for uplifting the status of king as vehicle of spiritual energy. The rulers of Ly dynasty of Vietnam (1010-1225) had more or less similar ideas; but the ruler was not God but possessed the spiritual energy of his domain. See K.W. Taylor, "Authority and Legitimacy in the eleventh century Vietnam" in D.G. Marr and A.C. Milner, eds, *Southeast Asia in the 9th to 14th centuries* (Singapore, 1986), P. 143.
289   D. Daweewarn, *Brahmanism in Southeast Asia* (New Delhi,

different names such as Rudra, Sankara, Pasupati, Ugra, Isana, Mahadeva, Mahesvara etc in these inscriptions. Rich endowments were made to Siva by different rulers like Indravarman, Prakasadharma and Vikrantavarman. His consort or sakti also was worshipped as evident from the image of Bhagavati Kautaresvari in the temple of Pro-Nagar. The minor deities of Siva pantheon like Ganesa, Kartikeya and Nandin were also being worshipped. Visnu was known by different names Purusottama, Narayana, Hari, Govinda, Madhava and Vikrama. Some of the rulers like Jayarudravarman and his son Jayaharivarmadeva considered themselves as incarnations of Visnu. The icon of this God found from Bien Hoa in richly decorated. An image of Krsna depicting the mountain of Govardana has been found[290]. Icons of various Gods and Goddesses like Brahma, Laksmi, Indra, Sarasvati, Surya and Kubera have also been found from different places of Campa. The shrine containing the Bhadresvara *linga* was built around 600 C.E. in the city of Mi-son. The cubic shaped main body of the temple has decorative pilasters, which stress the perpendicular aspect of construction. This is similar to the shrine at Malot in Punjab[291]. The decorative motifs of the shrine are *makara torana* niches and *apsaras*. The *linga* temple of Po Klaun Garai, constructed by Simhavarman III has the original Simhavarmalingesvara. Prakasadharma (653-670 C.E.) built temples of Kubera and Valmiki in the seventh century C.E. In art and architecture of Campa, one finds influences of Java, Angkor and India.

The Sanskrit inscription of Campa give lot of

1992), pp. 52-53.
290   *Ibid*, P. 64.
291   A.K. Coomaraswamy, *History of Indian and Indonesian Art* (New Delhi, 1972), P. 196.

information about the literary activity of the region. These inscriptions are examples of use of rhetoric and prasody with great skill and proof of Mandakranta metre's earliest use outside India[292]. In one inscription of Mi-son, lines from Kautilya's *Arthasastra* dealing with qualities of a prince were copied verbatim[293]. A number of kings of Campa were well versed in the Vedas and other ancient texts. The ruler Jaya Indravarman IV mentions in his Mi-son stele inscription of 1170 C.E. that he was proficient in grammer, astrology and the philosophical doctrines. The *Bhargaviya* and *Naradiya dharmasastras* were studied by the rulers[294]. The Chams were very much familiar with the *Ramayana*. Temple dedicated to its author Valmiki is very rare in India but king Pnakasadharma constructed a temple for him at Tra Kien. The writers of the inscriptions also describe many episodes from the *Puranas*. In some of the epigraphs, use of names like Yudhistira, Duryodhana and Dhananjaya show familiarity with the *Mahabharata*.

The Cham society was matriarchial. But some of the practices of the people were affected by Hindu tradition : they cremated the dead and ashes collected in urns were dispersed in water. The Hindu calendar fixed the dates of important events. Widows did not marry again. In the royal families *sati* was prevalent as fourteen wives of Harivarman IV immolated themselves at the time of death of the king.

---

292   H.B. Sarkar, *Cultural Relations Between India and Southeast Asian Countries* (New Delhi, 1985), p. 286.
293   G. Maspero, *The Kingdom of Champa* tans by J. Embree, (New Haven, 1949), pp. 10-14.
294   Sarkar, n. 14, p. 286. These texts trace their origin from the *Manusamhita*. The misson inscription dated 1081 A.D says that the king Harivarmadeva was well versed in eighteen titles of law prescribed by Manu. *Ibid*, P. 182.

Beaf eating was a taboo. Yogic exercises were practiced[295]. The marriage was confined to one's own clan and the *brahmans* played an important role in the ceremony[296]. The picture of Cham society in the second half of fourth century C.E. could be known from the Chinese work, *Wen-hsein T'ung-K'ao*, which states that royal dress, ornaments and rites of mourning were similar to India[297]. In ancient Campa, women were keeping the upper part of body bare like the women of ancient India and the sculptural art of two regions attest to this[298]. Some of the practices like letting loose an elephant, when these is no heir to the throne are akin to India[299].

Orissa and Campa

The Jaina *Uttaradhyayana Sutra* mentions that since the time of Mahavira, the Chams were visiting the port of Pithunda of Kalinga for religious and commercial purpose. A story describes that a merchant from Campa named Palita got married locally and while returning to his homeland from Kalinga in a ship, his wife gave birth to a son named Samudrapala[300]. This legend throws some light on the contact between the two religions. In the same Jaina text, relationship between Orissa and Campa from the second century C.E. onwards has been mentioned. The capital of Kalinga in the second half the fourth century C.E. was Simhapura. The same place name Simhapura was capital of Campa for sometime. Similarity with the script of Kalinga

---

295 Cady, n. 7, P. 107.
296 Daweewarn, n. 11, pp. 216-17.
297 Sarkar, n. 14, p. 13 and p. 157.
298 *Ibid.*
299 Daweewarn, n. 11, P. 218.
300 N.K. Sahu, *Odiya Jatira Ithihas*, Vol. I, in Oriya (Bhubaneswar, 1977), P. 385.

is found in the Cho-Dinh and Hon-Cut inscription of king Bhadravarman. According to some scholars these along with Mi-son stele inscription has been written in Brahmi script of southern India[301].

The Brahmanical religion prevailed in Campa with the worship of Hindu trinity. Monuments were erected in honour of deities. Mi-son was known as Hindu temple city because of eight temples in that place. The Cham temple scheme consists of a main shrine in the centre and secondary ones placed on either side. All shrines were arranged on a square terrace and above these rose three towers. The window-openings were of exquisite design having 'baluster-shaped mullions' like the Rajarani temple of Bhubaneswar[302]. Visnu was known by various names and Purusottama was one such name. Prakasadharma constructed a temple for Purusottama at Duong Mong. Jagannatha of Puri temple is worshipped as Purusottama. In the Kautara region of southern Campa, Sakti worship was prevalent. The Goddess Yapu Nagara or Bhagavati Kautaresvari had a temple in Po-Nagar. This was built by Vicitrasagara in eighth century. Later on temples were added to the brick building. The main sanctuary contains the image of Goddess Bhagavati replacing the original *linga*. In an inscription of Harivarman I it was mentioned that the temple had remained empty and he installed a new image. Later day kings made donations to the Goddess. Bhgavati was worshipped at Bankada near Banpur, the capital of Kongoda of ancient Orissa[303]. The decorative motifs of Mi-son group of temples include *makara torana* (crocodile

---

301 Sarkar, n. 14, P. 169.
302 P. Brown, *India Architecture Buddhist and Hindu Periods*, (Bombay, 1971), P. 192.
303 Sahu, n. 22, P. 404.

shaped archways) niches. This reminds one of beautifully carved *makara* heads in the archways in front of Muketsvara temple of Bhubaneswar. The dancing Siva balancing on the back of bull in some Cham icons are very much akin to the same types of images of eastern India.

(B) CAMBODIA
Political and Cultural Developments

Cambodia in its heyday corresponded to modern Cambodia, a part of Cohin-China and lower valley of the Mekong river in the basin of Tonle Sap. This country of Indo-Chinese Peninsula was bounded on north-east by Laos, South Vietnam on south-east, gulf of Thailand on the south and on north-west by Thailand. The majority of the people were Khmers, ethnically related to Mons of lower Myanmar. During the earliest or pre-Angkorean centuries of Khmer history, there were two successive kingdoms : Funan from second to sixth centuries and Chenla from sixth to the eighth centuries. The Chinese chronicles provide important information about the origin of Funan. It was founded by Indian *brahmana* Kaundinya, who married the local female chieftain. In the early history of Cambodia, there was no fixed centre of political power. The rulers promoted authority by legitimizing their rule through *brahmans* and proving their worth in the battlefield. The effectiveness lasted the lifetime of the ruler. In the early centuries of Christian era, small principalities arose across the map of Southeast Asia. Funan was one. The term 'multiplicity of centres' is more appropriate as O.W.Wolters says "greater unities were very fragile consequences of the prowess of an individual ruler[304]". There was in existence an "indigenous,

---

304 For study of nature of state in early period, see H. Kulke, *Kings and Cults, State Formation and Legitimation in India and*

prehistoric 'pre-state' structure[305]". The coming of Indian cultural influence was convenient for the rulers, who used it to buttress their political authority. This process of cultural interaction later on resulted in affecting not only elite but also people in their socio-religious life.

The Chinese envoys K'ang T'ai and Chu Ying, who visited Funan in middle of third century C.E. and a Sanskrit inscription of third century C.E. throw light on Funan[306]. K'ang T'ai had recorded a legend, which mentioned the coming of Indian *brahmana* Kaundinya (Hun-tien) to Funan. Earlier Kaundinya had in a dream visualized God giving him a bow and asking him to go on high sees. Next day he went to a temple and found the bow. He then boarded a ship and reached Funan, which was being govrned by the *naga* princess Soma (Lin-Ye). She was defeated by Kaundinya, who had the divine bow and got married to him. Then he governed the country from capital Vyadhapura or city of hunters[307]. This first dynasty by next generation was completely indigenous as there was no Indian women. The same legend appears in Campa and Kedah. It was given a status of legitimization with ancestry from India as well as local. The reference to moon, water and serpent had indigenous roots and even the word *naga* was from vocabulery of pre-Aryan, who had cultural affinity with people of Southeast Asia[308].

Southeast Asia (New Delhi, 1993), pp.264 ff.
305 *Ibid*, P. 265.
306 G. Coedes, *The Indianized States of Southeast Asia* (Honolulu, 1965), pp.37-38.
307 According to *Manusamhita* (X.8), issues of such marriage between high caste man and low caste women would be a nisada or a member of hunter community, hence the name of capital as city of hunters. See Sarkar, n. 14, P.135.
308 I.W. Mabbett, "The Indianization of Southeast Asia : Re-

After Kaundinya, his descendants ruled Funan. Under Fan Ch'an, its territory extended upto southern Vietnam, central Thailand and portion of Myanmar. He had a powerful navy. The importance of Funan as a seafaring and trading nation is proved by the port of Oc eo, situated near Cambodian-Vietnamese border. Upto sixth century C.E., trade routes between India and China passed through Funanese coast. Embassies were sent to India and China. The envoy Su Wu after a sea voyage arrived in the mouth of Ganga and afterwards went to the capital of a Murunda prince[309]. He came back with an Indian companion, who later on met the Chinese envoys K'ang T'ai and Chu Ying. When Fan Hsun was the ruler, relations with China deteriorated as Funan allied with Campa against Tonking, which was under Chinese domination. According to the Chinese chronicles, Chant'an (Candan), who became the ruler in 357 C.E. was paying tribute to China.

The second phase of Funanese history begins with arrival of second Kaundinya from the kingdom of P'an-P'an of Malay Peninsula. The Chinese chronicle *Liang Shu* mentions that Chia Ch'en-ju (Kaundinya), a successor of Candan heard the divine voice to rule over Funan and he changed laws in Funan in confirmity with practice in India[310]. His arrival in Funan, then being welcomed by people proves the high regard in which Indian *brahmans* were held. His successors with easily recognizable

---

flections on Historical Sources" in *Journal of Southeast Asian Studies*, VIII 2, 1977, P. 146.

309   Coedes, n. 28, P. 41.
310   P. Wheatley, *The Golden Khersonese* (Kuala Lumpur, 1961), P. 48.

Sanskrit names enlarged the Indian cultural elements. At the time of Jayavarman, the Indian monk Nagasena reached Funan. The king sent him to China in 484 C.E. to offer presents to the Chinese emperor. Nagasena had mentioned some of Funanese customs like worship of Siva, existence of mountain God cult and presence of Buddhism. Kulaprabhavati, the queen of Jayavarman in her inscription in the southern province of Takeo had invoked Visnu in the prefatory stanza. Rudravarman was the last king of Funan and sent various embassies to China between 517 and 539 C.E. He despatched the monk Paramartha or Gunaratna to China with two hundred and forty bundles of Buddhist texts[311]. He was from Ujjayini and living in Funan. The dominant religion of Funan was Hinduism but the Buddhist constituted an important community.

By the sixth century C.E., an all sea-rotue developed between India and China. The shift from coastal trade route coincided with appearance of conquerors from the mid-Mekong area, Bhavavarman and Mahendravarman[312]. Both the brothers' career was focussed toward the rice-growing areas of Mekong basin rather than maritime trade. The separate tradition for the new kingdom traced its origin from the sage Kambu Svayambhuva and the daughter of *Nagas* Mera and the state was called Kambuja after the sage[313]. The Chinese call it Chenla. The rulers built *lingas* of the mountain God Siva-Girisa. The kings came to be deified. There was also the tradition of getting princesses married to *brahmans* coming from India[314]. Beginning his

---

311 Sarkar, n. 14, P. 153.
312 Taylor,n. 3, P. 159.
313 R.C. Majumdar, *Kambuja Desa* (Madras, 1944), P. 19.
314 At the time of Isanavarman (617-635 A.D.), a royal princess married Durgasvamin of Daksinapatha and the daughter

career in southeastern Cambodia, Jayavarman II occupied northwestern part, the future site of Angkor. The *brahmanas* performed the consecration ceremony for the new ruler in a nearby mountain. Thus Jayavarman II became the ruler of a new state without being subordinate to anybody. Angkor dynasty was established in 802 C.E.

the *Devaraja* cult was introduced by the new ruler. Influences from India, megalithic culture of Southeast Asia, Chen-la, Campa, Indonesia and China could be discerned in the *devaraja* cult[315]. *Devaraja* means the 'king of Gods' which is God Siva himself. The famous temple mountains and royal *lingas* were dedicated to Siv himself. *Devaraja* cult was not same as the cult of royal *lingas*, which were erected by kings on the temple mountains that were unique of Angkor architecture[316]. The Saivite cult of royal *lingas* was later on represented on the famous Angkor Wat. Jayavarman II established his capital on Mahendra mountain and invited a *brahmana* named Hiranyadama from Janapada to perform some tantric rites[317]. Saivism is conected with tantricism and the *brahmana* performed ritual according to tantric texts. The object behind the ceremony was that Cambodia would not show allegiance to Java and the ruler would be consecrated as universal ruler or *cakravartin*. Hiranyadama consecrated the *linga* on Mahendra mountain and a movable image or *calanti*

---

of Jayavarman I and his queen Jayadevi, Sobhajaya got married to Saiva *brahmana* Sakrasvamin of Madhyadesa. C. Coedes, ed, *Inscriptions du Cambodge*, referred in Sarkar, n.14, P. 154.

315 H. Kulke, *The Devaraja Cult* trans by I.W. Mabbett (New York, 1978), pp.1-2.

316 *Ibid*, pp. 3-4.

317 P.C. Bagchi, *Studies in Tantra* (Calcutta, 1920), pp. 2 & 18.

pratima of this ws prepared and 'venerated as *devaraja*'[318]. The untramelled political authority of the new ruler was asserted.

Jayavarman II was succeeded by Jayavarman III. They were followed by Indravarman and Yasavarman I. The *brahmana* Sivasoma was mentor of Indravarman. Yasovarman I was a great builder. The successive rulers in different ways contributed to cultural life of Angkor. At the time of Suryavarman I, Lopburi region of Thailand came under his authority. Suryavarman II (1113-45 C.E.) extended his domain in Malay Peninsula and northern Cham territory. He constructed the famous edifice of Angkor Wat dedicated to Visnu Jayavarman VII (1181-1218C.E.) established his authority over Campa, northern Laos and southern Myanmar. He founded the new capital city of Angkor Thom and in the centre of city constructed the Mahayana temple of Bayon. He was the last important king of Angkor. There was constant Thai pressure in late thirteenth and early fourteenth centuries. In the fifteenth century, Angkor was abandoned in favour of sites in the vicinity of Phnom Penh for maritime trading contacts. Though the Khmer empire came to an end politically, some of the Angkorean features in social and cultural domain influenced the new states that were established on the ruins of Angkor.

The Cambodian civilization in Funan, Chen-la and Angkor periods witnessed a good deal of Indian influence. The Khmers accepted some of Indian cultural elements and adapted it according to their necessity. The legend of Kaundinya was mixed with indigenous myth of moon, serpent and water to give the rule of kings legitimization. Erection of pesonal royal *lingas* on top of mountains was

---

318   Kulpe, n. 37, P. 32.

a blending of autochthonous mountain cult with Hindu beliefs. Siva with the *linga* as his icon were moulded to the local tradition of prior cults like earth gods and the Cambodian inscription of pre-Angkorean times make reference to 'god of the stone pond'[319]. Siva in his *linga* form was connected with *devaraja* cult. He has been also identified with Brahma. There was also prevalence of a Saivite sect known as Pasupatas. The Hindu gods of trinity, Brahma, Siva and Visnu were known to the people. Brahma was not popular and only one icon of him has been discovered at Prasatsamrong. The three chief deities of Angkor were Siva, Visnu and Buddha. Probably Buddha had replaced Brahma in the Cambodian context. Siva was being worshipped under different names such as Bhadresvara, Sambhu, Girisa and Tribhubanesvara.

The cult of Visnu flourished in Cambodia Visnu had been shown resting on the serpent Anantanaga in the Kusi Cheng temple. Images of the God with his traditional attributes have been found pertaining to Funan period. The sculptural art representing Siva became more developed at the time of Angkor. The record of Jayavarman's queen Kulaprabhavati mentions the myth of Sesanaga, the serpent on whom Visnu reclines in rest. She also constructed a temple for the God[320]. The inscription of his son Gunavarman also displays Vaisnavite devotion. He commemorated the foot-prints of Visnu at Thopmoi, which came to be known

---

319 J.G. De Casparis and I.W. Mabbett, "Religion and Popular Beliefs of Southeast Asia before C. 1500" in Tarling, n. 1, P. 283. In the Ba Phnom site, where sacrificial rituals were addressed to a Goddess, who was amalgamation of indigenous Me Sa with Indian, Mahisasuramardini, *Ibid*, P. 284.
320 G. Coedes, "A new inscription from Fuhnan" in *Journal of Greater India Society*, IV, 1937, P. 120.

as *cakratirthasvami*[321]. Visnu was worshiped as Puskaraksa, Puspavatasvamin and Trailokesvara in Chenla[322]. The kings like Yasovarman, Indravarman, Suryvarman II etc were patrons of Vaisnavism. Angkor Wat was a magnificient Visnuite edifice. There was a reference to *Visnugrhas* in the Angkor Thom inscription, which were place of residence of the *Vaisnavas*. Visnu along with Siva was worshipped as Hari-Hara, Hari-Sankara and Sankara-Narayana. There was also *bhakti* cult of the Pancaratha sect and an inscription of the time of Jayavarman I refers to a priest of this sect. In the tenth century C.E. this sect occupied an important position in Cambodia. In the inscription during the reign of Rajendravarman (944-961 C.E.), the fourfold emanation (*caturvyuha*) of Visnu had been referred. Besides the Siva and Visnu, there were number of brahmanical Gods and Goddesses like Aditya, Ganesa, Indra, Sarasvati etc prevailing in Cambodia.

The Mahayana faith came to Cambodia from the Srivijayan kingdom as well as India. As early as fifth century C.E., Buddhism was prevalent in Funan. Its king Jayavarman sent an embassy to China with presents like the image of Buddha. His son Rudravarman made an invocation to Buddha in one of his inscriptions. I-Ching, the Chinese pilgrim had mentioned that Buddhism was prevalent in Funan. The Siemreap inscription of 791 C.E. makes reference to the image of Avalokitesvara. Quite a few Buddhist monks from India were residing and Nagasena's visit to China had been referred earlier. Suryavarman I gave much emphasis to Buddhism and he had the posthumous title Nirvanapada. His inscription at Prah Khan invokes both Siva and Buddha. The Khmer term Esvara for God appeared

---

321 Daweewarn, n. 11, P. 32.
322 M.M. Ghosh, *History of Cambodia* (Calcutta, 1968), P. 59.

in Saivite cult of Mahesvara and Mahayana Buddhist cult of Lokesvara[323]. The Theravada school of Buddhism reached its pinnacle of glory at the time of Jayavarman VII with construction of Bayon temple in Angkor Thom. In 1225 C.E., the Chinese visitor Chou Ta-Kuan mentions the importance of saffron-clad Theravadin monks, who were reciting Pali texts to new entrants in monasteries and they were leading a simple life[324]. The rulers of Angkor were influencing the life of Buddhist *sangha* by endowments.

The *brahmans* were playing an important role in the religious life of people. In Cambodia, the chief priest or *purohita* had a powerful influence on the royalty. This sacerdotal office passed from uncle to nephew in the maternal line, which was an example of indigenous matrilineal social system. The kings were seeking to ally itself to a particular priestly family by matrimonial alliance: Sobhajaya, daughter of Jayavarman I got married to *brahmana* Sakrasvamin. The sister of Jayavarman V, Indralaksmi was married to Divakarabhatta, who was an expert on Vedic sacrifices. The *brahmans* were advisors to the king and performed important rituals for royalty. Indravarman I's spiritual mentor was Sivasoma, who had studies the religious texts under the famous Sankaracarya of India[325]. The *brahmana* Hiranyadama conducted the consecration of Jayavarman II, the founder of Angkor dynasty. The role of Indian *brahmans* Kaundinya I and Kaundinya II had been referred earlier. After the king, the *brahmans* were next to be honoured. The royal guru was known as *Sivakaivalya* and he and his family

---

323 L.P. Briggs, *Ancient Khmer Empire* (Philadelphia, 1951), pp. 24-26.
324 Chu Ta-Kuan, "Memoirs sur les - Coutumes du Cambodge de Tcheou Ta-Kouan", referred in Cady, n. 71, P. 101.
325 R. C. Majumdar, *Greater India* (Bombay, 1948), P. 55.

alone could perform the ceremony associated with *devaraja* cult[326]. Hiranyadama taught *Sivakaivalya* the tantric texts like Vrah Vinasikha, Nayottara, Sammoha and Sirasched[327] in connection with installation of royal God.

Inscriptions from Cambodia attest to prevalence of competence in Sanskrit. The royalty was well versed in that language. Rhetorical and literary conventions were well known to writers of epigraphs, which were unique contribution to Sanskrit literature. They were also well acquainted with Indian epics, *kavyas* and *puranas*. The inscriptions refer to the *Vedas, Vedantas, Smritis* etc. In the inscriptions, there are references to the *Manusamhita* and verses from it were reproduced in verbatim. There was study of Sanskrit literature under Yasovarman I, who composed a commentry of *Mahabhasya*. His Baray inscription gives reference to Indian authors like Vatsyayana, Bharavi, Gunadhya, Visalaksa etc[328]. Princess Tilaka was known as Vagesvari Bhagavati on account of her knowledge and queen Indradevi was very erudite Sanskrit scholar[329]. Suryavarman I was a proficient Vedic scholar. The study of astrology (*horasastra*), archery (dhanurveda), medicine (ayurveda) and music (gandharvavidya) was also there in Camboda. The *Ramayana* and *Mahabharata* were popular epics in Kambuja. An inscription of sixth century C.E. says that copies of these epics were dedicated by the *brahmana* Somasarman before Tribhuvanesvara for daily recitation[330]. Some of the episodes from the *Ramayana* and

---

326 Daweewarn, n. 11, P. 48.
327 Sarkar, n. 14, P. 285.
328 *Ibid*, P. 275.
329 R.C. Majumdar, *Inscriptions of Kambuja* (Calcutta, 1953), no. 173 and 182.
330 *Ibid*, No. 13.

Mahabharata were portrayed in the bas-reliefs of Bhavajnana temple. The scholars like Sivasoma, Vagisvarapandita and Kavindrapandita were expert in study and recitation of these epics[331]. Some of the Buddhist texts like *Pratityotpadana, Brahmaghosa* and *Sadaharma-arsabha* were studied in Angkor. The teacher of king Jayavarman V, Yajnavaraha was proficient in Buddhist doctrines. Inscriptions in Pali also prove popularity of Hinayana Buddhism in royal circles. The Buddhist *Jataka* stories were also very popular.

Many of the Sanskrit words had been absorbed into old Khmer relating to geographical names, names of divinities and persons, administrative terms and terms relating to calendar and number[332]. The widely prevalent place names were Sivapura, Visnupura, Yasodharagiri, Sivapada, Visnupada etc. Some of the names of divinities attest the significance of indigenous cults : Jayasrestha, Lingapurasana and Nagasthana. The various names of Siva like Utpanesvara, Akalesvana and Amratakesvara are not common in India but were prevalent in ancient Cambodia. The administrative terms in old Khmer were *Kulapati* (chief of temple), *gramapala* (guardian of village), *rajakulamahamantri* (minister of royal welfare), *rajakarya* (administration), *rastra* or *desa* (country), *sasana* (royal order) etc. The Saka era was prevalent in ancient Cambodia. Inscriptions refer to era, year, month, fortnight, *tithi naksatra* etc. Some of the terms were *sankranta* (new year), *pratisamvatasara* (every year), *candradivasavara* (Monday) etc. Though there are seven days in a week, the Khmer calendar has a thirteen-monthh year. For calculation, the Khmers developed their own written script and used a counting system based on units of five. Some of the Indian terms were changed in

---

331   Sarkar, n. 14, P. 284.
332   For details see, Daweewarn, n. 11, pp. 200-212.

the Khmer version : garuda (*krut*), guru (*kru*), Ma-Ganga (*Mekong*) and nagar (*nokor*). In the inscriptions, old Khmer was used for description of foundations and enumeration of servants; whereas Sanskrit was used for royal genealogies, panegyries for kings and donors of various categories.

Orissan Cultural Contact

Orissa's connection with Funan was through diplomatic relationship between two regions. At the time of Funanese king Fan Chan (225-250 C.E.) an Indian visitor had arrived in the court of the king. Afterwards the king sent his relative Su-Wu as ambassador to the court of Murunda ruler in India. He embarked at the port of Chu-li in Malay Peninsula and went by sea reaching the mouth of Ganga. Su-Wu arrived at the port of Tamralipti and met the king, who had the title of Mou-luan. The Murundas had set up an independent kingdom in eastern India with Pataliputra as capital after the decline of Kusanas. They became prominent in Kalinga after the Satavahanas in second and third centuries C.E. The Murunda rule over Kalinga could be attested from the discovery of a gold coin from Sisupalgarh[333]. On the obverse of it, the name of the king is read as Dhamadamadhara (Dharmatamadharasya), who received Su-Wu[334]. The king presented him with four horses. There were regular export of horses from the port of Tamralipti to Funan and Ko-Ying kingdom located in

---

333 The Murunda rule over Kalinga is full of polemics. Sahu stronglyy believes in the theory of Murunda rule. See N.K. Sahu, *History of Orissa*, Vol. I (Bhubaneswar, 1964), p.418 ff. For an opposite view, see B.N. Mukharjee, "The Theory of Kusana rule in Orissa" in *The Journal of Orissan History*. I, 1980, pp.1-2.

334 B.B. Lal, "Sisupalgarh" in *Orissa Historical Research Journal*, XV, 1967,pp.51-55.

Java-Sumatra region. This trade was being monopolized by Yueh-chih or Kusana traders from Vanga region[335]. So, it is not unlikely that Kalinga was involved in this trade. Moreover, the people of Kalinga and neighbouring region of Vidarbha were using the port of Palura as point of departure to Southeast Asia. Kaundiny I might have gone to Funan from the contiguous region of Vidarbha and Kalinga. The Kaundinyas, a Vedic tribe, had their homeland in Kaundinyapur in Vidharva.

Saivism had become popular in ancient Cambodia. He was worshipped under different names like Mahesvara and Tribhubanesvara. Somasarma, the brother-in-law of Chenla ruler Mahendravarman (600-611 C.E.) installed a statue of Tribhubanesvara in a temple. Sasanka, the ruler of Karnasuvarna had constructed the Tribhubanesvara Siva temple at Ekambra Ksetra in Kalinga. This contemporary installation of same God could be a pointer to the close relationship between Orissa and Cambodia. The Buddhist monk Nagasena had mentioned that Mahesvara was worshipped at the top of Motan mountain. Shortly before 500 C.E., the Gangas of Kalinga were worshipping Siva Gokarnasvamin as tutelar deity on Mahendra mountain[336]. Worship of Gokarnasvamin and Mahesvara belonged to same time. Probably Motan mountain was another name of Mahendra mountain of Kalinga. The founder of Angkor dynasty had established his capital at Mahendra mountain,

---

335   B.N. Mukherjee, "New Evidences of Contacts of Ancient Vanga (in Eastern India) with South-East Asia" in *Bharati*, XX, 1993-94, P. 3.

336   H. Kulke, "Royal Temple Policy and the Structure of Medieval Hindu Kingdoms" in Anncharlott Eschmann and others eds, *The Cult of Jagannath and the Regional Tradition of Orissa* (New Delhi, 1985), P. 130.

where the *brahmana* Hiranyadama had performed the tantric rites in connection with *Devaraja* cult in 802 C.E. So, it could be inferred that the existence of Mahendra mountain and worship of Siva in both the regions point to close cultural relationship between Orissa and Cambodia. During the time of Isanavarman I (611-635 A.D) foot-prints of Siva were installed, which finds a referernce in the Phnom Bayang inscription of 624 A.D[337]. The followers of Pasupata sect worshipped the foot-prints as evident from the foot-prints of Siva temple constructed by Vidyavisesa in Saka tirtha of Cambodia. In India, worship of Siva's foot-prints is rare except in places like Ranipur-Jharial of western Orissa.

Vaisnavism flourished in ancient Cambodia. Gunavarman, son of Funanese king Jayavarman (484-514 C.E.) commemorated the foot-prints of Visnu and constructed the Cakratirthasvami Visnu temple at Thap-moi in Plain des Joncs. In Orissa, Puri is known as cakratirtha and Lord Jagannatha is Cakratirthasvami. In medieval Orissa, the kings were sons and viceroys of Visnu-Jagannatha and they were deified as moving Visnu or *Calanti Visnu*. Two largest temples dedicated to Visnu of India and Southeast Asia were constructed by rulers whose predecessors were followers of Siva. Jagannatha-temple in Puri by Codagangadeva and Angkor Wat by Suryavarman II. The institution of worshipping moving images or *calanti pratima* was prevlent in Orissa and Cambodia. In some of the festivals of Jagannatha temple, the Sudarsana *ckra* (disc) as *calanti pratima* was carried around the city[338]. In Angkor also, *calanti pratima* of *linga* that was consecrated on Mahendra mountain by Jayayvarman was made and venerated as *devaraja* by successive

---

337 Daweewarn, n. 11, P. 25.
338 Kulke, n. 58, pp. 89-90.

rulers[339]. Therefore, cultural affinity to an extent was there between both the regions.

The Khmers had excelled in the field of art and architecture with their stone vault, decorative details, pyramidal mass, splendid lintel stones, carved figures and bas-relief depicting scenes from Indian mythology. Though some of the Khmer monuments had Indian origin, local touch was always there. The walls of the monuments of early period had been engraved with sscenes from Indian mythology, but it had been decorated according to Cambodian model. There was also remarkable evolution of temple architecture with the addition of galleries, pyramidal construction in several stages and lofty central towers. The richness of architectural design is found in the temple of Banteay Srei constructed by the preceptor of Angkor king Rajendravarman II (944-968 C.E.), Yajnavaraha. It consists of a three tower-shrines on a single terrace with Siva as the main deity. The *sikharas* in the shape of curved arches over the doors are similar to the Orissan temples. In the Banteay Srei and Preah Khan temples, the bullioned openings are very splendid and are akin to temples of Bhubaneswar[340]. In Angkorean sculptures the round eye brows and deep plump lips are of Orissan variety[341].

Angkor wat built by Suryavarman II is one of the most perfect architectural complexes of the world. This Visnu temple with its five towers, three floors, walls and mots symbolizes the cosmos, topped with mount Meru, which is abode of Gods. The whole area is rectangular in shape enclosed by a colonnaded wall. Angkor wat has more than

---

339 Kulke, n. 37, P. 37.
340 Brown, n. 24, P. 184.
341 H.G. Wales, *The Mountain of God : A Study in Early Religion and Kingship* (London, 1953) pp. 182ff.

two square kilometres of bas-reliefs representing episodes from the *Ramayana* and *Mahabharata* and pictures of life of local people. These are considered to be pinnacle of Khmer art. The five towers of central temple were symbolic of peaks of mount Meru. Incarnations of Visnu are portrayed on an elaborate frieze relief. On the whole, Angkor wat was a blending of different styles with indigenous innovation. In open part of terrace on each side of entrance halls small shrines were there, which were similar to *pancharatha* (division of shrine tower into five vertical segments) pattern of Orissan temples.

(C) LAOS
Political and Cultural developments

Situated in the heart of Indo-Chinese Peninsula, the land-locked country of Laos is sorrounded by China in the north, Vietnam in the east, Cambodia in the south and Thailand and Myanmar in the west. Due to its very location, Laos has been a buffer state between its neighbours and a place for conflicting interests. Asia's fourth largest river, the Mekong flows through Laos. Except for the Mekong valley along the border of Thailand, most of Laos is characterized by rugged land and mountainous terrains. The largest single ethnic group is valley La of Tai stock. Originating from Yunan in southern China, the Tai people had moved to south along the plains of middle Mekong by seventh century C.E. Upto fourteenth century C.E., the parts of Laos were under different political entities. The vassal state of Funan, Kambuja had its capital at Sresthapura in the Bassac region of southern Laos[342]. The central and

---

342   P.P. Mishra, *Laos : Land and Its People* (New Delhi, n.d.), P. 3.

upper regions of Laos were occupied by Chenla ruler Jayavarman I (657-681 C.E.). After the capture of Nan Chao kingdom by Kublai Khan, there was reinforcement of earlier Lao migrants to capture power in the Luang Prabang region.

The first unified state of Lan Xang (million elephants) was established by Fa Nagum in 1353 C.E. with the help of Angkorean king Jayavarman. His kingdom extended from Spisong Panna in the upper Mekong to northern Cambodia[343]. Fa Nagum's queen, who was daughter of Jayavarman was responsible for converting the people to Hinayan Buddhism. In 1470s, Le Thanh Ton of Vietnam attacked Lan Xang and sacked Luang Prabang. Later the capital was shifted to Vientiane by Settathirat (1548-1571 C.E.). At the time of Souligna Vongsa (1637-1694 C.E.), the greatness of Lan Xang was once again revived. But after him the kingdom was fragmented. Luang Prabang, Vientiane and Bassac became splinters of Lan Xang. Though there were frequent quarrelling between the three, there was a sense of local pride and Lao people endeavoured to maintain their separate identity from Thais and Vietnamese.

As far as Indian influence was concerned, Hindu and Buddhist practices came to Laos in the early centuries of Christian era through Chinese, Khmers and Thais[344]. It is difficult to have an exact idea of the period of beginning of cultural contact between India and Laos due to absence of historical records. According to local tradition, a Buddhist shrine (That) was built in Laos during Asoka's time. The

---

343   *Ibid.*

344   P.P. Mishra, "Cultural Contribution of India to South-East Asia : A case study of Laos" in *Proceedings of the Indian History Congress*, 56th Session, 1995 (Calcutta, 1996), P. 870.

Ourangkharittan chronicle mentions that That Luang of Vientiane was earlier built by a Buddhist monk Phra Chao Chanthaburi Pasithisak to keep Buddhist relic brought from Rajgir in India[345]. From about first century onwards, the Lao living in southern part of China had set up principalities. The Chinese imperial power had extended southwards along the Indo-Chinese coast and there was constant pressure on these principalities by China. In 69 C.E. King Luang Limao of Muong Ngai Lao principality was influenced by Mahayana Buddhism from China. The Chinese Emperor Mingti had brought from India the image of Buddha and *Tripitaka*. According to the tradition mentioned in *Pongsavadan Lao*, the Chinese defeated the Laotian king, who had been deeply influenced by Buddhist culture[346]. Then the Laotians migrated to Nanchao in Yunnan and established a powerful kingdom under Sinhanara, whose successors ruled upto the middle of seventh century. These kings came under Indian cultural influence.

The next stage of Indianization in central and southern Laos was through the Khmers. The Indianized state of Funan began to disintegrate in the middle of sixth century and its vassal state Chenla centred at Sresthapura in southern Laos began to exert pressure on Funan. The Chenla rulers had claimed descent from the *brahmana* Kaundinya. Brahmanism became quite popular in Laos. Saivism and Vaisnavism became favourite creeds. There was decline of Hinduism in fourteenth century in Laos. Buddhism was in ascendancy. Laos was beginning to emerge as a unified state. The people of Laos were

---

345 Virachitch Keomanichanh, *India and Laos* (New Delhi, 1979), P. 58.
346 *Ibid*, P. 22.

converted to Hinayana Buddhism because of the Khmer princess and Jayavarman urged Fa Nagum to observe the teaching of Buddha in his dealing with the subjects. Fa Nagum received from his father-in-law a statue of Buddha, Pali scriptures and a mission of monks under Phra Mahapasaman[347]. The statue called Prabang was installed at the capital of Fa Nagum, which was named as Luang Prabang afterwards. Fa Nagum's son Thao Oun Muong built Buddhist monasteries and a copper image of Buddha was installed in the newly constructed Wat Manorm. Lan Kham Deng, his successor constructed some more Buddhist temples. Another king Photisarath, who had built Wat Visoun became a Buddhist monk in 1525 C.E. His son Setthathirath (Jayajetthadhi-raja) transferred the capital to Vientiane, where he built a famous shrine for emerald Buddha. His greatest contribution was That Luang built in 1566 C.E. over an old *stupa*. The Dutch traveller Van Muysthoff, who visited Laos in 1641 had written that Laos was full of "worshipped places and schools of Buddhist culture and art"[348].

The extent of Indian cultural influence could be known from the recurring of word 'Om', while invoking a particular spirit. The world of Laos is full of wandering spirits and souls of the dead known as *phi*. The life is one among several incarnations and past deeds shape the present life. One invocation says :

"Om, oh White herb;

I use the talisman of the White Angel:

Om, I invoke the power of Phra In,

....

---

347   P.L. Briggs, *The Ancient Khmer Empire* (Philadelphia, 1951), P. 253.
348   Virachitch, n. 67, P. 118.

Om, Maha Saming:
I invoke the Great Genius of living being"[349].

The *phi* cult was so popular that the rulers constructed sanctuaries for the deities. One such was Wat Phu Champassak built on the hill known as *Linga parvata* by Phya Kammatha, who offered to the deity a pair of virgins and a bowl of alcohol as sacrifice once in a year. This practice was later on substituted by the sacrifice of buffalo. The belief was that good fortune could come to life by offering flowers, candles, incense and blood of animals. Buffalo sacrifice, a common practice in many Indian temples was prevalent in Vientiane and Luang Prabang till 1975.

The prevalence of Hinduism also could be known from the numerous inscriptions found in Laos. On the top of Phou Lokan hill, a Sanskrit inscription mentions the erection of *Siva linga* by king Mahendravarman[350]. Another inscription of second half of fifth century compares the King Sri-Devanika with Yudhisthira, Indra, Dhananjay and also with Indradyumna[351]. Eulogizing the merits of Kuruksetra, the inscription records that the King planned to establish a new Kuruksetra in Laos as the former was a *mahatirtha* (a great place for pilgrimage)[352]. It is evident that Devanika was familiar with Sanskrit literature and ritualistic texts. The stele inscription of Jayavarman I at Wat Phu temple containing Bhadresvara Siva mentions that

---

349 Phimmasone Phouving, *Kingdom of Laos* (Saigon, 1959), pp. 36-37.
350 B.C. Chhabra, *Expansion of Indo-Aryan Culture During the Pallara rule* (Delhi, 1965), P. 69.
351 R.C. Majumdar, *India and South-East Asia* (Delhi, 1979), Pp. 179ff.
352 Mishra, n. 66, P. 872.

the hill was named as *Linga Parvata*. An inscription dated 835 C.E. refers to Sresthapura as a holy place because it was associated with Siva worship. The eleventh century inscription of Jayavarman VI records that the mother of king's court pandit Subhadhra, Tilaka has been compared with Goddess Sarasvati because of her learning[353].

In art and architecture, the impact of various Indian styles is clearly marked. The concept is Indian, but in the choice of pattern and other details indigenous touch is given. The different types of Buddhist icons found in Laos were in conformity with Indian canons. Artists represented Buddha in *Bhumisparsa* and *Abhay mudra*. Indra on Airavata and Visnu on Garuda were specimens of Hindu religious art of Wat Phu temple. An image of Laksmi standing on a lotus over the dome is from Wat Pra temple. The statue of Parvati on the door of Wat Aram, images of Garuda and Naga of Wat Pa Rouck, figure of aquatic animals at That Luong and representation of *dvarapala* at the entrance of various shrines prove strong Indian influence. The two main types of Lao monuments are *Wat* (monastery, temple, Pagoda) and *That* (*Dhatu*, edifice for putting relics). Wat Pa Rouk and Wat Ban Tan display close affinity with Gupta temples. Richly decorated door and window panels of Wat Nang show close affinity with Indian styles. The Wat Phu Champassak is the best example of Indo-Khmer influence. Another noteworthy feature of Lao architecture is presence of Hindu and Buddhist icons in the same monument. The Wat Pra contains images of Laksmi as well as Buddha.

Sanskrit and Pali made deep inroads into the script, language and literature of Laos. Majority of the Lao inscriptions had been in Sanskrit. The wide prevalence of Sanskrit influenced immensely the classical Lao script,

---

353   Virachitah, n. 67, P. 118.

language and literature. Lao script was introduced by King Rama Kampheng of Sukhodaya in 1283 C.E., which marked the common origin of Thai and Lao alphabets. In the same year Pali scriptures from Sri Lanka were introduced resulting in greater influence of Pali. One type of Lao script known as *Toua-Lam* is considered sacred and it is used for transcribing Pali[354]. In Lao languae, there are about sixty percent of words having Sanskrit and Pali origin. There are many Lao words having Indian origin like : *Kumara* (Kumara), *Pativat* (Prativada), *Pathet* (Pradesh), *Prom* (Brahma), *Pranam* (Pranam), *Rusi* (Rsi), *Shanti* (Santi), *Sri* (Sri), *Sut* (Sutra), *Setthi* (Sresthi), *Youvatnari* (Yuvanari), *Sabha* (Sabha), *Champa* (Campa), *Nang Mekhala* (Mani Mekhala), *Nang Thorani* (Devi Dharani), *Praya Nak* (Nagaraja) etc. The true classical Lao poetry is formed by translation of Indian poems, and Lao verses follow the metrics of Indian prosody[355]. In folk songs, dramas and theatres, themes from Indian literature are in abundance. The Lao folklore had been influenced by Indian themes. Development of religious song of Buddhist monks encouraged many stories becoming popular both in prose and poetry. In the classical Lao dance one can find gestures and movements showing strong influence of various Indian dance forms.

The *Ramayana* is very popular in Laos. The country was earlier known as Lava, the son of Rama. Story of Rama or *Phra Lak Phra Lam* with its fundamental human value and social idea has contributed to the cultural life of people. The Lao have adopted the stories of *Ramayana* as if it had

---

354   *Ibid*, P. 146.

355   Raghuvira, "The Literature of Lava" in L. Chandra and others eds, *India's Contribution to World Thought and Culture* (Madras, 1970), P. 488.

happened in Laos. Names, titles and geographical settings were given local colour[356]. Rabahnasvn (Ravana), Rama and Bari (Valin), the three princes of same line were ruling over Lanka (Langasuka), Kururathahnahgan (Jambudvipa) and Kasi (Kasi in northern part of Laos) respectively[357]. Rama and Laksmana were not the sons of Dasaratha but of Viruppakhah, the king of Jambudvipa. Bari (Valin) and Sugip (Sugriva) were sons of Dattahartthah (Dasaratha). The genealogy of the Lao version of *Ramayana* is a process of adoption. Valin and Sugriva were treated with equal importance as Rama and Laksmana. A new parentage of Rama had been created. Nan Sujata incarnated herself on the lap of Ravana in the form of Sita. In the marriage of Sita, the *Gvay Dorabhi* mentioned the acceptance of overlordship of Rama by one hundred and one kings who had come to lift the bow. The important aspect of introduction of the *Ramayana* was that freedom of choice conditioned its growth on independent lines reflecting environment and culture of Laos.

The majority of Lao stories were derived from the *Pancatantra*. It was translated into Lao language by Phra Samgharaja Vixula Mahaviharathipati in 1507 C.E. of Wat Vixula Mahavihan. The *Pancatantra* stories written by Visnu Sarma of Orissa[358] became very popular in Laos. The Lao version consisted of five *Pakon* (Prakarana); Nanda, Manduka, Pisaca, Sakuna and Samgha. The narrator of

---

356 S. Sahai, *The Phra Lak Phra Lam*, Part-I (New Delhi, 1973), P.xiii.

357 S. Sahai, *Ramayana in Laos : A Study in the Gvay Dvorabhi* (Delhi, 1976),pp.3-4.

358 S.C. Behera, "Home-Land of Visnu Sarma" in *Indian Historical Quarterly*, XXXVIII, 1962, pp. 160-167.

the stories was queen Tantai Mahadevi, which was the Sanskrit alteration of *Tantravaya* or weaver of tales. The collection of stories called *Mulla Tantai* (Mula-tantra) were used as commentries of law. *Molam* literature had been inspired by beauty of nature, prowess of Indra and wonders of paradise. Sirimangala's *Mangalasutta*, another Lao text was well known in Myanmar and was mentioned in the *Sasanavamsa*[359]. The popular Lao poem *Sin Xay* had its origin in the *Panasajataka*. The *Jatakas* like *Dadhivahana*, *Janakakumara, Vessantara, Vidhurapandita, Vimalaraja* etc were translated into Lao and became very popular. The Lao historical literature had been replete with Indian characters. The *Nitan Khun Borom* dipicting events upto 1571 C.E. mentioned that the son of Indra was sent from heaven to establish the kingdom of Lan Xang. Another Lao chronicle *Nitan Praya Cuong Lun* was about the history of Lava kingdom. Life of Buddha and sixteenth century Lava kings formed the subject matter of *Uranganidana*.

In daily life, rituals, customs and public ceremonies traces of Hindu influence are still present. The people of Laos invoke the names of Siva, Visnu and Indra in their prayer to Buddha. After the death of a member of family, rest perform rituals in the presence of *brahmana*. The sacrifice of buffalo at Wat Phu might have been influenced by the custom of animal sacrifice in some of the temples of India[360]. In the *Baisai*[361] ceremmony, the chief called Brahma is chosen from village elders and performs Buddhist and Hindu rites on occasions like New Year, marriage, arrival of important visitors, promotion of government officials etc. The form of greeting to learned persons and religious

---

359 Sarkar, n. 14, P. 293.
360 Mishra, n. 64, P. 5.
361 The term *baisai* is etymologically derived from *brahmana*.

teachers is by joining hands at the level of heart, which is very much akin to *Pranam*.

Orissa and Laos

The Orissan style is one of several Indian types that contributed to development of art and architecture in Laos. Architecture of That Luang show close affinity with medieval temples of Orissa. The pillars of Wat Phra Keo also have been influenced by the Orissan pattern. The inscription of second half of fifth century compares. King Sri Devanika with many personalities including Indradyumna. The legend relating to Indradyumna speaks of Jagannatha temple built by him which later or disappeared on sands. The existence of Purusottama in Puri before the great temple was built is attested by inscriptions and later works[362]. When the Jagannatha temple was built, earlier temple built by Indrdyumna was in a delapitated condition. So, mentioning of name Indradyumna in the said inscription suggests Sri Devanika's acquaintance with Orissa. The *Pancatantra* stories written by Visnu Sarma of Orissa was very popular in Laos. There is a reference to best type of elephants of Kalinga in the Titibha Dampati story[363]. Visnu Sarma had been honoured by the Mathara king of Kalinga, Anantasakti Varman. In daily life and public ceremonies, traces of Orissan influence are still found. The custom of buffalo sacrifice at Wat Phu might have been influenced by tradition of animal sacrifice in some of the temples of eastern India. This might have been also an indigenous custom. The practice was discontinued in 1975 after communist takeover of Laos. Certain similarities with Orissa could be

---

362 H.V. Stietenwon, "Early Temples of Jagannath in Orissa : The Formative Phase" in Eschmann, n. 58, P. 64.
363 Behera, n. 80, P. 162.

marked in rituals performed at the time of birth and death in Laos[364]. After the death of a family member, rest perform rituals in the presence of *brahmans*. It is believed that the soul (*Khuan*) of the dead would go to heaven if the relatives perform rituals for him[365]. In the *baisai* ceremony, the *brahmana* performs Buddhist and Hindu rites on occasions like New Year, arrival of important visitors and marriages. The people of different parts of India perform certain rituals with the *brahmana* during marriage, New Year etc. Even the habit of betel-chewing among people of Laos reminds one of this common practice prevalent in Orissa and other parts of India.

---

364   Author's Field Trip to Laos.
365   Virachiteh, n. 67, P. 131.

CHAPTER-V

Orissa's and Malayo-Indonesian Region

The region now designated as Malaysia consists of Peninsular Malaysia along with Sabah and Sarawak in north-western Borneo. Separated from the Malay Peninsula by the straits of Malacca, the Indonesian archipelago comprises of group of islands like; Sumatra, Java, Bali, Borneo, Celebes Moluccas, Flores etc. The Malay Peninsula along with the Indonesian islands are called the Malay world. In Southeast Asia, the Malay people inhabiting Malaysia, Indonesia and the Philippines is the largest ethnic group. Originating from southern China, this southern Mongloid group replaced the indigenous Australo-Melanesian population. The Proto-Malays brought the elements of neolithic culture around 2500 B.C.E. and deutro-Malays introduced bronze and iron around 300 B.C.E. The latter group spreaded all over island Southeast Asia with a common culture and related language.

The region had a rich pre-historical heritage. Discovery of artefacts and metallurgical objects have pushed back the cultural history. Between 4000 and 1000

B.C.E., the neolithic mode of technology appeared. Bronze and Iron made its appearance from 500 B.C.E. onwards. There is also evidence of traders from this region playing important role in the Indian Ocean. Megaliths have been found in north Sumatra, Nias, Suluwesi (Celebes) and Borneo. Puppet shadow theatre, *batik* work in textiles, a monetary system and knowledge of navigation - all these were known to Javanese before they came into contact with Indians. By the beginning of Christian era, the Malays had reached a high level of civilization. When Indian trade was intensified with a demand for goods of this region, the Malays were politically, economically and culturally receptive to elements of Indian culture.

(A) MALAY PENINSULA
Political and Cultural Developments

The Chinese sources refer to states situated in the Malay Peninsula in early centuries of Christian era. They were Tun-hsun, Ch'ih-t'u, P'an-p'an, Tan-tan and Langkasuka. Tun-hsun's existence was from first century C.E. and it was maintaining contact with Tonking, India and Parthia[366]. Located on the two stores of Isthmus of Kra, it was connected with trans-Peninsular networks. There was a confederacy of five kings in Tun-hsun, who were vassals of Funan[367]. A large number of Indian traders, *brahmans* and Buddhists were residing in the kingdom. The local people were also giving their daughter in marriage to the *brahmans* and they were staying in Tun-hsun afterwards[368].

---

366 Devahuti, *Malaysia in Historical Perspective* (Madras, 1980), P. 7.
367 P. Wheatley, *The Golden Khersonese* (Kuala Lumpur, 1961), P. 16.
368 Devahuti, n. 1, P. 7.

The kingdom of Ch'ia-t'u (Red-earth land) was situated in the area of north-eastern Malay. The Chinese text *Ch'ih'-t'u kuo chi* attest the presence of Buddhist and *brahmans*, who were venerated. In the said Chinese text mention of Sanskrit terms for administrative officials are there : *dhanada* (giver of good things), *karmika* (representative), *kulapati* (chief of family), *nayaka* (chief), and *pati* (master)[369]. Life of common people were also depicted in the same text, "It is customary for all persons to pierce their earlobes and cut their hair... It is the custom to worship Buddha but greater respect is paid to Brahmans... For a wedding an auspicious day is selected... Then the father, holding the girl's hand, delivers her to his son-in-law... On the death of a parent or brother (the mourner) shaves his hair and dresses in plain clothes... piles firewood around the corpse, he then sets fire to the pile... but when the king is cremated, his ashes are preserved in a golden jar and deposited in a temple"[370]. It is quite obvious that Ch'ih-t'u kingdom was subject to strong Indian influence. But the king's funerary treatment was a pre-Aryan Asiatic tradition and this also became custom for mortuary temples. A Chinese embassy headed by Ch'ang-Chun came to the royal word in 608 C.E.[371]

Situated in the area of Bay of Bandon on the east coast of Malay Peninsula, P'an-p'an was on trade route between India and China. The Chinese text *Wen-hsien T'ung-k'ao* says that numerous *brahmans* came in search of wealth and they were a favoured lot of the king[372]. Even his ministers were from Kalinga region of India. The chief ministers were

---

369 Wheatley, n. 2, Pp. 26ff.
370 G. Coedes, *The Indianized States of Southeast Asia* (Honolulu, 1965), P. 78 and P. 294.
371 Wheatley, n. 2, pp. 26-28.
372 *Ibid*, P. 49.

known as *Po-lang-so lan, K'un-lun-ti-yeh, K'un-lun-po-ho* and *K'un-lun-po-ti-so-kan* and the Chinese text mentioned that in the vernacular *K'un-lun* and *Ku-lung* had the same sound so that one could say either[373]. This Ku-lung is no other than Keling-Kalinga[374]. From P'an-p'an the *brahmana* Kaundinya II went to Funan. There were Buddhist monasteries in P'an-p'an and diplomatic relationship with China started from 424 C.E. The state of Tan-tan was situated in the region of Trengganu and its ruler sent to China gifts like tooth relic of Buddha, painted stupas and leaves of Bo-tree[375]. The first century C.E. state of Langkasuka was near Patani having access to Gulf of Thailand. Its ruler Bhagadatta established diplomatic relationship with China in 515 C.E.[376]. Langkasuka had been referred by Chinese travellers I-tsing and Hiuen-tsang[377]. It was controlling trade routes to the east and ruins of a Siva temple have been found from this place. Another state called Tamralinga was located between Chaiya and Pattani with its centre in Ligor region. The kingdom was already in existence in second century C.E. as evident from Buddhist canon *Niddesa*, where Tamraling has been referred as Tambalingam[378]. Located directly across Bay of Bengal, and on trans-Peninsular route to east, Kedah (Katah in Sanskrit) was a well protected habour. It figures prominently in Indian literature like the Tamil *Pattinappalai* of second-third century C.E., *Agni Purana, Kaumudimahotsava* and in Arab geography. Kedah and

---

373 *Ibid*
374 H.B. Sarkar, *Cultural Relations Between India and Southeast Asian Countries* (New Delhi, 1985), P. 143.
375 Wheatley, n. 10, pp. 52-53.
376 Coedes, n. 5, P. 511.
377 Devahuti, n. 1, P. 25, f.n.23.
378 Coedes, n. 5, P. 39.

another port named Takupa had yielded rich archaeological relics showing evidences of influence from various parts of India. The Chinese sources also mention Pahang, which was famous for supplies of tin and gold.

The Malay Peninsula with its ports assumed importance in trading network involving Rome, India and China. Ships of Roman empire were coming to Southeast Asia from Indian Ocean and they were calling in the port of Takupa (Takkola) and to the port of Klang further south. After the collapse of Roman trade the merchants were going through Kedah to southern Thailand and from there to Campa by way of northern Thailand and Kambuja. The trade routes of Indian traders were across Kedah, Palembang, east Java and West Celebes, where icons of Amaravati school of art have been found. One important site in the Malay Peninsula is Kuala Selinsing on the Perak coast, which has yielded beads of carnelian, crystal and glass and a seal dated to 400 C.E. with Sri Visnuvarman inscribed on it[379]. The trading activity in the region started around second century C.E. Ceramic and glass remains have been found from another trading centre, Pengkalan Bujang. The Hindu influence also could be marked from Bukit Batu Lintang and Kedah Peak dated to eigth century C.E. Among the sculptural evidences from the Peninsula are a fourth century C.E. icon of Visnu and a *linga* dated to fifth century C.E. from Chaiya. The Buddhist votive inscriptions dated to fourth century are found from Kedah. The Buddhagupta slate inscription from Muda estuary had an exquisite Buddhist *stupa* and a prayer inscribed by a sea captain for safe voyage. Buddhagupta was a resident of

---

379 H.P. Ray, "Early Maritime Contacts Between South and Southeast Asia" in *Journal of Southeast Asian Studies*, XX, 1989, P. 53.

Raktamrttika, identified with Rajabidanga on the banks of Bhagirathi river, which formed Ganga river's flow in ancient times[380]. In the site near Takupa were found three statues and an inscription in Tamil with reference to merchant guild known as *Manikkiramam*[381]. All these evidences point to existence of trading centres for overland and overseas commerce. The centres had presence of Indian community. The Malay Peninsula was well-organized politically and administratively. Trade in beads, discovery of Buddhist votive tablets and finding of Hindu icons point towards strong Indian influence. Cultural interaction between Malay Peninsula and India started from pre-historic times.

Sri Vijaya

The rise of kingdom of Sri-Vijaya with its capital at Palembang in south-eastern Sumatra was a consequence of decline of Funan and inability of Chenla to function as intermediary in East-West trade. Gaining control over the two important maritime passages, i.e., the straits of Malacca and the Sunda straits, Sri-Vijaya's control extended to rich hinterland of Kedah and Perak. Unlike the Javanese states dependent upon agricultural products for consumption and export, Sri-Vijaya's power was based upon maritime commerce. Sumatra's topographic advantage made the port of Palembang an important regional entrepot. Taking initiative in direct maritime trade between southern China and West Asia, the Sumatrans substituted local products for established items of trade. The new source of wealth set in motion during the last half of the seventh century reached

---

380   *Ibid*, pp. 53-59.
381   I.W. Mabbett, "The 'Indianization' of Southeast Asia : Reflections on the Historical Sources", *Journal of Southeast Asian History*, VIII, 2, 1977, P. 152.

an important phase when its ruler achieved a position of dominance in the region. Though detailed evidences of Sri-Vijaya's extent and organization is lacking and it has been characterized as 'loose association of trading ports' or as a 'chronological expression'[382], the fact remains that upto the second half of thirteenth century, it was a major power in Malayo-Indonesian world.

The Chinese traveller I-tsing during his six month's stay in Sri-Vijaya in 671 C.E. had mentioned that it was an important Buddhist centre and Palembang was a flourishing port[383]. There was brisk trading in the port in Indian textiles, Chinese porcelains, jade and silk and spices from Moluccas. Thirty-five ships arrived from Persia (Iran) alone during I-tsing's six-month stay. He sailed to India in a ship owned by the Sri-Vijayan king. The rulers sent several missions to China and the Chinese monks came to Sri-Vijaya to study with Indian monks. In late seventh and early eighth centuries, Sri Vijaya, emerged as a 'polity with pyramidal network of loyalities among Malay rulers', whose common interest was maritime commerce oriented profit[384]. The kingdom was controlling both sides of the straits of Malacca as evident from the Ligor inscription dated 775 C.E. on the Malay Peninsula, which commemorated the foundation of a Buddhist sanctuary by the Sri-Vijayan ruler.

In mid-ninth century, a prince of Sailendra dynasty of Java, Balipatra became the ruler of Sri-Vijaya, who founded

---

382 H.A. Lamb, "Early History" in W. Gungwu, ed, *Malaysia : A Survey* (Melbourne, 1965), pp. 99 ff.
383 H.A. Giles, *Record of Buddhist Kingdoms* (London, 1962), P. 76.
384 K.W. Taylor, "The Early Kingdoms" in N-Tarling, eds, *The Cambridge History of Southeast Asia*, Vol I (Singapore, 1972), P. 174.

a Buddhist monastery in Nalanda. At the end of tenth century, Sri-Vijaya's relationship with Java deteriorated and the expedition against Java in 1016 C.E. resulted in the destruction of the capital. At this time, the Colas of south India as an expanding maritime power resented Sri-Vijaya's attempt to dominate and tax ships passing through the straits. The major expedition against Sri-Vijaya by Rajendra-coladeva I (1012-1044 C.E.) is dated 1025 C.E. and the Tamil *prasasti* vividly described it[385]. But by 1060's relationship had improved and Tamil merchants once again became active. During the twelfth century, there was expansion of Chinese shipping, which reduced the dominance of Sri-Vijaya. The local ports began to deal directly with the Chinese. Palembang's status declined. In the thirteenth century, Ayuthia and Majapahit reduced the authority of Sri-Vijaya. There was also spread of Islam resulting in setting up of small Muslim principalities. Ultimately the Sri-Vijayan kingdom broke up.

Buddhism flourished in Sri-Vijaya due to patronage of its rulers. The Chinese traveller I-tsing had described importance of Palembang as Buddhist centre, where more than thousand priests were residing and lotus shaped golden vessels were being offered to gold and silver Buddhas. I-tsing translated Buddhist texts into Chinese and had brought 500,000 stanzas of *Tripitaka* from India. The Chinese pilgrims like Yun-ki, Ta-tsini, Tcheng-kou etc

---

385   K.A.N. Sastri, The *Colas* (Madras, 1984), pp. 211-219. The *Prasasti* mentions that the king of Kadaram (Kedah), Sangrama-vijayottungavarman was defeated. Places like Sri-Vijaya (Palembang), Pannai (east coast of Sumatra), Mayirudingam, Ilangasoka (Langkasuka), Talaittakkolam (Takola), Madamlingam (Tamralingam), Ilamuridesam (northern tip of Sumatra) etc come under Cola attack. See *Ibid*, pp. 212-13.

stayed in Palembang learning Sanskrit and Kouenlouen, a script of Kalinga[386]. In the hinterland, the Buddhist advisers of the king were making contact with local aristocracy and encouraging them to hold Buddhist ceremonies and to take part in religious functions in Palembang. Though adherents of Buddhism, the rulers took recourse to indigenous beliefs : one of the stone inscriptions depicted local Malay water oath with Buddhist icon[387]. The Indian motif of seven-headed cobra as protector of Buddha was effective as power of snakes was called to protect the domain by the Malay rulers earlier. A funnel was there on the stone, form where water drained out at the time of oath-taking. An inscription of 775 C.E. from east coast of Malay Peninsula depicted the construction of a monastery at the site by the ruler, who was a patron of the snakes[388]. So, there was a blending of traditional image of power (snake) and external influence (Buddhism). The Sri Vijayan rulers built monuments in areas as far away as Canton in China and Negapattan in east coast of south India. The construction of a monastery was undertaken at Negapattam by Sri Vijayan ruler in 1006 C.E. named Cudamani-varmadeva and was completed by his son, Maravijayottungavarman. Dharmakirti was the greatest Pali scholar of his times. He was the head of Sri Vijaya clergy, for whom the Thai king had a built a monastery, the Lankarama. The Buddhist scholar Atisa, who reformed Tibetan Buddhism studied under Dharmakirti from 1011 to 1023. Apart from Buddhism, Indian influence was there through Sanskrit language. Some of the inscriptions were in Sanskrit and this language was popular in Sri-Vijaya.

---

386   Sarkar, n. 9, P. 266.
387   K.R. Hall, "Economic History of Early Southeast Asia" in Tarling, n.19, P. 201.
388   *Ibid*, P. 202.

The Chinese pilgrims were advised to halt in Palembang to study Sanskrit[389]. In I-tsing's report on Sri-Vijaya, one finds a glimpse of customs and traditions of people. Indian influence could be marked in customs like : removal of footwear before Gods and superiors, washing of hands after meals, appeal by the priests to dead spirits etc. The Hindu practices self-immolation, cutting of one's flesh and throwing one's body to Ganga or into a funeral pyre were criticized.

Relations with Orissa

The people of Kalinga had maintained trade relationship with mainland and inland Southeast Asia from its prosperous ports like Tamralipti, Palura, Pithunda, Che-li-ta-lo, Kalinganagara etc. Elements of Indian culture were there in Tun-hsun of Malay Peninsula in early centuries of Christian era and the Chinese texts refer to five hundred families of merchants and more than thousand *brahmans* fromm India. Taking into account Kalinga's maritime activity in this period, it could be assumed that some of the above Indians might have been from Kalinga. From sites like Kuala Selinsing on the Perak coast and Kalumpong island large quantities of beads of carnelian, crystal and glass have been found. The beads are reported from Orissan sites like Sisupalgarh, Manikpatna and Sambalpur[390]. Even the name of Goddesses are associated with semi-precious stones : Manikesvari (Goddess of ruby),

---

389 K.A.N. Sastri, *History of Sri-Vijaya* (Madras, 1949), pp. 250-51.
390 Collared beads and crystalline quartz have been found from Sisupalgarh and Sambalpur respectively. See, R.E.M.Wheeler and others, "Arikamedu : an Indo-Roman Trading-station on the east coast of India" in *Ancient India*, 2, 1946, reprint 1983, P. 97 and P. 123.

Pannesvari (Goddess of emarlad) and Samelsvari (Goddess of Wealth). The prevalence of Kouenlouen script in P'an-p'an and Sri-Vijaya also points to the cultural contact with Kalinga. It has been mentioned earlier that the script had been derived from Kalinga. When the Chinese speak of Kun-lun, (Kouenlouen) the term denoted ethno-linguistic entity. There was expansion of Mahayana Buddhism in Sri-Vijaya in the seventh century. This with its tendency towards tantric mysticism of Vajrayana gained acceptance. On occasion of founding a public park in 684 C.E., the king Jayanasa in his prayer (*pranidhana*) expressed ideas about enlightenment that was in line with Mahayanist Sarvastivada[391]. In 775 C.E., is sanctuary of Buddha and the Bodhisattvas Padmapani and Vajrapani was built at Ligor by the king of Sri-Vijaya. In seventh and eighth centuries, Orissa was a centre of Vajrayana. In Ratnagiri, Mahayana and Vajrayana flourished. Tantric Buddhism developed in Orissa and according to some authorities it was birth place of Buddhist tantricism[392]. The tantric images like Marichi, Kurukulla, Lokesvara, Urdhvapada-Vajravarahi etc have been found from Orissa. The naming of public park by Jayanasa as Srikssetra assumes importance. Sriksetra was another name for Puri, where the Jagannatha temple was later on built[393]. Therefore, it would not be wrong to say that certain elements of Orissan culture influenced the Malay world.

---

391   Coedes, n. 5, P. 34. Presence of tantricism in Sumatra could be attested from the fact that in 714 A.D. Vajrabodhi, introducer of the doctrine in China halted in Sri-Vijaya. *Ibid*, P. 297, f.n. 33.
392   N.K. Sahu, *Buddhism in Orissa* (Cuttack, 1988), pp. 141 ff.
393   Sri Ksetra's antiquity and religious significance has been dealt in Chapter III.

(B) Java
Political and Cultural Developments

Amongs the islands of Indonesian archipelago, Java is fourth in area. It is separated on the west by Sunda strait and from Balli on the east by Bali strait. Central location among myriads of islands, fertile soil capable of sustaining a large population, command over alternate trade routes between the East and West through Sunda straits, access to spicies and sandal wood of archipelago, large fertile plains and rainfall suitable for growing rice etc - all these factors made Java dominant power in the region. The cultural accomplishment of the region included use of outrigger canoes, wet-rice cultivation, *wayang* or puppet shadow theatre, *garmelan* orchestra, *batik* work in textiles and megalithic tradition. Before coming into contact with Indians, the Javanese society was already developed. The slab graves of Java had produced irone, bronze, glass and carelian beads[394]. The beads originated from India and Indian traders probably were present in the region as early as 2000 years ago[395]. A Hindu king Devavarman had sent an embassy in 132 C.E. to China[396]. A more definite picture of Indian penetration in the region could be found from group of four Sanskrit inscriptions discovered in the region commanding Sunda strait. These stone inscriptions[397] dated to mid-fifth century C.E. depicts a picture of developed statehood in early Java. The king Purnavarman is eulogised

---

394 P. Bellwood, "Southeast Asia before History" in Tarling, n. 19, P. 132.
395 *Ibid*, P. 133.
396 R.C. Majumdar, *India and Southeast Asia* (New Delhi, 1979), P. 19. But nothing definite is known about this. There is no evidence to argument that Java was Indianized by 132 A.D. See Coedes, n. 5, P. 18.
397 Coedes, n. 5, pp. 53-54.

as Lord (Isvara) of the city (nagara) of Taruma, whose predecesor Pinabahu was euolused with royal title of king of kings (rajadhiraja). He was observing brahminic rites and did irrigation works. Puranavarman's footprints had been compared with Visnu's footprints and that of his royal elephant with Indra's elephant Airavata[398]. His kingdom was not centralized as it has been mentioned in the inscription that he was ruling over his own *nagara* as his enemies (*ari*) in their own cities. It cannot be said definitely about the king's place of origin. He might have been an immigrant from India or an indigenous Malay prince. But the fact remains that Purnavarman came under Indian influence. In the fifth century C.E., the Chinese pilgrim Fa-hien reached west Java from Sri Lanka. He writes that Hindu cultural influence was more than that of Buddhist[399]. He sailed for Canton in 413 C.E. in a ship with 200 Hindu merchants. The inscription of Kutei in Borneo (Kalimantan) dated to about 400 C.E. refers the name of the ruler Mulavarman, who performed a sacrifice and donated 20,000 cows to *brahmans*. Prevalence of Saivism could be known from sacrificial posts (*yupa*) associated with inscriptions. The Sanskrit inscriptions of western Borneo dated to sixth century show Buddhist influence.

Ho-ling in central Java was a coastal centre having interaction with China in fifth century. The kingdoms that arose in central Javanese rice plains in sixth century was based on a system in which one centre was establishing superiority over other regions. Ho-ling's early history

---

398   B.R. Chatterji, *History of Indonesia* (Merrut, 1967) pp. 6-7.
399   Giles, n. 18, P. 78. A Kashmir Prince Gunavarman was responsible for introducing Buddhism in Java by 423 A.D. He converted the members of royal family to Buddhism. See, Chatterji, n. 33, P. 7.

relates to a woman leader Sima and sending embassies to China. It was a centre of Buddhist culture in the seventh century and local scholar Jnanabhadra (Joh-na-poh-to-lo in Chinese) translated Buddhist texts along with the Chinese scholar Hui-ning, who had come to Ho-ling in 664-65 C.E.[400]. In Javanese history upto seventh century a system developed where sawah-cultivated sections of central and eastern Java rose into prominence. In spite of adoption of Indian cultural elements, traditional pattern survived. Buddhism prevailed. On the stele of the Tuk-mas inscription of mid-seventh century, there were Visnuite symbols like conch, disc, mace and lotus. From eighth century onwards, a repetitive pattern of rise and fall of kingdomswas witnessed. There was considerable shifting of power between central and eastern Java. Mataram, Sailendra, Kediri, Singhsari and Majapahit were some of the important kingdoms that emerged.

Sanjaya was a Saivite king who established himself at Mataram in central Java. His Cangal inscription of 732 C.E. reports the consecration of a *linga* on a mountain in Kunjarakunja[401]. He was the founder of Mataram dynasty and established the first known genuine kingdom in Javanese history, calling the state as *rajya*[402]. The Saivite temples on the Dieng plateau attest to Indian influence, prowess of the rulers and artistic abilities of artisans. The Prambanan group of temples dedicated to Hindu trinity are best examples of artistic achievement of the Mataram rulers. After Sanjay, Raka (Raja) Panangkaran become the ruler

---

400   Sarkar, n. 9, P. 266.
401   H.B. Sarkar, ed, *Corpus of Inscriptions of Java* Vol.I, (Calcutta, 1971),pp.15-24.
402   H. Kulke, *Kings and Cults, State Formation and Legitimation in India and Southeast Asia* (New Delhi, 1993), P. 311.

in 760 C.E. Then followed kings like Panungalan, Varak, Patapan and Pikatan. Patapan, inspite of a matrimonial alliance with the Sailendras acquired the latter's kingdom in 872 C.E. The rulers of Bali and western Borneo came under the suzerainty of Mataram. Mataram also participated actively in trade and commerce. In the end of tenth century, it was at its peak in political and economic strength.

From about the middle of eighth century to the middle of ninth century Sailendras were predominant in central Java. One of important dynasties of the region, their cultural legacy is best remembered by the magnificient monument of Borobudur. The Sailendras were patrons of Mahayana Buddhism. Borobudur became the central point for legitimizing their rule. Bhanu (752-775 C.E.) was the first ruler of the dynasty, then followed by Visnu (Pancapana), Indra and Samaratunga (812-832 C.E.). Under the Sailendras, a full-fledged kingdom had come into existence. An inscription of 782 C.E. mentions the consecration of a Manjusri image by a Sailendra ruler (Pancapana) to protect his *desa* (state or country). Pancapara also bore the title of maharaja. The Sailendra rulers made bid for supremacy in the Indo-Chinese Peninsula. Tonking, Campa and Chenla were raided. The founder of Angkor, Jayaraman II ended the Sailendra supremacy in 802 C.E. The Mataram ruler Pikatan had married the daughter of Samaratunga, Promodavardhini. He usurped the kingdom of his father-in-law in 832 C.E. Samaratunga's infant son Balaputra later on fled to Sri Vijaya, where he became the ruler.

The relations between Mataram and Sri-Vijaya deteriorated over the port facilities around the straits of Malacca. In the ensuring contest, the ruler of Mataram, Dharmavamsa was defeated in 1006 C.E. Meanwhile Sri-Vijaya became weak after Cola invasion and Dharmavamsa's heir Airlangga was consecrated as a king in 1019 C.E. Under him Mataram became powerful once again. The kingdom was divided into Kediri and Janggala after his death. Kediri became an important maritime power profitting greatly from the Mediterrnanean area's demand for spices. The Javanese traders went upto southeast coast of Africa for trade[403]. In 1129 C.E. the Chinese recognising the dominance of Kediri, gave the ruler Kamesvara title of king. The Chinese writer Chou-Chu-fei in 1178 C.E. referred to the leading maritime powers of Asia like the Arabs, Kediri and Sri-Vijaya[404]. The last ruler of Kediri, Sarvesana II was murdered by Ken Angrok in 1222 C.E. One of the important source materials for Javanese history from thirteenth century onwards, the *Pararaton* vividly describes the circumstances leading to Angrok's capture of power. The dynasty established by Angrok was known as Singhasari, whose greatest ruler was Kertanagara (1268-1292 C.E.). The Javanese epic poem *Nagarakertagama* written by Buddhist monk Prapanca in 1365 C.E. begins from Kertanagara. He like his father Visnuvardhana patronised the synthesis of indigenous religious traditions, Saivite and Mahayana Buddhist. Kertanagara was an aspiring empire builder, who made the rulers of Bali, south-west Borneo, the Moluccas etc his vassals and in 1290 brought Sri-Vijaya under his domain. But on the wake of Mongal invasion he was killed by a subordinate ruler Jayakatong of Kediri. At the time of Kertanagara's death, Java was a prosperous kingdom. Marco Polo described Java in 1292 C.E. as a prosperous kingdom and mentioned, "Indeed, the treasure

---

403   Chatterji, n. 33, P. 24.
404   B. Harrison, *South-East Asia : A Short History* (New York, 1966), P. 46.

of this island (Java) is so great as to be past telling"[405].

Kertanagara's son-in-law Raden Vijaya ascended the throne of Majapahit in 1294 C.E. after getting rid of Jayakatong. For next century, Majapahit claimed suzerainty over most of insular and Peninsular Southeast Asia. The prime Minister Gaja Mada's (1330-1364 C.E.) vision and skill was responsible for Majapahit's moment of glory. It became greatest political and maritime power. A chronicle of Samudra-Pasai, *Hikayat Raja-Raja Pasai* attests to power of the kingdom and its sound economic condition[406]. The Majapahit had an extensive international trade dealing with Myanmar, Cambodia, Thailand, China and India. Bubat became the cosmopolitan city where foreign merchants resided. But the kingdom was becoming weak politically due to civil wars between 1401 and 1406. A rebel prince named Paramesvara left Majapahit and carved out a small principality at Malacca. In 1411 he was converted to Islam with the new name Megat Iskander Shah. By 1428, Majapahit lost control over western Java. Malacca became the main diffusion centre of Islam. The trader-rulers of many small states converted themselves to Islam. A coalition of Javanese coastal communities attacked Majapahit and by 1528 the royal family took asylum in Bali. The Muslims that brought downfall of the kingdom were local people and no outside Muslim power was involved.

It has been mentioned earlier the prevalence of Hinduism and Buddhism in the early centuries of Christian era. There was a blending of Indian cultural elements with indigenous traditions. Brahmanism affected the life of people in Malao-Indonesian world in many ways. Many

---

405 H. Yule, trans, *The Book of Ser Marco Polo* (London, 1903), pp.272-74.
406 Hall, n. 22, P. 218.

forms of brahmanical religion affiliated to the Hindu trinity were practised by the Javanese. In Java, there was a great flowering of architecture and sculpture. The temple or *candi* is not only a religious shrine of a deity but a mausoleum housing the ashes of the dead king. It was a legacy of indigenous ancestor-worship. The ruins of Mataram capital at Prambanan bears testimony to many *candis* dedicated to Brahma, Visnu and Siva. There are eight main temples with three rows of minor shrines. The main temples are dedicated to Brahma, Visnu, Siva, Nandi etc. Scenes of *Ramayana* are depicted on the relief sculptures and there are *kala-makara* motifs. The Prambanan reliefs, unlike Indian counterparts depict besides main characters, attendants and subsidary figures amidst a tropical scene of trees and shrubs. Upper body of all figures including women is bare. The *Viradha-vadha* (killing of the *gandharva* reborn as *rakshasa*) scene on the relief is unique. Episodes like cremation of Dasaratha and Ravana's corpse lying on funeral pyre depict originality. The special effect of the temples is rich decoration. Architectural remains of Dieng (Dihyang) plateau date from early eighth century. The name of *candis* are borrowed from characters of the *Mahabharata* : Arjuna, Srikandi, Puntadeva (Yudhisthira), Bima, Ghatotkaca etc. *Sikharas, kala makara* and *caitya* window niches are unique in this group. In the Dieng plateau, images of Siva, Durga, Ganesa, Visnu and Brahma are found. The mounts of chief Gods are having human form and only heads of a bull, swan and beak of a bird indicate the mounts of Hindu trinity. Dieng plateau was a place of pilgrimage rather than a temple town. There are no trace of dwelling houses. The Sailendras, who were patrons of Buddhism also built brahmanical temples like *candi* Banon having images of Visnu and Agastya. The chief monuments of Singsari period include *candi* Kidal

(Siva) with pyramidal roof. Saiva-Buddhism syncretism could be found in *candi* Jawi, where in the central cell a Siva image with Buddha on top of it is there. The *candi* Singasari itself has yielded icons of Hindu pantheon. Amongst the monuments of Majapahit, the finest one is the Saiva temple complex of Panataran. The richly ornamented bas-reliefs depict scenes from the *Ramayana* and *Krsnayana*, which were designed in *wayang* like style. Apart from the images of Hindu trinity, icons of various Gods and Goddesses like Ganesa, Karttikeya, Durga, Indra, Varuna, Kubera etc are found. The icons of Ardhanarisvara, Bhairava, Bhattaraguru, Yama, Hariti, Surya, Candra, Kamadeva are lesser in number. The presentation of skull ornaments in Ganesa images is a speciality in Java.

The Sailendra kings strongly patronized Buddhism, which is reflected in art and architecture. *Candi* Kalasan dated 778 C.E. was dedicated to Tara. Enormous *kala makaras* are there in the entrance and niches. The *makara torana* arches are exquisite in design. Nearer to Kalasan complex, the storeyed *vihara* type of building known as *candi* Sari is situated. *Candi* Sewu (a thousand temples) at Prambanan is a large complex consisting of one large temple in the middle and sorrounded by four rows of 250 small temples. The whole complex is marked by order and beauty. Various deities of Buddhist pantheon are assigned to its proper place. Representing the highest genius of the Sailendra period, the Buddhist *stupa* of Borobudur was begun by Visnu in 778 C.E. and completed in 824 C.E. during the reign of his grandson, Samaratunga. Borobudur was selected as Mount Meru of kingdom of Sailendras to construct on it a miniature cosmos dedicated to Buddha. Representing nine previous lives of Buddha before he attained Buddhahood, nine terraces were carved out of a single hill. Long series of reliefs occupy the lower terraces depicting the life of Buddha. On the open circular terraces there are many bell-shaped *stupas*. At the top of the monument is a large *stupa* of plain stone. On each square terraces, the flight of steps go through a gateway, which are adorned with Buddha images. In Borobudur, the Javanese artisans made changes in traditional sculptural pattern of India. The faces are of Javanase people engaged in different occupations. Dress, jewellery, musical instruments, furniture, utensils etc are indigenous. The nearby *candis* of Mendut and Pawon were dedicated to ancestor worship which were very much important to indigenous beliefs. Figures of Kubera, Hariti and Pancika adorn the walls of *candi* Mendut. Images of Boddhisattvas and Tara are there on the triple panels. Image of a sedant Buddha represents the highest level of Indo-Javanese art.

Indian literature left a deep impact in Malayo-Indonesian world. The inscriptions before ninth century like epigraphs of Mulavarman, Purnavarman and Sailendra rulers were in Sanskrit. From ninth century onwards inscriptions were mainly written in Old Javnese. The golden period of Indo-Javanese literature was from 925 to 1400 C.E. and works produced in the period were :I) *Veda* and *Puranas* ii) Agama and *Dharmasastras, Nitisahitya* and *Sasana* iii) *Kanda* or grammer iv) Itihas v) genealogical stories vi) *tantri* or fables[407]. The *Bhuvanakosa* is a yoga text of tantric order. Various doctrines of the Saiva theology are discussed in the *Brhaspatitattva*. The *Rajapatigundala* deals with statecraft. Impact of Sanskrit rhetoric (*alankara*) on Old Javanese literature also was there. Themes taken from Indian epics known as *kakavin* formed an important element in Old Javanese language and the greatest work in this

---

407   [42]Sarkar, n.9, p.297.

category was *Bharatayuddha*. The *Tantri Kamandak* was based on Indian *Pancatantra* and *Hitopadesa*. The Old Javanese *Ramayana* is a famous work of Indo-Javanese literature. It was written by Yogisvara. Connected with several texts, temples and *wayang* stories, the *Ramayana* has influenced the social life of the people. The different versions of this epic are, *Rama Kling, Ramayana Sasak, Serat Kanda* and the Malay *Hikayut Seri Rama*. The *kakavins* dealing with the *Mahabharata* related stories are *Arjunavivaha, Harivijaya, Krsnantaka* and *Navaruci*. The mystic elements of Vajrayana are dealt in works like *Sang Hyang Kamahayanikan* and *Sang Hyang Kamahayanikan Mantranaya*.

From eleventh century onwards, Old Javanese sources mention presence of three religious communities (tripaksa) : the Saivites, Buddhists and Rsis or *mahabrahmans*[408]. In court of the kings, royal consecration (*abhiseka*) and funerary rites (*sraddha*) were two important ceremonies. The former was present even in the time of Puranavarman in fifth century, who dated his Tugu inscription in twenty-second regnal year. Presence of priests from the three religious communities was an example of deviation from Indian texts. In the *sraddha* ceremony, participants included not only members of royal family but also high officials, dancers, musicians etc, which was in contrast to the Indian ceremony confined to close relatives[409]. The ceremony was observed on full moon day unlike in India where it was conducted on dark half of the month. Tantric rites were also performed by monks and *brahmans*. The reference to God Haricandana in Javanese inscriptions is another novelty of

---

408 *Nagarakertagama*, 81-1-4 referred in J.G. De Casparis and I.W. Mabbett, "Religion and Popular Beliefs of Southeast Asia before c. 1500" in Tarling, n. 19, P. 305.

409 44 *Ibid*, P.307.

Javanese religious life. Imprecation formulas found at the end of Old Javanese charters are also examples of blending of Hinduism with traditional Austronesian beliefs. Worship of mountains and rivers was another indigenous practice, which was prevalent in pre-Aryan India also. As Aryanization spreaded, these were incorporated to brahmanical fold. So it is not surprising that in Java, Austronesian cults were in harmony with Indian cultural elements.

Indian influence was not confined to rituals only. From early times to eleventh century, a group of monks and ascetics resided in Dieng plateu. An archaic form of brahamnism prevailed[410]. The *Nagarakertagama* mentions existence of an influential Vaisnava community and there were Vaisnava foundations. Many *kakavins* were written pertaining to Visnu and some of the royalty were devotees of that God. His consort Laksmi became a Goddess associated with fertility in rice fields and in west Java she is still worshipped under the name Ni Pohaci Sargyang Sri. Rituals pertaining to ricefields is an admixture of traditional and Indian beliefs. The Javanese believe in a life force present in human beings and rice. In the famous *Caitra*[411] festival held at trading centre of Bubat of the Majapahit empire, the *brahmans* and Buddhist monks invoked the blessing of God for royal house's prosperity. Entertainment followed and presents were offered to the king. Afterwards the scene shifted to the royal centre and the speech of the king made

---

410 [45]*Ibid*, P.308.
411 [46] According to the Hindu calendar the month of *Caitra* correspond to March/April. The very same *Caitra* suggest Hindu influence. For details of the festival, see Casparis and Mabbett, n. 43, pp. 219-20.

it clear that wet-rice cultivation was very much important to his legitimacy. Even after coming of Islam, the Javanese culture retained some of the Hindu Buddhist elements. As late as early nineteenth century, people in Java did not take Islam seriously and some observed the Hindu taboo on beef eating. In the puppet shadow plays, the themes of Indian mythology are represented. Indonesia is replete with names having Sanskrit origin. In a letter to Pandit Nehru, the erstwhile President of Indonesia Dr. Soekarno wrote that India and Indians were "linked to us by ties of blood and culture which date back to the very beginning of our history. And at this very moment of writing the first ship to take rice to India is being loaded at the port of *Probolinggo* which is made of two words *Purva* and *Kalinga*"[412].

Borneo (Kalimantan) occupied a special position as it was a halting place for sailors to and from the straits of Malacca and Indo-China. The Kutei inscriptions of Mulavarman dated 400 C.E. attests to formation of an early kingdom. There was prevalence of Saivism as the name Vaprakesvara of the inscription suggests [413]. Siva images of a later period were found in Kutei. The images of Nandi, Linga, Ganesa, Durga etc have been discovered from various places of Borneo. From Genung Kombeng in Kutei, icons of Siva, Ganesa, Karttikeya, Mahakala etc have been found and a small golden statue of Visnu have been excavated from Muara Kaman [414]. Of the Buddhist images,

---

412   Quoted in D. Daweewarn, *Brahmanism in Southeast Asia* (New Delhi, 1982), P. 275.

413   In foundation ritual of kings like Jayavarman II of Angkor and Sanjaya of Mataram, *lingas* of Siva (*isvara*) were consecrated on a hillock (*vapra*).

414   Daweewarn, n.47, P. 187.

the important find-spots are from Genung Kombeng and Sambas. The Bukti Mas hill in northern Borneo has yielded a stone Ganesa, gold lion, a Persian gold coin and ornaments like necklaces, a phallic pendant, a fillet, four beads, and rings with inset gems, engraved motif and letters[415]. The conch and fish designs on the rings are popular Hindu-Buddhist motifs. After coming of Islam, Malaysia retained some of Hindu-Buddhist beliefs. Indra's thunderbolt symbol was there on the arrmlets of sultans of Malay. Astrology influenced the organization of palace area of these rulers. In the shadow-plays (*wayang Kulit*), the opening ceremony invokes not only to Allah but also to deities of Hindu pantheon. In many of the modern Muslim miracle (*kramat*) sites, Saivite relics are still present[416]. A liberal tradition prevails in whole Malayo-Indesian world and Islam is characterized by its catholicity.

Relations with Orissa

Orissa's relationship with Malayo-Indonesian world is attested by evidences like archaeology, incriptions similarity of names, art and architecture. Several traditions of the region also speak of people of Kalinga migrating to the region and establishing kingdom. Though legends could not be taken as historical proof, they point to acquitance of Malays with the Kalingans. Taking into account other evidences, it could be safely presumed that, people of

---

415   Devahuti, "India, Malay and Borneo-Two Millennia of Contacts and Cultural Synthesis" in L. Chandra and others eds, *India's Contribution to World Thought and Culture* (Madras, 1960), P. 528. A ring bore letters a-ra-kta in Nagari characters resembling Orissan script of 12th and 13th centuries. *Ibid.*

416   *Ibid.*, P. 525.

Orissa came to the Malayo-Indonesian region, established trade relationship and in the process left some imprints of Orissan culture. Archaeological excavations in both the regions have thrown new light on the cultural contact. The sites like Kuala Selinsing and Pengkalan Bujang in Malay Peninsula and graves of Java have yielded carnelian beads. In north-west Java, the Buni complex site has thrown new evidence in the form of Indian rouletted ware of the first and second centuries of Christian era [417]. Sites around Sulawesi and Sulu Seas have also yielded carnelian beads. Rouletted ware have been discovered from Sisupalgarh and Manikpatna in Orissa and archaeological sites of Mantai, Kantarodai and Anuradhapur citadel in Sri Lanka. The discovery of rouletted ware from Orissa, Sri Lanka and Indonesia is a testimony of maritime network linking these regions. Whereas the northern black polished ware point to north Indian contact, the rouletted ware had primarily east and south Indian contacts. This had distribution focussing around the Bay of Bengal but extending upto the coasts of Java and Bali[418]. The discovery of beads from different sites in Malayo-Indonesian region and Orissa are also pointer to trading contact between the two regions. Shasmalla's coins have been found form Polonnaruwa in Sri Lanka, Manikpatna in Orissa and Kotchina in Sumatra. Presence of five hundred families of Indian traders in the Tun-hsun kingdom on the shores of Isthmus of Kra assume

---

417 P. Bellwood, "Southeast Asia before history" in Tarling, n. 19, P. 133.

418 Martha Prickett, "Sri Lanka's Foreign Trade Before A.D. 600 : Archaeological Evidence" in K. M. De Silva and others, eds *Asian Panorama : Essays in Asian History, Past and Present* (New Delhi, 1990), pp. 169-170.

significance in view of the trade between India and Malay world. Some of these traders might have hailed from the region of Orissa.

The people of Kalinga played an important role in establishing cultural contact with Java. Kling is a generic term used for people of Indian origin. The word is derived from Kalinga and the term *Orang Keling* means people of Kalinga origin. Several traditions prevalent in Indonesia mention people of Kalinga coming to Java, Sumatra and Bali and residing there[419]. These speak of commercial and cultural contact of Kalinga with Java. A legend speaks of twenty thousand families being sent by the pricne of Kling to Java and these 'people prospered and multiplied'[420]. However, they continued to live in an uncivilized state till God blessed them with a prince named Kano in the Saka era 289. The three generations of kings ruled for a total period of four hundred years. At the same time another principality named Astina came into existence under Prince Pulasara. He was succeed by Abiasa and the latter by Pandu Devanatha. The reign of the three princes amounted to one hundred years. Another ruler Jaya Baya, who wrote this account later on removed the seat of government from Astina to Kediri[421]. According to this legend the rule of Kano started in the year 211 C.E. and his successors ruled for four hundred years, i.e. upto 611 C.E. The Kutei inscription of Mulavarman dated 400 C.E. speak of three generation of rulers and the first local leader was Kundunga. Kano and Kundunga might have been the same person. Moreover, some affinity is there in the script Mulavarman's inscription and Kalingan script.

---

419 T.S. Raffles, *History of Java*, Vol II (London, 1830), P. 69.
420 *Ibid*, P. 73.
421 *Ibid*., P. 69.

The legend becomes accurate when it refers to Jaya Baya. He was successor of Airlangga and ruled from 1135 to 1157 C.E. He is hero of Mpu Panuluh's *Harivamsa* and his reign produced the famous Old Javanese work *Bharatayuddha*, the story of great battle in the *Mahabharata*. For this reason, the legend has taken ancestors of Jaya Baya from the characters of the *Mahabharata* like Pandu, Abiasa (Vyas), Pulasara (Parasara) and place Astina (Hastina). The *Sejarah Melayu* or *Salahat as Salatin* refers to the story of Kalinga Vichitra, who descended from heaven and appeared at Palembarg in eastern Sumatra. He became the ruler of the region. Brushing aside the events mentioned in legends not conforming to historical authencity, it may be said that people of Kalinga came to the Malay-Indonesian region, established commercial contact and probably helped the local chiefs in building political entities.

According to the T'ang histories like *Chiu T'ang Shu* and *Hsin T'ang Shu*, Ho-ling kingdom of Central Java (640-818 C.E.) extended from sea to sea and it was an important centre for Buddhist studies. It was also known as Walaing. Ho-ling was the Chinese transcription of Kalinga [422]. Envoys were sent to China in 640, 648 and 666 C.E. The Chinese pilgrim Hui-ning translated the Sanskrit texts of the Theravada into Chinese under the direction of Jnanabhadra, a resident of Ho-ling. In the history of Tang dynasty it has been mentioned that the people of Kalinga took as their ruler a powerful lady named Sima. But the Chinese had not adopted in seventh and eighth centuries *ho* to transliterate *ka* of a foreign language, hence Ho-ling

---

422   J. Gonda, *Sanskrit in Indonesia* (Nagpur, 1952), P. 19. See also Sarkar, n.9, P.173 and P. 236.

kingdom was not the Chinese equivalent of Kalinga [423]. The Canggal inscription of king Sanjaya dated 732 C.E. refers to the consecration of a *linga* on a mountain in a *desa* called Kunjarakunja. It was believed that the area was located in Kalinga, which was famous for elephants. There is also an identical name in south India between Trancore and Tinnevelly, where the sanctuary of sage Agastya was located. But Sanjaya built the sanctuary in Kedu Plain of Java itself. Regarding the origin of 'Sailendra dynasty, one theory linked them with Pandyas of south India claiming descent from Siva. They assumed the title *minankit Sailendra* meaning Lord of the mountain and used carp as their emblem [424]. There is another view putting an Orissan background for the Sailendras. Their origin is traced to the Sailodbhabas of Kongoda region. Hard pressed between the Bhaumakaras of Utkala and Gangas of Kalinga, they migrated to Suvarnadvipa through the sea-port of Palura [425]. The Kalingans who had migrated to Java earlier might have helped new migrants in carving out a kingdom. Another historian holds the view that the Sailendras migrated from Kalainga or nearby region and extended their hold in lower Myanmar and Malay Peninsula [426]. After the establishment

---

423   Y. Iwemoto, "On the Ho-ling kingdom" in *Proceedings of the First International Conference on Tamil Studies* (Kuala Lumpur, 1968), P. 59.

424   Sarkar, n. 9, P. 207. Sarkar credits Sri Sailam rulers in establishing the Sailendra dynasty, *Ibid*, pp. 217-219.

425   H.K. Mahatab, *History of Orissa*, Vol I (Cuttack, 1981), P. 182.

426   Majumdar, n. 31, P. 28. He says in another place, "Gangas, Sailodbhabas and the Saila dynasties may all be the source of name like Sailendra". See, R.C. Majumdar, *Suvarnadvipa* (Dacca, 1937), P. 2.

of Sailendra supremcy, the Javanese inscriptions mention names like Kling or Kalinga. So, the argument is concluded by saying that some royal prince of Sailodbhabas established the Sailendra dynasty. But the Sailendras were Buddhists, whereas the Sailodbhabas of Orissa were not patrons of this faith. Moreover, the mountain cult and consecration of *linga* on it were indigenous beliefs. The kings like Mulavarman, Jayavarman II, Sanjaya etc performed this ritual in connection with foundation of their kingdoms. So, there is no conclusive evidence to prove the Orissan origin for the Sailendras.

In spite of the fact that Orissan link could not be established with Kunjarakunja, Ho-ling and origin of Sailendras, the inscriptions of Malay Peninsula and Indonesian archipelago point towards Orissa's close association with the region. The mid-fifth century Tugu inscription of Purnavarman mentions that the river Candrabhaga was regulated by a canal of fifteen kilometres in length. He is credited with many irrigational works also. The river Candrabhaga was connecting sea at Konarka in Orissa. So, Purnavarman was familiar with Kalinga. The king Jayanasa of Sri-Vijaya constructed a public park in his capital Palembang in 684 C.E. and named it Sriksetra. This assumes importance as Sriksetra was another name of Puri, where the Jagannatha temple was built. The religious significance of the place has been dealt in Chapter III. The Javanese inscriptions dated between ninth and eleventh centuries also prove the contact between Orissa and Java. The *candi* Kalasan inscription of 778 C.E. by king Panangkarana refers to the "lion of kings making repeated request to future kings : this bridge of religion which is the common property of (all) men should be protected by you at all times" [427]. The similarity of this passage could

---

427 Sarkar, n. 36, P. 86.

be found in plates of Somavamsi kings of Orissa, Govind Candra of Kanauj and Kadamba inscription of Nilagiri. The Kuti copper plate inscription of Java dated 840 C.E. speaks of porters and servants in the inner apartments coming from Kling (Kalinga), Kmir (Khmer), Karnaka (Karnataka) Cempa (Campa), Singha (Sri Lanka) and Malayata (Malabar)[428]. The records of king Airlangga of Mataram dynasty refers to foreign merchants coming to his kingdom bringing different commodities. These were from regions like Kalinga, Aryya, Gauda, Cera etc. The name Kalinga is mentioned first which shows the importance of the region. A river in East Java was known as *Kali* Keling or river Kalinga and an inscription of 1194 C.E. from the same region mentions *Jurn* Kling or chief of Kalinga people[429]. In the Majapahit kingdom, a charter from Jiju of Surabaya region refers to king Girindravardan as *Bhatare* Kling or lord of Kling and an inscription of 1447 C.E. describes his wife Kamalavarnadevi as queen of Kalingapura[430]. So, it may be inferred that two principalities of the name Kling and Kalingapura were there across river Kalinga. It may be mentioned here that one of the districts of Java was called *Desa* Buddha Kling or land of Buddhist Kalingas[431].

Certain names also point towards close affinity between Orissa and Indonesia. In a folklore of Indonesia, there is the story of king Jomojaja, who got a divine weapon. He also saw in a dream about Goddess Mahisasuramardini. The name of the king bears similarity with Orissan king Janmejaya. But this similarity alone does not prove

---

428 *Ibid.*
429 *Ibid,* Vol. II, P. 210
430 *Ibid.*
431 J.Crawford, "On the Existence of the Hindu Religion in the Island of Bali" in *Asiatic Researches,* XIII, 1979, P. 153.

anything regarding the cultural influence from Orissa. The argument that the name Borobudur is derived from Lord Balabhadra of Puri temple does not deserve any merit. In the Kutei inscription of Mulavarman dated 400 C.E., there is a reference to illumination of *Akasdvipa*. The lighting of lamps during the month of *Kartika* (October-November), which is favourable to sea voyage is an important ritual in Orissa. In west Java, Goddess Laksmi is still worshipped as promoting fertility in rice fields. She is known as Ni Pohaci Sangyang Sri. At the time of harvesting in Orissa paddy is worshipped and it is known as Laksmi *Puja*. Puri was named as Sriksetra after advent of Laksmi (Sri); so name Sri for Laksmi in Orissa and name Ni Pohaci Sangyang Sri of Java point towards cultural affinity.

The various styles of Orissan art have influenced in varying degrees art and architecture of Indonesia. In the Javanese *candis*, the three main components are basement, body and roof. It is generally three tiered structure crowned by a *stupa* for Buddhist temples and *amalaka* for Hindu *candis*. The relief depicted on walls are from Indian religious texts and Javanese shadow play. In the Dieng plateau, temples belonging to first half of eighth and ninth centuries are one of the oldest. In Orissa also there is a Panca Pandava temple in Ganesvarapura belonging to Ganga period. The *candi* Bima of this group has stepped tiers that are akin to the *sikharas* of Orissan temples. The system of placing *parsva devatas* in the Dieng group are different from Indian temples except the icon of Durga in the form of Mahisasuramardini occupying northern niche as in several temples of Orissa [432]. The temple complex of Loro Jonggrang at Prambanan

---

432 H.Santiko, "Technological Transfer in Temple Architecture from India to Java" in *Utkal Historical Research Journal*, V, 1994, pp. 37-38.

belonging to ninth and tenth centuries are renowned for its *Ramayana* panels. The temples were brahmanical in origin with Siva being the most important deity. Influence of Orissan style is prominent in some of the shrines and deities of Hindu trinty [433]. In the Siva temple known as *candi* Loro Jonggrang and Brahma temple at Prambanan, *Ramayana* scenes are carved on inner side of balustrade showing indigenous character regarding body physique, garments and treatment of different episodes [434]. Representations of *Ramayana* scenes in Siva temples are found on Kailas temple (Ellora), Sas temple (Nagda), Simhanatha temple (Baramba, Orissa) etc [435]. The Svarnajalesvara temple built by Sailodbhabas bear several scenes from the *Ramayana*. The sculptural rendering of episodes from *Ramayana* are found in Varahi temple of Chaurasi, Satrughnesvara temple of Bhubaneswar and Sun temple of Konark. The *chaitya* windows form an important part on the decoration of temples of Orissa. The niches endosed by these contain important cult images. The *kala-makara* heads of arches and *kirtimukhas* at the crown are common decorative motifs of Orissan temples [436]. These motifs are found in Dieng group of temples and *candi* Kalasan of Java.

---

433 A. Ghosh, "India and Indonesia" in *Our Cultural Fabric, India and Southeast Asia : A Study in Cultural Relations* (New Delhi, 1979), P. 7.
434 Kaml Giri, The Ramayana Scenes in Indian and Indonesian Art, A Thematic Comparison in Bharati, XX, 1993-94, pp. 123ff.
435 *Ibid*, P. 127.
436 *Makara* is mythical crocodile-like creature. *Kirtimukha* motif shows the head of a lion-like creature with beads coming out from its mouth.

The greatest representative of Javanese art and architecture is the famous Buddhist *stupa* of Borobudur. Some of the sculptured images of Buddha shown similarity with its counterpart from Orissa. The *Dhyani* Buddhas arranged along the four facade reminds one of massive heads of Buddha at Ratnagiri [437]. Tapering halo of Buddha in *bhumisparsamudra* found in Ratnagiri and Borobudur are very much akin. In the vicinity of Borobudur the *candi* Mendut is located, whose exterior walls show nine sculptured Bodhisattvas sitting on lotus. They are not dissimilar to the same type of images of Lalitgiri and Kendrapara of Orissa [438]. On the rear of outer walls, a Bodhisattva image is supported by a lotus and its stem flanked by the *nagas*. This combination of lotus and serpent could be found in monastery of main shrine two images carved on a single stone number two of Ratnagiri. In the gateway and sorrounded by children are present. The armour clad male figure on the south is holding a spear and the female on the north is dressed like a Roman matron. The whole scene is like Kubera and Hariti seated in *lalitasana* pose at the entrance of Ratnagiri monastery [439]. In the main shrine, there are three massive stone statues : a Buddha in *dharmacakramudra* flanked by two Boddhisattvas. The same type of triad is there in Ratnagiri. Another *candi* nearby known as Bayon temple has stepped tiers resembling with the *sikharas* of Orissan temples. Moreover, the holding

---

437   D.P. Ghosh, "Relations between Buddha images of Orissa and Java" in *Modern Review*, November 1993, P. 503.
438   Joanna Williams, "The Bird of Hariti : Some Questions about the Buddhist iconography of Orissa and Java" in *The Journal of Orissan History*, I, January 1980, P.22.
439   *Ibid*, P. 23.

of a Javanese *kris* (dagger) by the door-keeper of the Parsuramesvara temple of Bhubaneswar amply testifies to the widespread contact between Orissa and Java [440].

(C) BALI
Historical Development

Situated between Java and Lombok, the island of Bali presents a picture of Hinduism and Buddhism that has survived to the present day. The initial trade contacts between India and Bali gradually developed into social and cultural influence from India, which paved way for a composite Balinese culture.Like the majority of inhabitants in Southeast Asia, Balinese belong to the biological grouping known as southern Mongoloid. The Balinese people had by early centuries of Christian era had flourishing local industries as burial sites have produced iron, bronze, glass and carnelian beads. Discovery of Indian rouletted ware of first and second centuries of Christian era from Sembiran have established the fact that Indian traders were coming to the region. The finds from Sembiran and Gilimanuk point towards a brisk trade linking Roman empire, India and Southeast Asia [441]. So, a society of early metal phase attracting traders from outside was there in Bali. The Indian influence began to spread with growth in trade. Till eighth century, Bali was ruled by a king of Kaundinya family. Ambassadorial relations were established with China. The Chinese texts mention Bali as Po-li. The Canggal inscription of king Sanjaya of Mataram dynasty mentions the conquest

---

440 P.P.Mishra, "Contact Between Orissa and Southeast Asia in Ancient Times" in *The Journal of Orissan History*, July 1980, P. 19.
441 Bellwood, n. 52, P. 133.

of Bali. The Javanese rule which began in 732 C.E. was over by the beginning of ninth century. A new dynasty was established by Sri Kesari Varmadeva [442]. The rulers were having the title of Varmadeva. The Mataram ruler Airlangga was son of Balinese king Udayana (989-1022 C.E.) and queen Mahendradatta. Airlangga exerted some sort of influence in Java by appointing viceroys. One such was Dharmavamsa Markataraja. In the last quarter of fourteenth century, Bali came under the rule of the Majapahit empire. There was influence of Javanese culture. After the downfall of the Majapahit empire, Bali declared its independence. A unitary government followed. The kingdom of Gelgel extended over whole of Bali, east Java and Lombok. The Balinese also incorporated some elements of Islam, which did not pose any threat to Balinese society. Later on was it divided ito nine kingdoms. Afterwards it came under the Dutch occupation.

Contact with Orissa
i) Archaeology

The archaeological excavations conducted in Balihave proved the beginning Indo-Balinese relations dating to early centuries of Christian era. Compared to Java, the contact started late. Yielding of rouletted ware, glass beads, semi-precious stone beads, pot sherds with Kharosthi characters etc from Bali were pointer to cultural contact between it and different regions of India. Gilimanuk in western coast of Bali has yielded bimetallic artefacts of both bronze and iron datable to first century B.C.E. The burial assemblage has produced early metal phase pottery and Indian type of

---

442   I.G. P. Phalgunadi, "A Fundamental Dictionary of Balinese Language and Culture" in *The South East Asian Review* XIX, 1994, P. 2.

gold foil funerary eye cover[443]. The site of Sembiran situated in north-eastern Bali on the district of Tejakula has yielded items datable to first and second centuries of Christian era [444]. The direct connection of traders from Indian coasts to Bali is an established fact after these discoveries. The X-ray diffraction analysis of the rouletted ware 'conclusively supports an Indian origin' [445]. This ware is widely distributed in India : Candraketugada, Alangankulam, Arikamedu, Sisupalgarh, Manikpatna and Anuradhapur. A trading network had developed between Sri Lanka, eastern coast of India and island of Bali. A potsherd with three characters of Kharosthi script have been recovered from the waterlogged basal deposit of trench number VII [446]. The local sherds found in Sembiran are akin to pottery from Gilmanuk. From Manikpatna in Orissa, a potsherd inscribed with Kharosthi has been found. Candraketugada and Tamrlipti have also yielded similar item. Monochrome glass beads were recovered from Sembiran. Carnelian and glass beads were found from Gilimnuk. The glass beads were of Indian origin. The Orissan sites such by Sisupalgarh and Manikpatna have yielded such glass beads[447]. So, Bali

---

443 Bellwood, n. 52, P. 133.
444 I.W. Ardika and P. Bellwood, "Sembiran : the beginning of Indian contact with Bali" in *Antiquity*, LXV, P. 221. The archaeological excavations conducted by I.W. Ardika in 1987 and 1989 yielded materials dating from 2800 years age upto 1500 years ago. Sherds totalling 45,000 pieces and 501 glass beads were found. See *Ibid*, pp. 222-23.
445 *Ibid*, P. 224.
446 *Ibid*, P. 225.
447 K.K. Basa, "Cultural Relations Between Orissa and South East Asia : An Archaeological Perspective" in P.K. Mishra, ed. *Comprehensive History and Culture of Orissa* Vol. I (New Delhi, 1997) In print.

in the early centuries of Christian era was located on a major trading route. The Indian traders visited these ports. Indonesian ships and traders were also active in the area. The coastal region of Bali was visited by both local and foreign traders.

ii) Religion

The Hindu-Buddhist religion prevailed in Bali. Unlike Buddha's predominance in the Malay Peninsula, Java and Sumatra, brahmanical religion was predominant in Bali. Siva is the elder brother of Buddha and on ceremonial occasions four Saivite and one Buddhist priest perform the rituals. To the common people, the saying is : He who is Siva is Buddha (*Ya Siva, Ya Buddha*)[448]. In spite of prevalence of Gods like Visnu, Brahma, Indra, Varuna, Ganesa and Krsna; Siva was the most powerful. He, as supreme deity has the attributes of both Visnu and Brahma. According to traditional belief, Bali was the centre of Universe and abode of Gods. Siva was the presiding deity. Another indigenous belief is acknowledgement of spirits or *butas* living in water, tree and hills. The benevolent spirits were to be befriended and evil *butas* to be appeased. Ancestor or *pitara* worship also was prevalent in Bali. Each house has a small temple for the purpose and religious ceremonies like *pegursi, galungan* and *kuningan* were held for the departed souls. In the worship, *ghrta* (clarified butter), *kusa* (grass-effigy), *madhu* (honey) and *tila* (sesamum) are offered. So in Balinese religious beliefs, both Hinduism and indigenous practices are intermingled.

Buddhism was introduced in Bali in early part of fifth century C.E.[449]. The *Purvaka Veda Buddha* contains the

---

448 Daweewarn, n. 47, P. 112.
449 Majumdar, n. 31, P. 197. According to the history of the

Buddhist priest's daily ritual and *Buddha Veda* mentions the death ritual. In Bali, there was Siva-Buddha tradition which regards Siva as elder brother withh age-old privileges and Buddha as younger one with ascetic qualities. In ceremonies, the consecrated water brought by a Saivite priest is mixed with that of a Buddhist. The practice of Buddhist priest is called *Yoga*, whereas that of a Saivite is known as *Bhakti*. Due to Javanese influence, there was worship of *Dhyani* Buddhas and Prajnaparamita. There was affinity between Orissa and Bali as regards Buddhism. Even a section of *brahmans* in Karangasam district regard themselves as *Brahmana-Bouddha-Kalinga*. The votive tablets with inscriptions and figures of Buddha and Boddhisattvas have been found from Bali and Ratnagiri and Avana in Orisa[450]. In the daily ritual of a Buddhist priest, God is addressed as Jagannatha, Suresvara and Rudra. According to *Veda Buddha* the daily ritual begins with following *slokas*,

Ksamasva mam Jagannatha sarvapapavinasanam sarvakaryapranadevam pranamami Suresvaram [451].

The name Jagannatha in above prayer is suggestive of Orissa's contact with Bali. In Orissa tradition, Adi Buddha is referred as Jagannatha. Probably Vajrajana Buddhism of king Indrabhuti of Orissa was introduced in Bali. He had written a tantric work *Jnanasiddhi*, where the first *sloka* refers to close association of Jagannatha and Buddha :

       Liang dynasty, Balinese king claimed that wife of Suddhodana hailed from Bali. *Ibid*.

450   K.S. Behera, "Ancient Orissa/Kalinga and Indonesia : The Maritime Contacts" in *Utkal Historical Research Journal* IV, 1993, P. 129.

451   T. Goudrian, "Sanskrit Texts and Indian Religion in Bali" in Chandra, n. 50, P.560.

Namaskrtya Jagannatham sarvajinavarareitam
Sarvabuddhamayam siddhivyapinam gaganopamam [452].

In Bali, Buddhist tantric cult was prevalent. A ninth century work *San Hyan Kamahayanikan* (the holy Mahayana system) teaches a tantric variety of Mahayana [453]. Tantricism developed in Bali due to influence from India as well as Java. In Bali, Siva also was worshipped as Jagannatha and priests chant *slokas* like, "Om Ksamam mam Sivadeva, Jagannatha hitamkara" [454]. So, there was some sort of *rapprochement* between Siva, Buddha and Jagannatha in Bali and in this influence from Orissa is marked. Like the famous Car festival of Puri, the Balinese carry three wooden Gods in a procession. The three are covered by masks resembling the three deities, Jagannatha, Balavadra and Suvadra of Orissa[455].

iii) Language and Literature

In the Balinese context, Veda means worship. There are no Vedas in Indian sense but parts of it [456]. The *Purvaka Veda Buddha* containing priest's daily ritual mentions that Vajrajana Buddhism as reformed by king Indrabhuti of Orissa was popular in Bali [457]. An account of daily

---

452   G.C. Tripathy, "Concept of Purusottama in the Agamas" in Anncharlott Eschmann and others, eds, *The Cult of Jagannatha and the Regional Tradition of Orissa* (New Delhi, 1986), P. 53.
453   Goudrian, n. 86, P. 556.
454   *Ibid*, P. 559.
455   I.G.P. Phalgunadi, "Hinduism in Bali" in *Southeast Asian Perspective*, I, June 1984, P. 41.
456   Goudrian, n. 86, P. 556. They are one pada of Savitri, a *sloka* to the sacred and five names of Siva in *Brahmastava*. *Ibid*.
457   N.K. Sahu, *Odiya Jatira Itihas* (In Oriya) Vol I (Bhubaneswar,

worship is found in the text known as *Veda-parikramasarasamhitakirana*. There are also regular series of texts containing hymns or *stotras* addressed to Gods and Goddesses of Hindu pantheon. The syllabae of Sanskrit alphabet containing Tantric *bijas* like grim, hrim, gmum etc were also known. In *Panaksama Bhatara*, there are *stutis* to be recited by Saivite priest in daily ritual. The eight divine qualities like, *dharma, jnana, vairagya, aisvarya* and their opposites were known to Balinese priests [458]. The recital of these qualities in daily worship had same function in India and Bali - a stage in invocation of deity. There are verses in Bali having semi-religious purpose which is similar to India - *Om Ahalya Draupadi Sita Dara* (for *Tara*) *Mondodari tatha panchakanya smarennityam* [459]. The protective *stuti* or kavaca found expression in *Ramakavaca* of 22 stanzas in Sanskrit. In the *Kawi* literature of Bali, the Indian classics provided basic inscription. The *Ramayana kakawin* was one of earliest literature in this genre. In the period between tenth to fifteenth centuries was the high watermark of *Kawi* literature. The Balinese poems like *Dukuh-Silandri, Basura and Jayaprana* bear Sanskrit impact. The *Brahmandapurana* and ten *parvas* of the *Mahabharata* are preserved presently [460]. Indian influence could be marked in composition of works on astrology. It is known as *wariga* in Bali and has influenced day to day life of a Balinese.

In course of centuries, the Sanskrit language influenced Balinese. It was used in court circles and religious ceremonies. There was prevalence of *Kawi* language after tenth century. The Blanjong inscription of Sri

---

     1974), P. 410.
458   Goudrian, n. 86, P. 559.
459   Majumdar, n. 31, P. 212.
460   Phalgunadi, n. 77, P.3.

Kesari Varmadeva was in *Kawi*. There was influence of Old Javanese also. Oriya and Tamil words had also crept into Balinese as initial trade links were established from these regions. Some of the words having similarities in Oriya and Balinese are stated below[461].

Oriya	Balinese	English meaning
borokuli	bokul	a kind of fruit
bou	bu	mother
chhuin	tui	a kind of vegetable
china(badam)	kacan (cina)	peanut
genda	gondan	snail
gua	buah	betel nut
muha	muha	face
para	dara	pigeon
Ruti	Roti	bread
sanja	sanja	evening

iv) Society

The maority of population of Bali are Hindus. It presents a unique social order characterized by four basic divisions of Hindu caste system. The Balinese follow the four fold division of society : *brahmana* (priestly class), *satria* (warrior), *wesia* (nobles) and rest of the population belonging to *sudra* caste. The first three castes known as *trivangsa* occupy a higher position than the *sudras*. Despite strict adherence to this rigid social order, inter-caste marriages were not uncommon. The the *trivangsa* also received special titles : *ida* for *brahmans*, *deva* to *satrias* and *wesias* received the title of *gusti*[462]. The *brahmans* were

---

461   *Ibid*, pp. 6-7.
462   H. Meinhard, "Ancient Indian Culture in Bali", in *The Journal of Greater Indian Society*, I, 1934, P. 119.

divided into two categories : *padande* and *pamangku*. The former were Siva worshipping priests enjoying a better privilege. They procure holy water and were expected to maintain a high moral order. The letter known also as temple priests were relegated to common status. They perform ceremonies in village and family temples and were often from lower castes. The female *brahmans* were known as *Idayus*. The *satrias* were warrior class and royal families belonged to this caste. Holding higher position, the *wesias* were influential community. The *sudras* known as *kaulas* were considered impure earlier. They maintained their separate identity. Untouchability was absent in Bali.

In festivals and day to day life, certain common Hindu practices are observed. In spite of influences from outside, the Balinese have never lost their indigenous practices. Balinese calenders follow five days a week and Saturdays are considered auspicious marked for worship of Sarasvati[463]. This is not found in India and the Indians do not consider *Amavasya* as auspicious like the Balinese. The new year or *Saka-Samvat* celebration is a week-long affair marked by various types of entertainment. The Balinese also celebrate festivals like *Sivaratri, Saraswati Puja* or *Odalan Sarasvati* and *Durga Puja (Page Wesi)*. In certain festivals influence of Orissa could be marked. The Orissan legends speak of merchants going to distant islands like Java and Bali. To commemorate that tradition, the people of Orissa take a dip in river water and float miniature boats with a candle burning inside it. This is celebrated in the month of October/November on the day of *Kartika Purnima*. On the banks of the river Mahanadi in Cuttack, large number of people congregate for this festival of *Bali Yatra* or Journey to Bali. The *Masakapam kepesih* ceremony of Bali is observed

---

463   Phalgunadi, n. 90, P. 51.

by floating of small boats having burning candles with the belief that the child is being sent to his original homeland in Kalinga [464]. The rites in a funeral ceremony are elaborate affairs in Bali. It is known as *Pitrayajna*. Some of the rituals like shaving of heads, offering food items like clarified butter, sesamum and honey and feeding to *brahmans* on twelfth day are found in Orissa and other parts of India. Along with other rivers, the Mahanadi river flowing in Orissa is considered sacred :

Om Ganga, Sindhu, Sarasvati, Vipasa Kausiki-nadi Yamuna, Mahandi Srestha Saryu mahati [465].

The Mahendra range of mountains along with Mahendratanaya river of Orissa are mentioned in Balinese *stutis*. As in Java, the Balinese worship of Sri Devi by the side of cornfields is akin to worship of Laksmi in month of *Margasira* (November-December) [466].

There are also similarities in food habits, manners and dress designs of both the regions. The thick flurd of cooked rice is called *peja* in Orissa and Bali and *arua* is uncooked rice made out of parboiled paddy [467]. The practice of cooking young leaves of drum-stick tree (*Maninga oleifera*) or *sajana saga* is an item of delicacy in Orissa and Bali. Some other common food items are : curry made out of flowers and stem of banana plant and cake made of rice-flour

---

464   *Ibid*, P. 41.
465   *Ibid*.
466   Laksmi is associated with paddy-worship in Orissa. She is also known as Sri. At the time of harvesting, housewives worship paddy. This happens in the month of *Margasira*. Paddy-worship has become synonymous with Laksmi-worship.
467   I.G.P. Phalgunadi, *Development of Hindu Culture in Bali, From Earliest Period to the Present times* (Delhi, 1991), P. 39.

known as *manda* and *endori pitha* in Orissa [468]. The habit of chewing betels and keeping the ingredients in a wooden box are found in both the regions. In home of a Balinese, the guests are offered betel leaf and nut as in Orissan homes. The practice of bending down and stretching right hand towards ground while passing along elders sitting on the way is a common behaviour in both the regions. Raising of folded hands as a common form of greeting is a practice both in India and Bali. The bridal dress and crown are similar in Orissa and Bali. Rounding of hairs by women in typical bun are alike in villages of Orissa and Bali. Even some of the ornaments and dresses of Balinese women resemble its counterpart found in Orissan sculptures. The famous Sambalpuri style of textile weaving hasinfluenced the tie and dye weaving known as *Patola* in Bali. In Balinese cremation textile, Orissan *Kumva* design are there. Bali is famous for various dance form and dramas, where themes of Indian mythology predominate. The *Lari-bubung* dance has its impact from eastern India [469]. In the *kecak* (monkey) dance and *barong* (tiger) dance of villagers, some influence of Orissan dances of tribals and *Paika* dance (a form of martial dance) could be marked.

v) Art and Architecture

Compared to Java, architecture did not reach the same height in Bali. Existing indigenous ideas, Indian impact from early centuries of Christian era and Javanese

---

468 Phalgunadi, n. 90, P. 42.
469 Prabha Nibasulu, "Daksina Purba Asia. Bises rup se Bali dvipa men Bharatiya sanskrutika parampara ka swarup" (In Hindi) in Manjushree Rao and others ed, *India's Cultural Relations with Southeast Asia* (Delhi, 1996),P. 83.

influence of from twelfth century onwards have created a unique pattern of Balinese architecture. The Balinese temple called *Pura* is dedicated to Hindu trinty. These are devoid of Hindu images in the sanctum sanctorium and idea of pre-historic megaliths might have influenced the Balinese mindin this regard. In Hindu house of villages, not only small shrines dedicated to Hindu deities are there, but also shrines for the spirit of local hills and great hill are present. Temples in Bali are temporary abode of Gods or *Pasimpangan* and they are also supposed to free people fom cycle of birth and death. The Vasuki temple complex dedicated to Siva was constructed with the belief that Bali is the centre of Universe and Mount Agung on which it was built represented Mahameru of the Universe. The *Pura* Lempuyang situated in eastern Bali was dedicated to Isvara. Brahma was enshrined in the temple of *Pura-*Andhakasha. Located in north-western Bali, Purnacak temple is dedicated to Visnu. Gateway in the entrance is heavily decorated. After it, the courtyard houses musical instrument and community feasts are arranged also. The second courtyard is the scene of council meetings and number of offering pillars are situated also. Placing of offering pillars has been influenced by Orissan style. In the third or innermost courtyard images of Hindu trinity are enshrined. This square chamber constituting cella owes its style to the Bhubaneswar temples of Orissa[470]. The standing male and female figures of *Pura* Sukhavana are akin to early Orissan art. The use of *Kirtimukha* motifs is a significant feature of Indo-Balinese art and the influence of Orissan temples like Vaital and Muktesvara is remarkable. The elephant cave or *Goa Gaja* at Bedhulu in Tubanan consists

---

470 H.B. Sarkar, *Some Contributions of India to the Ancient Civilization of Indonesia and Malaysia* (Calcutta, 1970), P. 115.

of a rock like an elephant's head, which has a passage under its trunk leading to a dark cell. The whole structure resembles the Tiger cave of Udayagiri in Orissa. There is also an image of Hariti sorrounded by seven children near the entrance deriving inspiration from the style of Ratnagiri figures. Several sculptures having a combination of four figures facing north, south, east and west have their origin from the Asokan pillar at Dhauli.

CHAPTR-VI

Conclusion

The material and cultural base of autochthonous societies of Southeast Asia was already developed at the time of contact with external forces. On this base was raised a superstructure, the mateerials of which was largely contributed by the Indians. An interaction between local and external cultures went on. A rapport was established and as acculturation proceeded, elements of Indian culture were absorbed. In course of time, its origin was forgotten. Some of the indigenous beliefs were in harmony with Indian traditions like worship of mountains, rivers and serpents. In fact, the pre-Aryan India and Southeast Asia shared many cultural traits that were similar. Many facets of life in India and Southeast Asia looked alike. They are interwined to such a degree that sometimes it becomes difficult to differentiate between them.

Orissa, as part of India contributed in a significant way to the above process. As a maritime power, it played an important role in dissemination of Indian culture in Southeast Asia. Since early times, overseas of trade of Orissa was carried by merchants venturing into distant lands. Its long sea-coast, dotted with ports like Palura, Pithunda, Kalinganagar, Dantapura, Tamralipti etc was exploited fully for establishing maritime contact. The people of Orissa were expert in maritime activities and even the art of navigation was there in the curriculum of Kalingan princes. Images relating to sea voyages are found in monuments of Puri, Konark, Ratnagiri and Bhubaneswar. Reminiscences of overseas commercial tradition are found in folklore and festivals of Orissa. The archaeological excavations have corroborated literary evidences of Orissa's interaction with Southeast Asia. Distribution of shouldered adzes, some tribals speaking languages belonging to Austric family, folk customs like erecting stone menhirs for dead etc have proved cultural affinity between Orissa and Southeast Asia that started in pre-historic times. From about third century B.C.E., Orissa was an important zone of trade and commerce as evident from yielding of rouletted ware, knobbed vessels, glass beads, semi-precious stones and potsherds from archaeological sites of Orissa. In course of time, along with trade and commerce, cultural relations were established. The Orissan culture had left deep imprints in many facets of life in Southeast Asia.

Orissa has maintained close cultural and trade relations with Myanmar because of geographical proximity. Cultural intercourse developed through traders and Buddhist missionaries. The Pyus, Mons and Burmans were influenced by Orissan culture. Their legends speak of coming of the two merchant brothers Tapussa and Bhallika from Utkala with eight handfuls of hairs from Buddha. These were enshrined in the Shwedagon pagoda of Yangon. Myanmar becaeme vital link in spreading Theravada Buddhism to other parts of Southeast Asia. Gold plates containing Buddhist texts in Pali have been found at Maungun. The style and language of these inscriptions belonging to fifth and sixth centuries are similar to epigraphs of Mathara and eastern Ganga kings of Kalinga. Influence from Orissa could be found in Mahayana Buddhism and tantric practices that developed in Myanmar. The names of ancient places of Myanmar like Kalingaratha, Ukkala, Sriksetra etc resemble closely Orissan geographical places. Sculptures and bas-reliefs of Shwezigon pagoda of Thaton show affinity with early medieval art of Orissa. The temple of Ananda along with Thatpinnyu and Nanpaya had terraces, spires and latticed windows of Orissan variety. Availability of brown glazed ware of Maratuan type from Manikpatna further attests cultural interaction between Myanmar and Orissa.

The archaeological excavation conducted in the last two decades have pushed back the period of cultural contact between Thailand and Orissa to pre-Christian era. The archaeological sites of Thailand like Ban Non Nok Tha, Ban Chiang and Ban Do Ta Phet have yielded items like glass beads, semi-precious stones, bronze bowls etc. Similar items have been unearthed from different places of Orissa. These are pointer to cultural contact betwen two regions. From the Chansen area in Thailand an Indian ivory comb had been found with *Srivatsa* motif, which is similar in design obtained from Hatigumpha inscription of Kharavela. There is also similarity between clay ear plugs of Tha Kae with Khandagiri and Udayagiri in Orissa. In temple architecture of Thailand, some influence of Orissa is marked. The twelfth century Wat Mahadhatu shows affinity to Bhubaneswar temples in detailed treatment. In the life and custom of Thai people, influence from various parts of India is clearly marked. The royal ploughing ceremony of Thailand is very much akin to the *Aksya Trutiya* festival of Orissa. In the *Loi Krathing* festival of Thailand, miniature boats with a burning candle inside are floated. This is very much similar to the *Boita Bandana* festival of Orissa.

Trade and commerce increased during the first two centuries of Christian era along the Asian sea route. One of the trade routes between India and China passed through the coasts of central and southern Vietnam. The famous port of Oc eo had yielded coins having *Srivatsa* motif, which appeared for the first time in the Hatigumpha inscription of Kharavela. According to Jaina texts, the port of Pithunda was being visited by the Chams since the time of Mahavira. Similarity with the script of Kalinga is found in the inscriptions of king Bhadravarman. The window-openings of Cham temples were of exquisite design like the Rajarani temple of Bhubaneswar. Bhagavati image of Po-Nagar temple and Purusottama temple of Duong Mong show cultural affinity of the Chams with Orissa. The decorative motif of Misson group of temples include the *makara torana* niches, which were not unlike the beautifully carved *makara* heads in the archways in front of Muktesvara temple of Bhubaneswar.

In the early centuries of Christian era, the Vidarbha-Kalinga tracts provided emigration of Indians to Cambodia. The Kaundinya clan living in the Vidarbha region played an important role in the kingdom of Funan. From the ports of Palura and Tamralipti, the Kalingans went to Cambodia. It is therefore not surprising that the Cambodian culture bears some imprints of culture of Orissa. Su-Wu, the Funanese envoy was received by the Murunda king of Kalinga, Dhamadamadhara. The Kusana traders of Vanga region were involved in exporting of horses to Funan and it was not unlikely that Kalinga was involved in this trade. Contemporary installation of Tribhubanesvara Siva temples in Chenla and Ekambra ksetra in Kalinga was a pointer to close relationship between Cambodia and Orissa. Worship of Siva on mountains named Mahendra, both in Cambodia and Orissa was not a coincidence. The foot-prints of Siva were worshipped by the Pasupata sect in Cambodia. In India it was rare except in places like Ranipur-Jharial of western Orissa. The existence of cakratirthasvami as a holy place and institution of moving image or *calantii pratima* in both the regions are evidences of Orissan impact in the field of religion. The *sikharas* in the shape of curved arches over the doors of tenth century Banteay Srei temple are similar to Orissan temples. The splendid bullioned openings of this temple along with temple of Preah Khan are akin to Bhubaneswar group of temples. On each side of entrance halls of the famous Angkor wat small shrines are there, which are very much akin to *Pancaratha* pattern of Orissan temples.

The land-locked country of Laos witnessed Indian cultural influence largely through the Khmers and Thais as parts of Laos were under different political entities. A Lao inscription of second half of fifth century compares king Sri Devanika with many personalities including Indradyumna. When the Jagannatha temple was built by Codagangadeva, the earlier temple constructed by Indradyumna was in ruins. The *Pancatantra* stories written by Visnu Sarma of Orissa was popular in Laos. In the Lao version the narrator of the story is Tantai Mahadevi. There is a reference to the best type of Kalingan elephants in the *Titibha dampati* story. The influence of Orissan art could be found in That Luang and Wat Phra Keo. Certain similarities with Orissa could be marked in rituals performed at the time of birth and death. The habit of betel chewing in Laos reminds one of this common practice prevalent in Orissa and other parts of India. Compared to other regions, evidences of contact with Orissa are few Laos. This could be due the fact that Laos was not in the trade-route of Indian merchants.

The people of Kalinga had maintained trade relationship with Malay Peninsular in early centuries of Christian era. According to the Chinese texts, there existed number of Indianized states like Tun-hsun, Ch'ih-t'u, P'an-p'an etc. The sites like Kuala Selinsing and Kalumpong had yielded large quantities of beads of carnelian, cryastal and glass. These were reported from sites in Orissa also. The prevalence of Kounlouen script in P'an-p'an also points to cultural contact with Kalinga. The Sumatran kingdom of Sri-Vijaya based on maritime commerce had extensive contact with outside world. Orissa as a centre of Vajrayana influenced its development in Sri Vijaya. Jayanasa in the year 684 C.E. built a public park and named it Sriksetra. It was another name for Puri, where the Jagannatha temple was built later on. Along with the Malay Peninsula, Orissa developed contact with Indonesian archipelago. This is reflected in archaeology, epigraphy, place names, religion, social custom, art and architecture of Malayo-Indonesian world. All the evidences point towards people of Orissa coming to the region. In the beginning, they established trade relationship and in the process left imprints of Orissan culture. Further, archaeological excavations in Orissa as well as Malayo-Indonesian region have shown new light on the cultural contact between the two regions. Discovery of rouletted ware from Sisupalgarh and Manikpatna i Orissa and Kopak Kendal and Cibutak in north-west Java proves contact between Orissa and Java. It had distribution focussing around the Bay of Bengal but extending upto the coasts of Java and Bali. Discovery of carnelian beads from Sulawesi, Sulu Seas and slab graves of Java is also pointer to trading contact. Presence of five hundred families of Indian traders in the Tun-hsun kingdom assume significance in this context. Some of these traders might have hailed from Kalinga.

Several traditions prevalent in Indonesia mention people of Kalinga coming to Java, Sumatra and Bali and residing there. Kling is a generic term used for people of Indian origin. The word is derived from Kalinga and the term *Orang Keling* means people of Kalinga. Although the legends cannot be taken as authentic, these along with other evidences point to coming of Indians and Kalingans were prominent among them. In spite of the fact that an Orissan background could not be established with Kunjarakunja, Ho-ling and origin of Sailendras, other evidences of Malayo-Indonesian region point towards Orissa's close association with these regions. The inscriptions of the region like Tugu inscription of Purnavarman, epigraph of Panangkarana, Kuti copper plate inscription and records of Airlangga prove contact with Orissa. A ring found in northern Borneo has letters resembling Orissan script. There are also names associated with Kalinga : *Kali* Keling (river Kalinga), *Jurn* Kling (chief of Kalinga people), *Bhatare* Kling (king of Kalinga) and *Desa* Buddha Kling (lord of Buddhist Kalinga).

The various style of Orissan art have left deep imprint on Indonesian art and architecture. The holding of a Javanese *kris* (dragger) by the door-keeper of Parasuramesvara temple of Bhubaneswar testifies the widespread contact between two regions. Temples of Dieng plateau take their names from characters of the *Mahabharata*. The *candi* Bima of this group has stepped tiers that are akin to the *sikharas* of Orissan temples. Durga image occupying northern niche in this group is similar to placing of *parsva devatas* in several temples of Orissa. Influence of Orissan style also is marked in some of the shrines and deities of Hindu trinity in Loro

Jonggrang temple complete. The *Ramayana* scenes are carved on inner side of balustrade in the Siva and Brahma temples of this group. The sculptural rendering of episodes from the *Ramayana* is found in Siva temples of Simhanatha in Baramba. Scenes from the *Ramayana* are there in Varahi temple of Chaurasi, Satrughnesvara temple of Bhubaneswar and the Sun temple of Konark. The common decorative motif of Orissan temples like *kala-makara* heads of arches and *kirtimukhas* at the crown are found in Dieng group of temples and *candi* Kalasan of Java. Tapering halo of Buddha in *bhumisparsamudra* found in Ratnagiri and Borobudur are very much akin. In the gateway of the main shrine of *candi* Mendut, two images carved on a single stone and sorrounded by children are present. The whole scene is like Kubera and Hariti seated in *lalitasana* pose at the entrance of Ratnagiri monastery. Combination of lotus and serpent in the Boddhisattva images of *candi* Mendut and Ratnagiri are alike. In the main shrine of *candi* there are three massive stone statues : a Buddha in *dharmacakramudra* flanked by two Boddhisattvas. The same type of triad is there in Ratnagiri.

The archaeological excavations conducted in Bali have proved India's contact dating to early centuries of Christian era. Yielding of rouletted ware, glass beads, semi-precious stone beads, potsherds with Kharoshi inscriptions from Gilimanuk and Sembiran prove the existence of commercial relations of Bali with eastern coast of India. A potsherd with Kharosthi inscription have been found from Manikpatna of Orissa. Glass beads have been found from Sisupalgarh and Manikpatna. In the sphere of religion, impact of Orissa is also clearly marked. The votive tablets with inscriptions and figures Buddha and Boddhisattvas are found from Bali as well as Ratnagiri and Avana in

Orissa. A section of *brahmans* in Karangasam district regard themselves as *Brahmana-Bouddha-Kalinga*. In the daily ritual of a Buddhist priest, God is addressed as Jagannatha also. In Orissan tradition, Adi Buddha is referred as Jagannatha. Siva also was worshipped as Jagannatha in Bali. So, there was some sort of *rapprochement* between Siva, Buddha and Jagannatha in Bali and in this impact of Orissa is marked. Vajrajana Buddhism of king Indrabhuti of Orissa was introduced probably in Bali. Like the famous car festival of Puri, the Balinese carry three wooden Gods in a procession covered by masks resembling Jagannatha, Balabhadra and Suvadra of Orissa. The worship of Sri Devi by the side of cornfields is akin to Laksmi worship in month of *Margasira* (November-December) in Orissa. *Bali Yatra* festival of Orissa and *Masakapam kepesih* ceremony of Bali are observed by floating of miniature boats with burning candles inside. The Balinese consider the river Mahanadi of Orissa as sacred. In the *stutis*, the Mahendra range of mountains along with Mahendra-tanaya river are mentioned.

The ancient culture of Bali has survived through *wayang* (shadow play) and *kain* (textiles). *Patola* design of Balinese textile with dyed warf and weft threads has been influenced by Sambalpuri style of weaving. Even in cremation textile, Orissan *kumva* designs are there. In the bridal dress and crown of both the regions, some similarity is found. Rounding of hairs by women in typical bun are alike in villages of Orissa and Bali. In the *kecak* (monkey) and *barong* (tiger) dance of villagers, impact of tribal dance and *paika nacha* (a form of martial dance) could be marked. There are also some similarities in food habits and manners in both the regions. *Peja* and *arua* denote thick fluid of cooked rice and uncooked rice made out of parboiled paddy respectively in both the regions. The habit of betel chewing and keeping the ingredients in a wooden box are found in both the regions. In homes of Orissa and Bali, betel leaf and nut are offered to guests. There are also words having similarities in both the regions. Art and architecture in Bali did not reach the same height as in Java. The Balinese temple called *pura* is dedicated to Hindu trinity. Placing of offering pillars and the square chamber consisting cella owe its style to Orissan temples. The standing male and female figures of *Pura* Sukavana are akin in dressing style of early Orissan sculpture. The elephant cave of Bedhulu in Bali resembles the tiger cave of Udayagiri in Orissa. There is also an image of Hariti sorrounded by seven children near the entrance deriving its inspiration from Ratnagiri figures. Sculptures having combination of four figures have their origin from the Asokan pillar at Dhauli. Some of the ornaments and dresses of Balinese women resemble its counterpart found in Orissan sculptures. The use of *kirthimukha* motifs in Balinese temples proves the impact of Orissan art.

The above evidences have made it abundantly clear the impact of Orissan culture in the art of writing, language, religion, festivals, art and architecture of Southeast Asia. In some areas, it was thoroughgoing and absent in other areas. Orissa played a dynamic role in the relations between two great civilizations, India and Southeast Asia. It was also an important zone of commerce with a developed maritime trade contributing in a major way to Indo- Southeast Asian trade. Through its prosperous ports, items of exports and knowledge of navigation, the people of Orissa considerably enlarged the area of trade in the Asian waters. From about third century B.C.E., Orissa developed maritime contact with Southeast Asia. When the Indianized kingdoms were established in first century C.E., Orissa's relationship was marked by commercial intercourse and cultural interaction. This phase continued upto the end of fifteenth century.

The overseas trade and cultural contact continued under the imperial Gangas (1035-1435 C.E.). With the accession of Gajapati monarchs (1435-1533 C.E.), this process received a set back. There was the onset of a period of decline. Internal troubles and foreign aggression did not create a suitable environment for overseas activities. Political instability, treacherous revolts and court intrigues became well known features of Orissan politics. In the early part of sixteenth century, Orissa was being encircled by hostile powers like Bengal, Vijayanagar and Golkonda. The weak successors of the imperial throne aggravated the problem. Agrarian production declined in this period and there was no surplus production. The famine and drought took heavy toll of life. There was also decrease in circulation of metallic currency. Economic growth was hampered due to conversion of currency to bullion and temple offerings. The arts and crafts got a set back. The hinterlands were not capable of supplying commodities to the ports, which had themselves lost pre-eminence of the earlier periods. Finally, at the time of Mukundadeva, Orissa fell easy prey to the armies of Sultan Sulaiman Karrni of Bengal in 1568 C.E. The successive rule of Afghans, Moghuls and Marathas for over two hundred years spelt eternal gloom in the shape of political disintegration and dismemberment. There was fragmentation of Orissan territory under the British, when parts of it remained under Bengal, Madras and Central provinces. Orissa's role in trading network of Indian Ocean was in a reduced scale. There was virtually no cultural interaction in this period. When the colonial powers began to extend their domination over Southeast Asia, there was shortage of labour. The British empire in Malay, Singapore and Myanmar was based on economic resources of India. A large number of Indian emigrants went to Southeast Asia as labourer, money-lenders and merchants. The role of Orissa was that of supplying labourers to the region. When the Indian National Army under Netaji was formed, some of the recruits were from Orissa.

Indian culture consists of plurality of traditions which evolved out of interaction between Sanskrit culture and particular lore of dominant groups. It spreaded to Southeast Asia due to endeavours of warriors, traders and priests along with local initiative. Both the Indianization and indigenization processes were not mutually exclusive. The attempt to accord importance either to Indians or Southeast Asians would result into a semantic controversy. Emphasis should be on interaction between Indian and indigenous cultures. The Southeast Asians were not passive recipients of Indian culture. They absorbed Indian elements into their indigenous cultural patterns after adapting it to their own necessities. There were some similarities between the way Indian culture spreaded in Southeast Asia and expansion of Indian culture in India itself. The 'Indianization' of Southeast Asia was an extension of 'Aryanization' in India. Therefore, many facets of life in the two regions look alike. Southeast Asia has preserved many of Indian cultural traits. Traces of India's past might be found in customs, religious life and monuments of Southeast Asia. The age-old bond of cultural ties should be renewed with fresh vigour. Southeast Asia has acquired a significant position in the present day after the end of cold war. India has been compelled to review and reorient its foreign policy objectives. Opening of India's economy have brought new hope for India playing an important role in the region. India is making attempts for greater interest at bilateral and multilateral levels. It is striving for also membership of Association of Southeast Asian Nations (ASEAN).

As far as Orissa's cultural influence is concerned, it played a dominant role upto the end of fifteenth century. It became prosperous in the past through maritime activities. Making sea-voyages to distant lands, the merchants established commercial relations. Consequently there was diffusion of Orissan culture in the region. The study of foregoing pages demonstrated clearly the role of Orissa in influencing some facets of Southeast Asian life. Archaeological findings, inscriptions, architectural designs, religious beliefs, customs and place names underline the role played by the Orissan people in Southeast Asian history and culture. On the indigenous cultural substructure was raised a superstructure, the elements of which were contributed by various zones of India including Orissa. The former President of Indonesia, Soekarno wrote to Pandit Nehru that Indians and Indonesians were linked by ties of blood and culture from very early times and the word India would remain a part of Indonesian. He added that at the moment of writing the letter the first ship to take rice to India was being loaded at the port of of Probolinggo consisting of two words, Purva and Kalinga and it was the place at which the first Indians, that is Kalingans arrived. This clearly sums up Indo- Southeast relations with due emphasis on the role of Orissa.

Select Bibliography

Primary Sources

(A) Original Texts and Translations
i) Buddhist and Jain Sources
Aryamanjusri mulakalpa, ed T. G. Sastri (Trivandrum, 1920).
Culavamsa, trans, W. Geiger, Vol. I and Vol. II (London, 1929-1930).
Dathavamsa, ed B.C.E. Law (Lahore, 1925).
Dipavamsa, trans, H. Oldenberg (London, 1879).
Jatakas, ed V. Fausball, Vol I-VI (Lodon, 1877-97).
Mahavamsa, trans W. Geiger (London, 1912).
Majjhima Nikaya, ed V.Trenekner and R.Chalemers (London,1888-89).
Uttaradhyayana Sutra, ed J. Carpenter (Uppasala, 1922).
Vinayapitaka, trans T.W. Rhys Davis and H. Oldenburg, Pt.I (Oxford, 1881-85).
ii) Sanskrit
Arthasastra of Kautilya, ed. R.P. Kangle (Bombay, 1969).
Bhagavata Purana, trans, Pandit Pustakalaya (Varanasi, 1963).
Brhatsamhita, ed. V.S. Sastri and M.R. Bhat (Bangalore, 1974).
Harivamsa ed, R. Kinjawadekar (Poona, 1936).
Mahabharata, ed, R.N. Dandekar (Poona, 1966).

Manasollasa of Somesvara, ed. G.K. Srigondekar, 2 volls, (Baroda, 1925-30).
Manusamhita, ed. G. Jha (Calcutta, 1939).
Matsya Purana Anadasrama Sanskrit Series (Poona, 1907).
Pancatantra, trans. A. William (Oxford, 1930).
Raghuvamsa of Kalidas, ed. H.D. Velankar (Bombay, 1948).
Ramayana, trans, H.P. Sastri, 8 Vols. (London, 1952-1959).
Satapatha Brahmana, trans. J. Eggeling, 5 vols (Oxford, 1882-1900).
Yuktikalpataru of Bhoja, ed, I.C. Sastri (Calcutta, 1917).
iii) Oriya
Bhagavata Purana ed, P.K. Mishra (New Delhi, 1989).
Deula Tola of Krusna Dasa, Orissa Jagannatha Co. (Cuttack, n.d.).
Jagannatha - Caritamruta, Divakaradasa (Cuttack, 1916).
Kaivartta Gita, Achyutananda Dasa
Madalapanji, ed, A.B. Mohanty (Cuttack, 1969).
Mahabharata of Sarala Dasa, ed. A.B. Mohanty (Bhubaneswar, 1965).
Samara Taranga of Brajanatha Badajena, ed. Sudhakar Pattanaik (Cuttack, 1960).
iv) Tamil
Manimekalai, ed U.V.S.Aiyar (Madras, 1921).
Silappadikaram, ed U.V.S. Aiyar (Madras, 1920).
v) Arabic and Persian
Hludud-al-Alam, ed, V. Minorsky (London, 1937).
Riyaz-us-Salatin of Ghulam Husain Salim; trans, M.A. Salam (Calcutta, 1902).
Tabakat-i-Nasiri, trans H.G. Raverty, Vol. I (New Delhi, 1970).
Tarikh-ul-Hind, trans E.S.Sachau (New Delhi, 1964).
vi) Burmese
Burmese sit tans 1764-1826, trans. F.N. Trager and W.J.Koering (Tucson, 1979).

Hmannan Yazawin, trans, P.M. Tin and G.H. Luce (Rangoon, 1960).

vii) Old Javanese

Arjuna Wiwaaha of Mpu Kanwa, trans Patricia B. Henry (Gaya, 1986).

Kalangwan, ed. P.J. Zoetmulder (The Hague, 1974).

Nagarakertagama of Prapanca, ed., T.G. Th. Pigeaud, 5 Vols. (The Hague, 1960-1963).

Pararaton, ed, N.J. Krom (Batavia, 1920).

Wangbang Wideya, ed. S.O. Robson (The Hague, 1971).

viii) Lao

Brah Ku'td Brah Ban, trans. S. Sahai (New Delhi, 1978).

Gvay Dvorabhi, S. Sahai (Delhi, 1976).

Phra Lak Phra Lam, trans. S. Sahai, Part I (New Delhi, 1973).

ix) Malaya

Sejarah Melayu, ed, W.G. Shellabear (Singapore, 1960).

Translation of Malay Annals, trans, J. Leyden (London, 1821).

(B) Palm Leaf Manuscripts

(a) Museum of Department of History, Sambalpur University.

Harivamsa, Achyutananda Das (Acc No.460).

Hitopadesa, Visnu Sarma (Acc No.739).

Kartika Mahatmy, Mahadeva Das (Acc.No.16).

Laksmi Purana, Balaram Das (Acc No.154).

Mahabharata, Sarla Das (Acc No.234).

Prastaba Sindhu, Dinakrushna Das (Acc No.756).

Prastaba Sindhu, Sri Krushna Das (Acc No.23).

Puja Archana Pothi, (Acc No. 1035).

Rasa Kallola, Dinakrushna Das (Acc No.798).

Sachitra Bhagavata, Brajanatha Badajena and Ghanasyama Badajena (Acc No. 66).

Tantra Pothi, (Acc No. 966).

Usha Vilasa, Sisu Sankar Das (Acc No. 65).

(B) Orissa State Museum, Bhubaneswar.
Usha Vilasa, Sisu Sankara Das (Cat No.Ext.1, 25, 318 and 319).

(C) Inscriptions
Casparis, J.G. de, *Selected Inscriptions from the Seventh to the Ninth Century C.E., Prasasti Indonesia*, II (Bandung, 1956).
Duroiselle, C. and Blagden C.O., *Epigraphia Birminica* (Rangoon, 1919-36).
G.H. Luce and P.M. Tin *Inscriptions of Burma*, 5 Vols. (Rangoon, 1933-56).
Jaiswal, K.P. and Banerjee, R.D., *Epigraphia Indica* (Calcutta).
Majumdar, R.C., *Inscriptions of Kambuja* (Calcutta, 1953).
Pigeaud, T.G. Th., *Java in Fourteenth Century : A Study of Cultural History*, Vol. III (The Hague, 1960).
Rajguru, S.N., *Inscriptions of Orissa*, 5 Vols. (Bhubaneswar, 1960-76).
Sarkar, H.B., *Corpus of the Inscriptions of Java* 2 Vols. (Calcutta, 1971-72).
Sircar, D.C., *Indian Epigrapy* (Calcutta, 1939).
Sircar, D.C., *Select Inscriptions*, Vol. I (Calcutta, 1965).
(D) Contemporary Travel Accounts, Diaries, Works etc.
Beal, S., trans, *Life of Hiuen-tsang* (London, 1911).
Certasau, A., trans *The Suma Oriental* of Tom Pires, trans (London, 1944).
Dames, M.L., ed, *The Book of Durate Barbosa* ed Vol. II (Liechtenstein, 1967).
Fitch, R., *Early Travels in India* (London, 1899).
Foster, W., ed, *A New Account of the East Indies* of A. Hamilton, 2 vols. (London, 1930).
Frederick, C., *The Principal Navigators, Voyages, Traffiques and Discoveries of the English Nation*. Vol. IV (New York, 1969).
Gerini, G.E., *Researches on Ptolemy's Geography of Eastern Asia*

(New Delhi, 1974).

Giles, H.A., *The Travels of Fa-hsien* (London, 1956).

Hirth, F. and Rockhill, W.W., *Chau Ju-Kua, His works on the Chinese and Arab Trade in the Twelfth and Thirteenth Centuries*, trans (St. Petersburg, 1911).

Latika Lahiri, I. Tsing's *Chinese Monks in India*, trans (Delhi, 1986).

Mc Crindle, J.W., *Ancient India as described by Ptolemy* (Calcutta, 1885).

Mills, J.V.G., trans., *The overall survey of the Ocean's shores* of Ma Yuan (Cambridge, 1970).

Schoff, W.H., ed., *The Periplus of the Erythraean sea*, ed (London, 1912).

Takakusu, J., I. Tsing's *A Record of Buddhist Religion as practised in India and the Malay Archipelago, 671-695* (Oxford, 1896).

Temple, R.C., ed, *Diaries of Streynsham Master, 1675-1680*, 2 vols. (London, 1911).

Temple, R.C., ed., *A Geographical Account of the Countries Round the Bay of Bengal, 1669 to 1676* of T. Bowrey (London, 1905).

Watters, T., *On Yuen Chwang's Travels in India* (New Delhi, 1961).

Yule, H., trans, *The Book of Ser Marco Polo, the Venetian, concerning the kingdoms and Marvels of the East*, 2 Vols. (London, 1875).

(E) Reports, Records, Bulletin etc.

Annual Report of Archaeological Survey of Burma.

Behera, S.C., ed, *Interim Excavation Reports* (Sambalpur, 1982).

Bulletin of Archaeological Survey of India, *Ancient India*, Vol. 2, 1946 & Vol. 5, 1949 (New Delhi).

Fawcett, C., *The English Factories in India* (New Series), 1670-1684, 4Vols. (Oxford, 1936-53).

Thaw, A., *Report on the Excavations at Beikthano* (Rangoon, 1968)

SECONDARY SOURCES
(A) Books and Monographs

Arasaratnam, S., *Merchant, Companies and Commerce in the Coromandel Coast*, 1650-70 (Delhi, 1986).

Aung-Thwin, M., *Pagan : the Origins of modern Burma* (Honolulu, 1985).

Bagchi, P.C., *Studies in Tantra* (Calcutta, 1920).

Basa, K.K., *Problems and Perspectives in Archaeology of Orissa* (Occasional Paper 4, Bhubaneswar, 1994).

Behera, K.S., ed, *Sagara O Sahitya* in Oriya (Cuttack, 1993).

Behera, S.C., *Rise and Fall of Sailodbhavas* (Calcutta, 1981).

Bhattacharjee, A., *Greater India* (New Delhi, 1981).

Birggs, L.P., *Ancient Khmer Empire* (Philadelphia, 1951).

Boner Alice and Sharma, S.R., ed, *Silpa Prakasa* (Leiden, 1966).

Bosh, F.D.K. *Selected Studies in Indonesian Archaeology* (The Hague, 1961).

Bosh, F.D.K., *Selected Studies in Indonesian Archaeology* (The Hague, 1981).

Brown, P., *Indian Architecture : Buddhist and Hindu Period* (Bombay, 1971).

Cady, J.F., *Southeast Asia : Its Historical Development* (New York, 1976).

Chandra, L. And others, eds., *India's Contribution to World Thought and Culture* (Madras, 1970).

Chatterji, B.R., *History of Indonesia* (Merrut, 1967).

Chaudhuri, S., *Trade and Commercial Organization in Bengal*, 1650-1720 (Calcutta, 1975).

Chhabra, B.C.E., *Expansion of Indo-Aryan Culture : During the Pallava Rule* (Delhi, 1965).

Coedes, G., *The Indianized States of Southeast Asia* (Honolulu, 1965).

Coomarswamy, A., *History of Indian and Indonesian Art* (New Delhi, 1972).

Cunningham, A., *Ancient Geography of India* (Calcutta, 1924).
Das Gupta, A. and Pearson, M.N. eds. *India and the Indian Ocean 1500-1800* (Calcutta, 1987).
Das, M.N., ed. *Sidelights on History and Culture of Orissa* (Cuttack, 1975).
Das, S.P., *Glories of Ancient India* (Sambalpur, 1964).
Daweewarn, D., *Brahmanism in Southeast Asia* (New Delhi, 1982).
De Silva, K.M., eds, *Asian Panorama : Essays in Asian History, Past and Present* (New Delhi, 1990).
Dehejia, Vidya, *Early Stone Temples of Orissa* (New Delhi, 1979).
Desai, W.S., *A Pagent of Burmese History* (Calcutta, 1961).
Devahuti, *Malaysia in Historical Perspective* (Madras, 1980).
Eschmann Anncharlott and others, eds., *The Cult of Jagannath and the Regional Tradition of Orissa* (New Delhi, 1985).
Ghosh, M.M., *History of Cambodia* (Calcutta, 1968).
Gian, G., *Tai Minorities in China* (Gaya, 1992).
Giri, G.N., and Mahapatra, N., *Dhanesvara Saudagara Suanga* in Oriya (Cuttack, 1901).
Glover, I.C., *Early Trade Between India and Southeast Asia* (Hull, 1990).
Gonda, J., *Sanskrit in Indonesia* (Nagpur, 1952).
Gosling, Bettty, *Sukhothai : Its History, Culture, and Art* (Singapore, 1991).
Gunguru, ed., *Malaysia : A Survey* (Melbourne, 1965).
Hall, D.G.E., *A History of South-east Asia* (New York, 1964).
Harrison, B., *Southeast Asia : A Short History* (New York, 1966).
Harvey, G.E., *Outlines of Burmese History* (Bombay, 1926).
Higham, C., *The Archaeology of Mainland Southeast Asia* (Canberra, 1989).
Imprints of Indian Thought and Culture Abroad (Vivekananda Kendra Prakashan, Madras, 1980).
Kantowsky, D. ed. *Recent Researches on Max Weber's Studies of*

Hinduism (London, 1984).

Kar, B.P., *Prachina Utkalara Jalayatra* in Oriya (Bhubaneswar, 1967).

Keomanichanh, V., *India and Laos* (New Delhi, 1979).

Kulke, H., *Kings and Cults, State Formation and Legitimation in India and Southeast Asia* (New Delhi, 1993).

_____, *The Devaraja cult* trans by I.W. Mabbett (New York, 1978).

Lyall, A.C., *Asiatic Studies* (London, 1882).

Mahatab, H.K., *History of Orissa*, Vol. I (Cuttack, 1981).

Majumdar, R.C., *Ancient Indian Colonies in the Far East*, I and II (Lahore, 1927) and (Dacca, 1937).

_____, *India and Southeast Asia* (New Delhi, 1979).

_____, *Hindu Colonies in the Far East* (Calcutta, 1944).

Majumdar, R.C., *Ancient Indian Colonisation in Southeast Asia* (Baroda, 1955).

_____, *Kambuja Desa* (Madras, 1944).

_____, *Greater India* (Bombay, 1948).

Marr, D. And Milner, A.C., eds, *Early Southeast Asia in the 9th to 14th Centuries* (Canberra, 1986).

Maspero, G., *The Kingdom of Champa*, trans by J. Embree (New Haven, 1949).

Mathew, K.S., ed., *Studies in Maritime History* (Pondicherry, 1991).

_____, *Mariners, Marchants and Oceans* (New Delhi, 1995).

May, R.L., *The Culture of Southeast Asia* (New Delhi, 1972).

Mishra, P.K., ed., *Comprehensive History and Culture of Orissa* Vol.I (New Delhi, 1997). In print.

Mishra, P.P., *A History of Contemporary Laos* (, New Delhi, 1999)

------------------, *Government and Politics of South East Asia* (New Delhi, 1992)

-------------., *Laos : Land and Its People* (New Delhi, n.d).

Mital, A.C., *An Early History of Kalinga* (Beranaras,1962).

Mookherjee, R.K., *A History of Indian Shipping* (London, 1912).
Morehead, F.G., *A History of Malay and Her Neighbours* (Hongkok, 1965).
Mukherjee, P., *The History of Gajapati Kings of Orissa*, 2nd ed (Calcutta, 1981).
Nag, K., *India and the Pacific World* (Calcutta, 1941).
Nayak, B.K. and Ghosh, S.C., eds., *New Trends in Indian Art and Archaeology* (New Delhi, 1992).
Om Prakash, *Dutch East India Company and the Economy of Bengal, 1630-1720* (Princeton, 1985).
Panda, S.K., *Medieval Orissa : A Socio-Economic Study* (New Delhi, 1991).
Pargiter, G.E., *Ancient Indian Historical Tradition* (London, 1913).
Phalagunadi, I.G.P., *Development of Hindu Culture in Bali, From Earliest Period to the present times* (Delhi, 1991).
Phouvong, P., *Kingdom of Laos* (Saigon, 1959).
Pillay, K.K., *South India and Sri Lanka* (Madras, 1975).
Raffles, T.S., *History of Java*, 3 Vols. (London, 1817, 1830).
Rajan, K.V.S., *Early Kalinga Art and Architecture* (New Delhi, 1984).
Rajdhoh, P.A., *Life and Ritual in Old Siam*, trans by W.J. Gedney (New Haven, 1961).
Rao, Manjushree and Others, eds, *India's Cultural Relations with Southeast Asia* (Delhi, 1996).
Risley, H.H., *Tribes and Castes of Bengal* (Calcutta, 1892).
Roy, N.R., *Brahmanical Gods in Burma* (Calcutta, 1932).
Sah, A.P., *Life in Medieval Orissa* (Varanasi, 1976).
Sahai, B., *The Ports of India* (New Delhi, 1986).
Sahu, N.K., *Buddhism in Orissa* (Cuttack, 1958).
_____, *History of Orissa*, Vol I (Cuttack, 1981).
_____, *Odiya Jatira Itihasa* in Oriya (Bhubaneswar, 1977).
Sardesai, D.R., *Southeast Asia : Past and Present* (New Delhi,

1981).

Sarkar, H.B., *Cultural Relations Between India and Southeast Asian Countries* (New Delhi, 1985).

_____, *Some Contributions of India to the Ancient Civilization of Indonesia and Malaysia* (Calcutta, 1970).

_____, *Trade and Commercial Activity of Southern India in the Malayo-Indonesian World* (Calcutta, 1986).

Sastri, K.A.N., The *Colas* (Madras, 1984).

_____, *History of Sri Vijaya* (Madras, 1949).

_____, *South Indian Influence in the Far East* (Bombay, 1949).

Sharma, R.S., *Perspectives in Social and Economic History of Early India* (New Delhi, 1983).

_____, *Ancient India* (New Delhi, 1981).

Smith, R.B. and Watson, W. Eds, *Southeast Asia : Essay in Archaeology, History and Historical Geography* (London, 1979).

Srinivas, M.N., *Social Change in Modern India* (New Delhi, 1972).

Stutterheim, W.F., *Indian Influence in the Land of the Pacific* (Weltevreden, 1930).

Tarling, N. Eds, *The Cambridge History of Southeast Asia*, Vol. I (Singapore, 1992).

Van Leur, J.C. *Indonesian Trade and Society : Essays in Asian Social and Economic History* (The Hague, 1955).

Vien, N.K., *Traditional Vietnam : Some Historical Stages* (Hanoi, n.d.).

Wales, H.G.Q., *The Mountain of God : A Study in Early Religion and Kingship* (London, 1953).

Weber, M., *The Religion of India,* trans by H. Gerth and D. Martindale (Glencoe, 1958).

Wheatley, P., *The Golden Khersonese : Studies in the Historical Geography of the Malay Peninsula before C.E. 1500* (Kuala Lumpur, 1966).

_____, *Nagara and Commandery : Origins of Southeast Asian*

Urban Territories (Chicago, 1983).
Wolters, O.W., *Early Indonesian Commerce : A Study of the Origins of Sri Vijaya* (Ithaca, 1967).

(B) Articles in Journals and Proceedings

Ardika, K.W. and Bellwood, P., "Semibiran : the beginings of Indian Contact with Bali", *Antiquity*, LXV, 1991.
Aung-Thwin, M., "The 'Classical' in Southeast Asia : The Present in the Past", *Journal of Southeast Asian Studies*, XXVI, 1995.
Bapat, P.V., "Cultural Migration from India to Countries in Southeast Asia", *Proceedings of Asian History Congress*, 1961 (New Delhi).
Behera, K.S., "Marittime Contacts of Orissa : Literary and Archaeological Evidence", *Utkal Historical Research Journal*, V, 1995.
Behera, P.k., "Sulabhadihi : A Neolithic Calt Manufacturing Centre in Orissa", *Puratattva*, XXII, 1992.
Behera, S.C., "Home-land of Visnu Sarma", *Indian Historical Quarterly*, XXXVIII, 1962.
_____, "Ancient Orissa/Kalinga and Indonesia : The Maritime Contacts", *Utkal Historical Research Journal*, IV, 1993.
_____, "Early Sea Voyages to Orissa", *Chilika Boita Bandana*, 1992.
Crawford, J., "On the Existence of Hindu Religion in the Island of Bali", *Asiatic Researches*, XIV, 1979.
Das, R.N., "Orissa Neoliths : A Typo-Technological Study" *Orissa Historical Research Journal*, XXXV, 3 & 4 No.
Desai, S.N., "Ramayana - An Instrument of Historical Contact and Cultural Transmission Between India and Asia", *Journal of Asian Studies*.
Deva, K., "The Rama Legend as Depicted in India and Indonesia", *Man and Environment*, XXI, 1996.

Donaldson, T.E., "Navigation and Maritime Goddess of Orissa", *Studies in History and Culture*, II, 1994.

Ghosh, D.P., "Relations Between Buddha Images of Orissa and Java" *Modern Review*, November, 1933.

Giri, Kamal, "The Ramayana Scene in Indian and Indonesian Art : A Thematic Comparision", *Bharati*, XX, 1993-94.

Gorman, C.F., "Hoabinhian : a Pebble-tool complex with early plant association in Southeast Asia", *Science*, CLXIII, 1969.

Iwamoto, Y., "On the Ho-ling kingdom" in *Proceedings of the First International Conference on Tamil Studies* (Kuala Lampur, 1968).

Jha, G.N., "Indo-Thai Relations : Problems and Prospects", International Studies, XVI, July-Sept, 1977.

Lal, B.B., "Sisupalgarh", *Orissa Historical Research Journal*, XV, 1967.

Lal, B.B., "Sisupalgarh", *Orissa Historical Research Journal*, XV, 1967.

Mabbett, I.W., "The Indianization of Southeast Asia," *Journal of Southeast Asian Studies*, VIII, 1 and 2, 1977.

Meinherd, H., "Ancient Indian Culture in Bali, *The Journal of Greater Indian Society*, I, 1934.

Mishra, P.K., "Influence of Brahmanism in Early Siamese Art", *Art and Archaeology International Conference on Thai Studies*, August 1984, Bngkok.

Mishra, P.P., "Contact Between Orissa and Southeast Asian Ancient Times", *The Journal of Orissan History*, I, July, 1980.

_____, "Orissa as reflected in Al-Biruni's Tarikhu'l Hind", *Proceedings of Orissa History Congress* XII, Jyoti Vihar, 1986.

_____, "Islam in Southeast Asia : A Case Study of Southern Thailand", *Asian Studies*, V, 1987.

_____, "Cultural Contribution of India to South-East Asia : A Case study of Laos", *Proceedings of the Indian History Congress*, 56th Session, Calcutta, 1995.

--------------, "Indo-Myanmar Relation: A case Study of Orissan Culture in Transit", *The Historical Review* (Calcutta, 1997).

-----------,"Critique of Indianization Theory", Full Article in *PIHC*, 58th Session, Bangalore (Aligarh, 1998).

_____,"The Orissan Art in Mainland Southeast Asia: A case study of Cultural Interaction, *New Aspect of History of Orissa* VIII, 1998 (Burla).

_____," Indo-Thai cultural relations", *Asian Review*, 10, 1999,(Hongkong)

_____," Rapprochement between Balinese and Orissan traditions", *XI Colloquium on Indonesian and Malay studies*, (Moscow, 1999).

_____," Rapprochement Between Thai Buddhism and Indian Traditions", *Tai Culture*, IV,1999(Berlin)

--------------, Orissan Art in Southeast Asia: A Case Study of Cultural Interaction", Full Article in *PHIC*, 61st Session, (Calcutta.2000)

--------------,"Urban Continuum in Orissa: Ports and towns in early modern period" , *Histoire Urbaine*, (Paris, June 2003)

Mohanty, H.B., "Development of a Port of Paradip", *Orissa Review*, XIV, 1957.
Mohapatra, K.N., "Po-lo-mo-lo-ki-li of Hiuen-Tsang's Account", *New Aspects of History of Orissa*, 1971.
Mukherjee, B.N., "New Evidences of Contacts of Ancient Vanga (In Eastern India) with South-East Asia", *Bharati*, XX, 1993-94.
Mukherjee, B.N., "The Theory of Kushana Rule in the region of Orissa", *The Journal of Orissan History*, I, July 1980.
Nandi, R.N., "Clients, Ritual and Conflict in Early Brahmanical Order", *Indian Historical Review*, VI. 1979-80.
Om Prakash, "The European Trading Companies and the

Merchants of Bengal", *Indian Economic and Social History Review*, I(3), 1964.

_____, "Dutch East India Company in Bengal; Trade Privileges and Problems, 1633-1712", *Indian Economic and Social History Review*, 9(3), 1972.

Patel, C.B., "Navigation and Maritime Tradition of Ancient Kalinga", *Chilika Boita Bandana*, 1992.

Patra, Benudhar. Early Maritime Contacts of Odisha with Indonesia and Sri Lanka. (New Delhi: 2017)

Pattanaik, A.P., "Daksina Purva Asiare Sanskrutika Upanivesa", *Utkala Prasanga*, XXXXII, 1986.

Pattanaik, J.K., "Palur Port Through the Ages", *Studies in History and Culture*, II, 1994.

Pattanaik. Sushil and Sarita Nayak. Proto & Early Historic Archaeology of Odisha. (New Delhi: 2024)

Pattanayak, A.K., "Identification of the Port of Che-li-ta-lo : A Review", *Utkal Historical Research Journal*, VI, 1995.

Phalgunadi, I.G.P., "A Fundamental Dictionary of Balinese Language and Culture", *The Southeast Asian Review*, XIX, Jan-Dec. 1994.

_____, "Hinduism in Bali", *Southeast Asian Perspective,* I, June, 1989.

Prusty, H. and others, "Dantapura, the Capital of Ancient Kalinga : A Reappraisal", *Studies in History and Culture* III, 1995.

Ray, H.P., "Early Maritime Contacts Between South and Southeast Asia", *Journal of Southeast Asian Studies*, XX, 1980.

_____, "An Interpretative Essay on Maritime History, *Journal of Indian Ocean Studies*, III, 1996.

Roy, P.K., "Karama, An Ancient Buddhist Site", *Orissa Historical Research Journal*, XXIV, 1981.

Santiko, H., "Technological Transfer in Temple Architecture from India to Java", *Utkal Historical Research Journal*, V, 1994.

Sinha, B.K., "Discovery of 'The Missing Link' in the Proto-History of Orissa", *Studies in History and Culture* II, 1994.

Sinha, S., "State Formation and Rajput Myth in Tribal Central India", *Man in India*, XXXXII, 1962.

Solheim, W.G., "New Lights on a Forgotten Past," *National Geographic*, CXXXIX, 1971.

Stephen, S.J., "Entrepot of Malacca in the trading world of Southeast Asia and Portuguese networks of overseas commerce with the ports of Tamil country in South India", *Journal of the Institute of Asian Studies*, XII, No. 2.

Sundaram, K., "The Vaisya Community in Medieval Andhra", *Journal of the Andhra Historical Research Society*, XXX.

Tripati, Sila. Shipwrecks Around the World: Revelations of the Past. (New Delhi: 2015)

William, Joanna, "The Bird of Hariti : Some Questions about the Buddhist Iconography of Orissa and Java", *The Journal of Orissan History*, I, Jan., 1980.

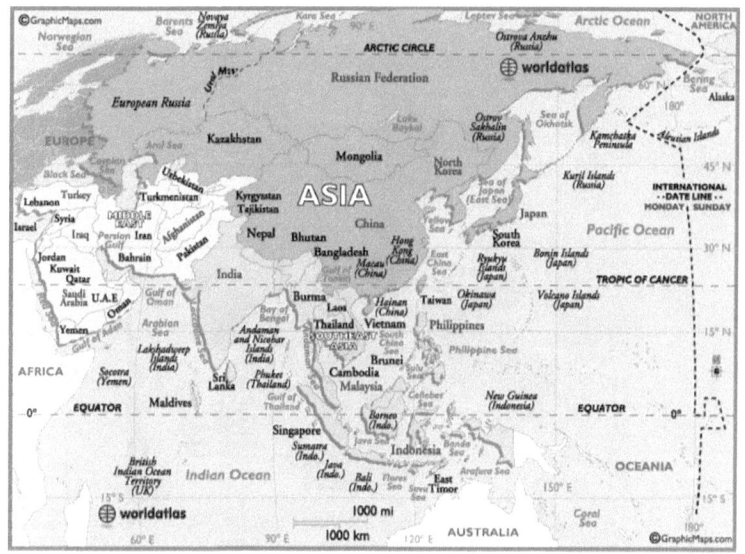

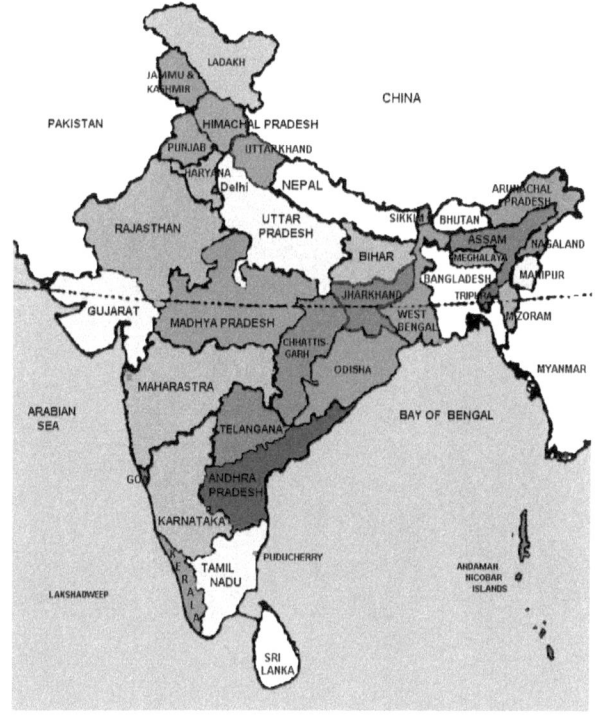

Kalinga and Southeast Asia: A Saga of Shared Civilizations | 251

Black Eagle Books

www.blackeaglebooks.org
info@blackeaglebooks.org

Black Eagle Books, an independent publisher, was founded as a nonprofit organization in April, 2019. It is our mission to connect and engage the Indian diaspora and the world at large with the best of works of world literature published on a collaborative platform, with special emphasis on foregrounding Contemporary Classics and New Writing.

www.ingramcontent.com/pod-product-compliance
Lightning Source LLC
Chambersburg PA
CBHW060556080526
44585CB00013B/581